Life Writing Outside the Lines

Designed as a contribution to the field of transnational comparative American studies, this book focuses on gender in life writing that exceeds the boundaries of traditional genres.

The contributors engage with authors who bend genres to speak gender as it manifests in multiple shapes in different geographic locations across the Americas, and especially as it intersects with race and migration, war and colonialism, illness and aging. In addition to supplying new insights into the established sites of auto/biographical production such as memoir, archive, and oral history, the book explores experimental mixed forms such as selfies, auto-theory, auto/bio comics, and autobiogeography. By combining multi-genre and multi-media perspectives with a multi-generational approach to life writing, the book showcases a spectrum of established and emerging critical voices, many of whom have been influenced by the work of Marlene Kadar, the Canadian life writing scholar, whose interventions have expanded the feminist and interdisciplinary methods of life writing studies.

Tracing the intergenerational relay of ideas, this collection fosters dialogue across the Western Hemisphere, and will be useful to those studying life writing exchanges between North America, Latin America, and the Caribbean.

This book was originally published as a special issue of *a/b: Auto/Biography Studies*.

Eva C. Karpinski is an Associate Professor in the School of Gender, Sexuality and Women's Studies at York University, Toronto, Canada. She is the author of *Borrowed Tongues: Life Writing, Migration, and Translation* (2012), and a co-editor of *Trans/Acting Culture, Writing, and Memory* (2013). She is currently working on a book project on multilingual life writing.

Ricia Anne Chansky is a Professor of Literature at the University of Puerto Rico at Mayagüez, USA. She is a co-editor of *a/b: Auto/Biography Studies*, editor of the *Routledge Auto/Biography Studies* book series, and a Voice of Witness Fellow. She has recent and forthcoming publications on disaster studies, pedagogy, and contested identities.

Life Writing Outside the Lines
Gender and Genre in the Americas

Edited by
**Eva C. Karpinski and
Ricia Anne Chansky**

Routledge
Taylor & Francis Group
LONDON AND NEW YORK

First published in paperback 2024

First published 2020 by Routledge
4 Park Square, Milton Park, Abingdon, Oxon OX14 4RN

and by Routledge
605 Third Avenue, New York, NY 10158

Routledge is an imprint of the Taylor & Francis Group, an informa business

Publisher's Note
The publisher has gone to great lengths to ensure the quality of this reprint but points out that some imperfections in the original copies may be apparent.

Disclaimer
Every effort has been made to contact copyright holders for their permission to reprint material in this book. The publishers would be grateful to hear from any copyright holder who is not here acknowledged and will undertake to rectify any errors or omissions in future editions of this book.

British Library Cataloguing-in-Publication Data
A catalogue record for this book is available from the British Library

ISBN: 978-0-367-35830-3 (hbk)
ISBN: 978-1-03-283887-8 (pbk)
ISBN: 978-0-429-34215-8 (ebk)

DOI: 10.4324/9780429342158

Typeset in Minion Pro
by codeMantra

To Marlene Kadar, who has inspired generations of life writing scholars

Contents

How Would You Teach It? **235**

Citation Information

The chapters in this book were originally published in the journal *a/b: Auto/Biography Studies*, volume 33, issue 3 (Autumn 2018). When citing this material, please use the original page numbering for each article, as follows:

Introduction
Introduction – Finding Fragments: The Intersections of Gender and Genre in Life Narratives
Eva C. Karpinski and Ricia Anne Chansky
a/b: Auto/Biography Studies, volume 33, issue 3 (Autumn 2018) pp. 505–515

Chapter 1
Cultivating Gullibility
Marlene Kadar
a/b: Auto/Biography Studies, volume 33, issue 3 (Autumn 2018) pp. 517–522

Chapter 2
Marlene Kadar interview with Sidonie Smith – May 15, 2017
Sidonie Smith
a/b: Auto/Biography Studies, volume 33, issue 3 (Autumn 2018) pp. 523–531

Chapter 3
The Work of Marlene Kadar
Eva C. Karpinski
a/b: Auto/Biography Studies, volume 33, issue 3 (Autumn 2018) pp. 533

Chapter 4
Mar and Me: Following the Traces
Linda Warley
a/b: Auto/Biography Studies, volume 33, issue 3 (Autumn 2018) pp. 534–541

Chapter 5
Marlene Kadar's Life Writing: Feminist Theory Outside the Lines
Julie Rak
a/b: Auto/Biography Studies, volume 33, issue 3 (Autumn 2018) pp. 541–549

For any permission-related enquiries please visit
http://www.tandfonline.com/page/help/permissions

Contributors

Rose Mary Allen was born in Curaçao and studied anthropology at the University of Nijmegen, the Netherlands. She obtained her doctorate at the University of Utrecht, the Netherlands. Allen has been conducting oral history interviews on the islands of the Dutch Caribbean, and is working as a freelance researcher and a part-time lecturer at the University of Curaçao, where she teaches Caribbean studies. She has authored and coauthored several curricula on issues of Curaçao culture and society for the University of Curaçao and other institutions. She has co-published, edited, and published several books and articles on the cultural and social history of Curaçao with special attention to cultural traditions, migration, gender studies, and cultural diversity. Allen has served as a representative of the government of Curaçao on numerous committees concerning cultural and gender issues. In 2015, she was awarded the Cola Debrot Prize, Curaçao's most prestigious national award in the area of culture, art, and science, for her research on oral history. She is currently a postdoc on the research project "Traveling Caribbean Heritage" (Royal Netherlands Institute of Southeast Asian and Caribbean Studies, University of Leiden and University of Curaçao) and a research project at the University of Amsterdam and University of Curaçao, "Cultural Practices of Citizenship under Conditions of Fragmented Sovereignty: Gendered and Sexual Citizenship in Curaçao and Bonaire."

Leonor Arfuch is Professor in the Social Sciences School at the Universidad de Buenos Aires, Argentina, and the Director of research on cultural studies at the Gino Germani Research Institute. She has been a Visiting Professor at the University of Essex, Universidad Autónoma de México, Universidad Pedagógica y Javeriana, and Pontificia Universidad Católica, among others. She has been awarded the UBA Thalmann Scholarship, the British Academy Professorship Award, and a Guggenheim Fellowship; she was Tinker Visiting Professor at Stanford University (2013). She is the author of several books, including *O espaço biográfico: Dilemas da subjetividade contemporânea*.

Helen M. Buss is Professor Emeritus of English at the University of Calgary, Canada. She is the author of several scholarly books, including *Mapping Ourselves: Canadian Women's Autobiography in English*, which won the Gabrielle

Roy Prize, and *Repossessing the World: Reading Memoirs by Contemporary Women*, winner of the Laure Jamieson Book Prize. She coedited, with Marlene Kadar, *Working in Women's Archives: Researching Women's Private Literature and Archival Documents*. As Margaret Clarke, she has published novels such as *The Cutting Season* and *Healing Song*. She has also published her memoir, *Memoirs from Away: A New Found Land Girlhood*.

Mark Celinscak is the Louis and Frances Blumkin Professor of Holocaust and Genocide Studies in the Department of History at the University of Nebraska Omaha, USA. He is also the Executive Director of the Sam and Frances Fried Holocaust and Genocide Education Fund at the University of Nebraska at Omaha, USA. He is the author of *Distance from the Belsen Heap: Allied Forces and the Liberation of a Nazi Concentration Camp*.

Ricia Anne Chansky is Professor of Literature at the University of Puerto Rico at Mayagüez, USA. She is a co-editor of *a/b: Auto/Biography Studies* and *The Routledge Auto/Biography Studies Reader*. She is the editor of the new *Routledge Auto/Biography Studies* book series as well as *Auto/Biography across the Americas: Transnational Themes in Life Writing* and *Auto/Biography in the Americas: Relational Lives*. She is a Fulbright Specialist in US studies who is currently working on a long-term public humanities project with Voice of Witness and the Humanities Action Lab. She has forthcoming publications in disaster studies, disaster pedagogy, diasporic studies, and contested national identities.

Rachel E. Dubrofsky is an Associate Professor in the Department of Communication at the University of South Florida, Tampa, USA. Her research is rooted in a critical cultural studies tradition, with a focus on digital culture (reality television, television, social media, film) and an emphasis on the role of surveillance and issues of race and gender. Some of her work has appeared in the journals *Critical Studies in Media Communication*, *Communication Theory*, *Communication, Culture & Critique*, *Feminist Media Studies*, and *Television & New Media*. She is the author of *The Surveillance of Women on Reality Television: Watching The Bachelor and The Bachelorette*, and the co-editor of the collection *Feminist Surveillance Studies*. She is currently working on a book, *Under Surveillance: Mediating Race and Gender*, which examines the cultural shift from older digital media to newer digital media with attention to how a context of surveillance situates racialized and gendered identities and bodies.

Ozlem Ezer obtained her BA in English Language and Literature at Boğaziçi University, Istanbul, Turkey; her MA in Women's Studies at the Middle East Technical University, Ankara, Turkey; and, her PhD in Gender, Sexuality, and Women's Studies at York University, Toronto, Canada She did her postdoctoral studies at GEXcel—Centre for Gender Excellence at Linköping University, Sweden. She is currently a Visiting Scholar at the Center for Middle Eastern Studies at the University of California, Berkeley. She collaborated with the Human Development Resource Foundation in Istanbul for the initial stages of her oral history project with Syrian refugee women between January and

July 2016. She will record further interviews with Syrian women activists in Europe and North America, and work on her book cn life stories, during her residency at the Center for Middle Eastern Studies.

Lauren Fournier is an artist, writer, and doctoral candidate in the Department of English at York University, where she is completing a Social Sciences and Humanities Research Council-funded doctoral project on autotheory as a contemporary mode of feminist practice across media. Her work has been exhibited in galleries and artist-run centers across Canada and the US, and in Berlin. Her writing has been published in *Canadian Art*, *Magenta*, *Journal of Comparative Media Arts*, *Canadian Journal of Woman Studies*, and *West Coast Line*. She is on the editorial committee of KAPSULA and the programming committee of the Feminist Art Conference in Toronto. Redundant information: any student associated with any graduate program at York can become a Graduate Associate at the CFR.

Julia A. Galbus is an Associate Professor and the Associate Chair of English at the University of Southern Indiana, Evansville, USA, where she teaches courses in American literature, autobiography, and literary theory.

Marlene Kadar is a Professor in the School of Gender, Sexuality, and Women's Studies at York University, Toronto, Canada. She has published extensively in the field of life writing, especially in relation to traumatic historical events, archival lives, and memory studies. She edited the genre-defining study *Essays on Life Writing: From Genre to Critical Practice*, which won the Gabrielle Roy Prize. She co-edited, with Helen Buss, *Working in Women's Archives: Researching Women's Private Literature and Archival Documents*. She has co-edited three volumes of life-writing theory: *Tracing the Autobiographical*, with Linda Warley, Jeanne Perreault, and Susanna Egan; *Photographs, Histories, and Meanings*, with Perreault and Warley; and *Working Memory: Women and Work in World War II*, with Perreault. She is currently writing a study of the social and cultural contexts of medical diagnosis and misdiagnosis. She also edited the award-winning collection *The Missing Line: Poems from Canadian Woman Studies*. For the past several years, she has been the editor of the Life Writing Series at Wilfrid Laurier University Press.

Eva C. Karpinski is an Associate Professor in the School of Gender, Sexuality, and Women's Studies at York University, Toronto, Canada. Her research focuses on women's life writing, feminist translation, and multilingualism. She is the editor of *Pens of Many Colours: A Canadian Reader* and has edited *Broken Dialogues*, a special issue of *a/b: Auto/Biography Studies*. She is the author of *Borrowed Tongues: Life Writing, Migration, and Translation*, and co-editor of *Trans/Acting Culture, Writing, and Memory: Essays in Honour of Barbara Godard*.

Linda M. Morra is a Professor of English at Bishop's University, Lennoxville, Canada. In 2016–2017, she served as the Craig Dobbin Chair of Canadian Studies at University College Dublin, Ireland. Her book *Unarrested*

Archives: Case Studies in Twentieth-Century Women's Authorship was a finalist for the Gabrielle Roy Prize. She edited Jane Rule's autobiography, *Taking My Life*, which was shortlisted for the Lambda Award, and co-edited, with Jessica Schagerl, *Basements and Attics, Closets and Cyberspace: Explorations in Canadian Women's Archives*.

Elizabeth Podnieks is a Professor in the Department of English and the graduate program in Communication and Culture at Ryerson University, Toronto, Canada. She teaches and researches in the areas of life writing, mothering, modernism, popular and celebrity culture, scholarly editing, and digital humanities. Her articles and chapters have appeared in *a/b: Auto/Biography Studies*, *Life Writing*, and *The Routledge Auto/Biography Studies Reader*, among others. Selected books include the monograph *Daily Modernism: The Literary Diaries of Virginia Woolf, Antonia White, Elizabeth Smart, and Anaïs Nin*; the edition *Rough Draft: The Modernist Diaries of Emily Holmes Coleman, 1929–1937*; and, the edited collection *Pops in Pop Culture: Fatherhood, Masculinity, and the New Man*.

Julie Rak is a Professor in the Department of English and Film Studies at the University of Alberta, Edmonton, Canada. She is a recipient of the Killam Professorship and the winner of The Hogan Prize. She is the author of *Boom! Manufacturing Memoir for the Popular Market*, the co-author (with Anna Poletti) of *Identity Technologies: Constructing the Self Online*, and the co-editor of *Life among the Qallunaat*, by Mini Aodla Freeman. She also edited *Auto/Biography in Canada*.

Candida Rifkind is a Professor in the Department of English at the University of Winnipeg, Canada. She specializes in graphic narratives and Canadian literature and culture. In addition to numerous articles, she has published *Comrades and Critics: Women, Literature, and the Left in 1930s Canada*, and co-edited a scholarly collection with Linda Warley, *Canadian Graphic: Picturing Life Narratives*. She currently holds a Social Sciences and Humanities Research Council Insight Grant to research contemporary graphic biographies and is planning a future project on Canadian women's graphic life narratives.

Manoela dos Anjos Afonso Rodrigues is an artist, teacher, and researcher working within experiences of displacement from the decolonial perspective. Her art practice is informed by feminist geography and border epistemologies. Individual and collective practices are in constant dialogue in her work, which draws on the politics of dislocation and conviviality. She is interested in art practice as an autobiographical place for confronting coloniality, exposing coloniality of being, and opening space for the decolonial self. She holds a PhD from Chelsea College of Arts, University of the Arts London, UK, and is an Assistant Professor in the Visual Arts College at the Federal University of Goiás, Brazil.

Sidonie Smith is Lorna G. Goodison Distinguished University Professor of English and Women's Studies at the University of Michigan, Ann Arbor, USA.

She is a past President of the Modern Language Association. She is one of the pioneers of women's autobiography studies with books such as *A Poetics of Women's Autobiography: Marginality and the Fictions of Self-Representation* and *Subjectivity, Identity, and the Body: Women's Autobiographical Practices in the Twentieth Century*. With Julia Watson, she co-authored *Reading Autobiography: A Guide for Interpreting Life Narratives*. Together, they have co-edited several groundbreaking collections, including *De/colonizing the Subject: The Politics of Gender in Women's Autobiography*; *Getting a Life: Everyday Uses of Autobiography*; *Women, Autobiography, Theory: A Reader*; and *Interfaces: Women's Visual and Performance Autobiography*. Her latest publication is *A Manifesto for the Humanities: Transforming Doctoral Education in "Good Enough" Times*.

Keila D. Taylor is a graduate student in the Department of Sociology at the University of Texas at San Antonio, USA, where she earned her BA in Sociology. Her research and scholarship focus on Black feminist theory, intersectional identities, and secularism. Her Master's thesis in progress is entitled "Life on the Margins: A Qualitative Approach to Identity Formation among Secular Black Women," which examines the manner in which self-identified nonreligious Black women navigate their social lives and shape their social identity without the direct influence and guidance of traditional Black theology.

Patrick Taylor teaches postcolonial thought and Caribbean literature, religion, and culture in the Department of Humanities and the graduate program in Social and Political Thought at York University, Toronto, Canada. He is currently working on constructions of whiteness in the anglophone Caribbean, focusing on Barbados. His recent publications include "From Planter's Daughter to Imperial Soldier and Servant in Britain's War" in *Working Memory: Women and Work in World War II* (edited by Marlene Kadar and Jeanne Perreault). A fellow of the Centre for Research on Latin America and the Caribbean, he directed the Caribbean Religions Project, an international, collaborative research and editorial project funded by the Ford Foundation and the Social Sciences and Humanities Research Council of Canada. He is the co-editor of *The Encyclopedia of Caribbean Religions* (with Frederick I. Case) and *Forging Identities and Patterns of Development in Latin America and the Caribbean* (with Joanna Rummens and Polo Diaz); the editor of *Nation Dance: Religion, Identity and Cultural Difference in the Caribbean*; and the author of *The Narrative of Liberation: Perspectives on Afro-Caribbean Literature, Popular Culture and Politics*, among other publications.

Kathleen Venema is an Associate Professor in the Department of English at the University of Winnipeg, Canada, where she teaches and publishes on Canadian literature and narratives of illness, aging, disability, and care. Her recently completed book, *Bird-Bent Grass: A Memoir, in Pieces*, is an interdisciplinary critical memoir that integrates creative, critical, and theoretical perspectives on the ways in which issues related to international development, spiritually grounded commitments to social justice, war, trauma, and loss associated with dementia's devastations are negotiated in epistolary discourse.

Linda Warley specializes in Canadian life writing, including texts by First Nations and Métis authors. She has co-edited, with Marlene Kadar, Jeanne Perreault, and Susanna Egan, *Tracing the Autobiographical*, and, with Perreault and Kadar, *Photographs, Histories, and Meanings*. She is also a co-editor, with Candida Rifkind, of *Canadian Graphic: Picturing Life Narratives*, which won the Gabrielle Roy Prize.

Preface

After Lives: A Reflection on the 2017 IABAA Conference

By Ricia Anne Chansky and Eva C. Karpinski

The publication of this book affords us an opportunity to reflect on the conference we convened at York University in 2017, "Lives Outside the Lines: Gender and Genre in the Americas." This was the third biennial meeting of the International Auto/Biography Association Chapter of the Americas (IABAA) and was shaped by a commitment to forging connections between some of the discourses and spaces of auto/biography studies that we found particularly relevant to the work of the chapter. Furthermore, the event allowed us to put into practice some of the feminist collaborative models and methodologies that we had been conceptualizing for some time, both individually and together. The conference was dedicated to our recently retired colleague—the Canadian life narrative scholar, Marlene Kadar—and running through the event was a consideration of the ways in which her research has impacted the field. Emergent from this interrogation of and reflection on Kadar's work were additional points that we would like to consider briefly: sustained mentorship and collaboration with emerging scholars; intergenerational exchanges; autotheoretical approaches; a commitment to multilingual, transnational relationships; and, the interrelations between gender and genre.

The conference began with a half-day seminar dedicated to mentoring emerging scholars that included workshops, discussions, and one-on-one conversations. Mentors and mentees were introduced prior to the event, and mentees were invited at that time to share with their mentors abstracts for dissertation projects, grant applications, conference presentations, or essays that were in progress. There were no additional fees incurred to participate in this workshop due to grant funding that we received in support of the event from the Social Sciences and Humanities Research Council of Canada.[1] Workshop topics were selected in accord with the leadership of the IABA SNS, the Student and New Scholar chapter of our umbrella organization, and included presentations by international scholars on the themes of methodological approaches, the study of gender and genre, interviewing, collaboration, and publishing, among others. Following the presentations and discussions, the approximately forty participants broke out into the predetermined pairs of emerging and senior scholars to discuss the previously shared abstracts. After the individualized mentorship sessions, the pairs were provided with lunch and invited to continue their discussions informally.

We were pleased to hear feedback responses from graduate students that this model worked to destabilize the hierarchical model of professor and student or established and emerging scholar while fostering a sense of inclusion.

One example of a successful mentorship relationship borne of this seminar lies in the one-on-one breakout sessions. A graduate student shared with her mentor an abstract for a prestigious postdoctoral position. The mentor continued to advise the graduate student on her application after the conference concluded and the submission was successful. The two continued to work together and have now co-authored a book chapter. Based upon examples such as this one, the many responses that we received from this portion of the proceedings, and our own observations of both the mentorship workshop itself and the post-conference relationships developed between many of the pairs, we feel strongly that such exchanges are paramount to the success of not only conferences, but the healthy longevity of a discourse community.

In a time in which education—and especially the humanities—is wrongly and nefariously under fire, mentorship and collaboration become a means of undermining a fraught exceptionalism, a way of putting our feminist practice ideals into play in meaningful ways. And, while it is oftentimes hard to imagine futures when we ourselves are caught up in the battles of the present, it is essential to make mentorship, collaboration, and inclusion central to our work every single day. In this case, we had to conceptualize the mentorship workshop in our initial planning stages and write it into our funding requests from the inception. Curiously, funding agencies do not typically expect the intersection of pedagogy and research in scholarly meetings, and mentorship is most commonly classified as a pedagogical undertaking, if recognized at all. In our experience as conference conveners, then, we note that organizing a mentorship activity from the initial planning stage; writing it into all funding proposals so as to eliminate participant costs; introducing mentors and mentees ahead of time; positioning the seminar at the very beginning of the event; providing the space for informal exchanges as well as more prescriptive ones; and, encouraging sustained interaction throughout the conference and afterwards contributed substantially to the success of the undertaking as well as to the well-being of emerging scholars in the field after the event ended.

This mentorship, however, was buoyed by the inclusion in the proceedings of several recently retired scholars who had completed collaborative undertakings with Kadar over the years. In conversation, one of these colleagues confided that she had recently been told that she was now "too old" to peer review submissions for a journal and was therefore hesitant to participate in the IABAA conference. This was a startling admission to us as we found that the intergenerational exchanges that unfolded around us were a boon to participants. These retired scholars were primarily second wave feminist activists who had fought for the right to even be present in academic circles and built together collaborative networks that forced open doors through which many of us entered academia: both in gender studies and area studies, subjects that are built on the study of narrated lives. While many contemporary projects have grown from the work done in this era, there does at times seem to be a trend to distance newer work from its precedents, although this is not an inclination unique to our field.[2]

A few possible reasons for this separation from past scholarship may be found in the relatively young age of auto/biography studies as a formalized research area, the demands of the era in which we live, and the precarity of scholars in the twenty-first century. We point to the 1985 conference convened by James Olney at Louisiana State University, the "International Symposium on Autobiography and Autobiography Studies," as the inception of the field as we know it today. The last thirty-five years of studying auto/biographical narratives on a global scale have been thrilling. There is simply so much to do. Human beings have developed endless ways in which to narrate the stories of their lives and lives that go beyond the human. In the last ten years, new media and modes of life narration have been developed through the Web 2.0 world: Facebook, YouTube, Twitter, Instagram, RPGs, blogs, dating websites, refugee mapping sites, and the list goes on and on. There are so many narratives and acts to engage with, study, and write about in this age of the auto/biographical boom. It stands to reason that with such a dazzling array of accessible life narrative texts there might be some disconnect between the foundational works of our field and the most current.

There are also new urgencies to understand and amplify the voices of the marginalized others. In a time laced with fear, hatred, and a resurgence of Eurocentric populism, many scholars of life narratives are focusing on the role of the reading witness and their own scholarly or editorial participation in the circulation of auto/biographical acts and narratives as sociopolitical activism. The impetus weighs heavily upon us to witness and facilitate the range and power of contemporary life narratives with the understanding that the life in the narrative may be one that is currently in jeopardy and therefore able to be assisted through our actions. How might discussing narratives of border crossings, for example, impact immigration laws and customs?

Furthermore, the precarious status of education in many nations has placed undue pressure on scholars to become breakout superstars of academia. A popular mass-market book, blog, or other research output that individuates an author from their peers can translate into public accolades that might lead to job security. A recognized separation from the perceived dusty academic who has fallen out of favor with many administrators, politicians, business elite, and media representations can signal a new kind of scholar that may have better success in a ruined job market and woefully underfunded institutions of higher learning. In light of this failing market, there are also increasing pressures to produce scholarship quickly and prematurely. It is now commonly understood that graduate students will need to publish at least one peer-reviewed essay in a journal in their field to be considered for a faculty position; assistant and untenured professors have frenetic publication requirements that hold strong amid increased teaching and service requirements; and, the precarity of contingent faculty labor comes with its own burdens to publish in the hopes of building a CV that will allow one to acquire a more stable job in academia.

While many scholarly meetings are very rightly forward facing—trying to parse through what might come next in a field—at times there can be an anti-historicizing bent that reflects these noted apprehensions of the fraught early years of the twenty-first century and the academy situated within this challenging time. In our own research community, we also note that the age of the field, richness and variety of life narratives available to us, and responsibilities to serve the people and communities that we are studying sometimes impede us from discussions that look both ways: those that remain forward facing while being rooted in the body of scholarship that already exists or those in tandem with historic texts that enliven and extend our studies. For us, the direct invitation to retired scholars to participate as plenary speakers had the effect of crafting a productive intergenerational exchange, one that augmented the work of our mentorship event and helped to extend it throughout the days of the conference.[3]

These scholars also needed funding to participate in the conference as their university bursaries were no longer active. This is another point that we articulated conscientiously in our grant funding applications from the get-go. We had to strive to build carefully a conference program that was well-balanced an inclusive and—as in the case of the retired scholar who told us that she was no longer a welcome peer-reviewer—we sometimes had to explain to invited scholars the relevance of their attendance within our conference design. From our perspective, an inclusive feminist practice model encouraged us to work to build these bridges between retired, established, and emerging scholars in order to have multifaceted intergenerational discussions across the work of the conference that will in turn lead to richer, deeper, and more nuanced scholarship.

One such presentation was Jeanne Perreault's self-reflexive piece that explored the ethics of representation by incorporating her private self into her scholarship. This plenary address, delivered on the second day of the conference, underscored for many of us the value of placing emphasis on the self as subject and the possible functions of an experiential "I" in life narrative theory. At times, this mode has proven problematic within feminist theory as critiques of experiential knowledge emerged in the backlashes against women's studies and second wave feminist practice. These criticisms tended to marginalize the work of scholars who situated the personal as theoretical, discouraging many researchers from pursuing this model. The autotheoretical approach, of course, has never disappeared from scholarship—especially evident in area studies. However, we recognize that a shift to the personal as theoretical is gaining momentum and acceptance in the wider spaces of academia, both in life narrative communities and elsewhere.

From our perspective, carefully constructed and contextualized inclusions of autotheoretical analyses lead to a transparency of intent; foster interconnectivity between scholar, life narrator, and reader (or receiver); and, potentially, construct a different sense of immersion in the scholarship and the primary text/s for these participants—life narrator, scholar, and reader (or receiver)—which can benefit the research community, pedagogical exchanges, and the outcomes of reading witnesses who may be moved to action on behalf of the narrator or communities discussed in the narrative. For Lauren Fournier, whose essay is included in this volume, autotheory as "contemporary feminist practice" holds the potential for "exposing the problematics of maintaining conceptual separations between self and theory," a division that may be read as particularly unnecessary within the field of auto/biography studies.

These intergenerational exchanges and multidirectional crossings were situated within the context of our organization's dedication to exchange within the Western Hemisphere, which inevitably led us to the challenges posed by multilingual encounters. Our multinational mandate provokes a need to explore the difficulties of establishing and maintaining transnational research networks when one has to rely on English as a lingua franca. In this respect, *a/b: Auto/Biography Studies*, the journal sponsoring this event as well as the other meetings of IABAA, has pioneered a policy of linguistic hospitality, which often consists in offering financial support for different forms of translation that facilitate multilingual communication. Historically, the journal has tried to remedy language barriers by providing live interpreting at IABA conferences, preparing translated versions of presentations for participants attending the conference, and ensuring in-house publication assistance for translated papers selected for post-conference special issues. In our case, a desire to create a multilingual space was built into the conference design, as we requested funding for translation in our grant application. Moreover, the conference website was multilingual, hosting abstracts in two or more languages.[4] We also invited presenters to share the transcripts of their presentations on our website for the duration of the conference, so that all participants could follow along more easily: a request to which many participants acquiesced. We further facilitated the translation of several papers into English ahead of time and likewise posted these on our website so that they might be referenced during the conference. The conference website, therefore, became a useful tool to respect the linguistic rights of presenters while furthering understanding and exchange. This digital support was offered in addition to providing multilingual moderators at the majority of panels.

The multilingual, multigenerational, and multidisciplinary character of our Toronto meeting was well-suited to exploring the problematics of gender and genre in life writing. The conference and the present collection that has grown from it are, of course, not the first instances when gender and genre have been put together and examined through each other in their mutual entanglements. The majority of prominent genre theorists, from Aristotle to Mikhail Bakhtin, and more recently Jacques Derrida, Tzvetan Todorov, and, specifically in relation to life writing, Philippe Lejeune, have considered genre to be genderless or gender neutral. By contrast, in addition to Kadar, among our participants we had such trailblazing theorists of the relevance of gender in auto/biographical genres as Sidonie Smith, Helen Buss, and Jeanne Perreault. Asking what difference gender makes, second wave feminists recognized gender as an important cognitive and affective filter, and taught us to see its often invisibilized work in all socially organized relations. Feminist literary scholarship not only perceived the absence of gender in genre as a sign of the hostility of certain genres to female and other illicit authorship, but also deconstructed genre's simultaneous dependence on gender exclusion and other exclusions of difference for reproducing sameness and continuity in the established order. As early as 1984, following Derrida's reflection on the (il)legitimizing and (de)stabilizing effects of the law of genre, British scholar Mary Jacobus applied the gender/genre lens to reading Wordsworth's autobiography and arrived at the conclusion that genre and gender function according to the same law of selective, not to say limited, intelligibility, which "puts a recognizable face on the page of literary history and thereby makes it readable, [allowing] us to find our own faces in the text rather than experience that anxious dissolution of identity which is akin to not knowing our kind" (57).

There have been fascinating trajectories in thinking about gender and genre since the 1980s, ones that often run into each other and cross paths. In both areas, new theories have moved away from rigid taxonomies towards a process-oriented view of genre and gender as fluid, dynamic, and evolving in response to their social and historical moment. We have come to understand generic and gender conventions as both regulating and regulated by common modes of perception and production of intersectional identities. Smith and Kadar, alongside other feminist critics such as Julia Watson, Françoise Lionnet, and Leigh Gilmore, among others, have been exploring the intersections of genre and gender in literary history and general poetics, pushing the boundaries of auto/biography still demarcated by the lingering hierarchies of European, bourgeois, white, male, literate, cisgendered, heteronormative, and able-bodied subjects. Feminist scholars have analyzed ideological motives behind the construction of certain subjectivities and bodies as normative while others as marginalized; recuperated forgotten or devalued work in non-traditional, non-canonical auto/biographical genres; and exposed the limits of traditional genres to contain certain ineffable, fractured, and fragmented gendered experiences related to the trauma of war, genocide, colonial violence, slavery, rape, poverty, and displacement. More recently, urgent attention has been given to exploring embodiments of illness and disability, as well as toxicity, pain, and death, in a world where the ecological and humanitarian crises raise fewer concerns than the state of market profits and resource extraction. The twenty-four panels and four plenary sessions assembled for our conference echoed and updated these concerns, enlarging their scope through additional focus on non-normative masculinities, neurodiversity, aging, trans lives, sex work, refugees and migrants, Black diasporas, activism, visual art, pedagogy, and popular culture.

However, as soon as the connection between genre and gender is denaturalized, and the gendered (male) bias of (traditional) auto/biography comes into focus in feminist criticism, vigilant scholars like Kadar see it as necessary to loosen the grip of gender on genre, opting instead for the unfixed, anti-normative, and inclusive term "life writing." Emancipating life writing from any prescriptive, regulatory norms and categories—be they androcentric or secondarily imposed by feminists—frays the borders, including geopolitical and conceptual, and opens the field to thinking genre and gender differently, not in terms of constraints but rather possibilities. Such disorientation is necessary and productive: multiplying genders across historical, local, transnational, and non-binary, or even posthuman, digital identifications expand the vast archive of life writing genres and reading practices. As we have learned by bringing together colleagues from across the Americas, this potential shift in the politics and aesthetics of knowledge production through life writing requires receptiveness to a democratizing, dialogic ethics of the cross-hemispheric, intergenerational, multilingual encounter.

As a result of these critical interventions, both genre and gender have been freed from essentialist connotations and viewed as assemblages of traces that never cohere into a seamless, ideal norm; moreover, an auto/biographical text is always a selection and composition of pieces of memory. But as in comics, where meaning-making happens in the space of the gutters, the auto/biographical incompleteness offers a similar pleasure of fleshing out a story through the work of imagination. For authors and readers of auto/biography alike, genre and gender have started to be recognized as performative sites of intelligibility and creative innovation, continuity, and necessary rupture. While, on the one hand, genre and gender impose a horizon of familiar expectations and thus serve to reproduce consensual, dominant realities, they are also available for re-combination and transformation. At the same time as they reveal and preserve established social patterns, shared affects, and agreed-upon truths, genre and gender constantly invite transgression and contamination, subversion and defamiliarization of their putative norms. What we also know from studying theories of genre and gender is that they rely simultaneously on recurrence and codification, and therefore, they may be said to have both a diachronic and synchronic existence, situating one always in a historical relation to one's predecessors and in a combinatory space of change. In this sense, the joint terrain of genre and gender is always already a terrain of intergenerational dialogue, of learning and contestation, of critical genealogies and possible futures.

If we believe Jacques Rancière that both genre and gender belong to "the repetitive tense of the institution" (170), life writing and lives that fall outside the lines disrupt this repetition and pose a direct challenge to the institutionalized norms of cultural, linguistic, political, and economic dominance that polarizes the North against the South and Center in the Americas. The present volume invites many of the same scholars who started these dialogues and asks them to look at the problem of gender and genre by engaging with a specific body of theories about life writing formulated by Marlene Kadar. It thus indirectly asks about a life of the text, in this case a literary critical text: how does it return to mark its trace in thinking done after its turn, by others who come to pick it up?

This question lies at the core of the tangled problematics of gender and genre as well. How are they passed across generations? How will they be challenged, modified, performed differently—because they must constantly be taken up anew and transmogrified, no matter how insistent the voices of tradition rising in the cause of their purity, continuity, and preservation. Such has historically been the law of genre and gender. The papers presented at the conference, some of which are included here, provide ample evidence of this necessary plasticity of gender(s) and life narrative genres through innovation and invention. On the one hand, they revisit established genres such as biography, memoir, testimony, letter, or spiritual autobiography, showing how they are remade to accommodate little known bodies and experiences and how they are remediated into film, photography, digital autoethnography, or graphic narratives. On the other hand, they create ever-expanding new inventories of auto/biographical genres by examining selfies, anecdotes, celebrity interviews, scrapbooks, poetry, rap, and autotheory, to name a few.

Kadar once described life writing as "the site of new languages and new grammars, sometimes blended non-white languages, including Native-Canadian and African-American styles and dialects" (152–153). We hope that the IABAA conference that has given rise to this volume can be seen as such an inclusive, multilingual incubator of ideas, a fertile ground for the emergence of the much desired intergenerational, cross-hemispheric dialogue on the unlimited possibilities of life writing. In a spontaneous manner, the format of our conference has evolved into a sui generis auto/biographical spectacle in a new performative genre, where open-call panel presentations were framed by morning and afternoon plenaries dedicated to personal recollections, generous anecdotes, and tributes by colleagues and graduate students, celebrating one particularly influential, feminist academic life and the traces it has left. What we have learned is that—whether conceived as a field of study, a genre, or a critical practice—life narrative is always spurred by its autotheoretical impulse, self-reflexively testing its own limits, proliferating connections, and opening up collaborative spaces.

Notes

1. This grant also covered the registration fees for all attending graduate students and allowed us to subsidize housing for them and many of our international guests.
2. We feel compelled to speak against such forgetfulness of earlier feminist contributions, although we do not presuppose to suggest canonization of any work of theory or criticism in particular. Rather, we encourage exploration of and engagement with a variety of foundational texts.
3. We made the decision to feature plenary panels throughout the conference rather than keynote speakers as a means of reinforcing our conceptualization of a feminist collaborative conference model.
4. All of the abstracts were translated into Portuguese for the benefit of the large contingent of Brazilian attendees, and many were also presented in Spanish. The Portuguese translations were prepared meticulously by the students of Professor Jennifer Sarah Cooper enrolled in the graduate program in translation at the Federal University of Rio Grande do Norte in Brazil.

Works Cited

Jacobus, Mary. "The Law of/and Gender: Genre Theory and *The Prelude*." *Diacritics* 14, 4 (Winter 1984): 47–57.

Kadar, Marlene. "Whose Life Is It Anyway? Out of the Bathtub and into the Narrative." In *Essays on Life Writing: From Genre to Critical Practice*. U of Toronto P, 1992, pp. 152–161.

Rancière, Jacques. *The Politics of Literature*. Trans. Julie Rose. Polity Press, 2011.

INTRODUCTION

Finding Fragments: The Intersections of Gender and Genre in Life Narratives

By Eva C. Karpinski and Ricia Anne Chansky

This special issue comes to fruition after a long and gratifying period of collaboration that has brought us together as colleagues straddling a geographic divide between Puerto Rico and Canada. All the papers included here originated at the third biennial conference of the International Auto|Biography Association Chapter of the Americas that we co-organized at York University in Toronto in May 2017.

The theme of the conference—"Lives Outside the Lines: Gender and Genre in the Americas"—refers to ceaseless flows and crossings that challenge the lines demarcating hemispheric and national borders, bounded identities, bodies, genres, and disciplines as well as language separations— the shifts that characterize multiple and heterogeneous practices of contemporary life writing, biography, and autobiography. Our aim was to investigate fluid representations and intersectional theorizations of the impact of gender, class, racialization, sexuality, ethnicity, Indigeneity, ability, age, and other aspects of social being and embodiment on different possibilities of telling and showing lives. IABAA 2017 set the stage for transnational and interdisciplinary explorations across the north-south and humanities–social sciences polarities. We are cognizant of the different research practices, lexicons, and rhetorical norms specific to particular regions. Unlike its South American counterpart, North American auto|biography studies tends to be humanities and literature based, drawing less on social sciences' engagements with autoethnography, oral history, narrative, and biographic qualitative research methods, which have seen a significant ascendance in recent years. In bridging these disciplinary divides between disparate locations of the Americas, the participants were able to exchange ideas on transnational and decolonial, queer and trans practices of gender and embodiment; life writing and pedagogy; hybrid, multimedial, and multimodal forms of life writing; alternative archives; the connections between archive, fragment, and trace; meta-approaches to feminist self-representation; intersections of illness narratives and biopower; and the entanglements of testimony, trauma, and public memory.

Taking place in Canada, the IABAA conference in 2017 at the same time afforded a reorientation of the field through Canadian genealogies and the presence of such major Canadian scholars of life writing as Marlene Kadar, Helen Buss, Jeanne Perreault, Julie Rak, Eleanor Ty, Linda Morra, Sarah Brophy, Linda Warley, and Candida Rifkind, all of whom have done important work building on the strength of Canadian feminist literary theories and criticism. While the conference set out to explore the multiple lines that gendered lives in the Americas cross, it was especially dedicated to celebrating the achievements of Kadar, a noted Canadian feminist studies and life-writing scholar whose research interests cluster around theoretically, epistemologically, and ethically complex issues of gender and genre. Accordingly, the first part of this issue is devoted to exploring Kadar's impact and influence on her colleagues, collaborators, and former students, whom we invited to reflect on the significance of Kadar's work for their own professional development and for the advancement of theories and methods of life-writing study. We also encouraged other contributors, whose essays were selected through an open call for papers, to situate themselves vis-à-vis Kadar's interdisciplinary legacy, which served as a focal point for life-writing scholarship from across the Americas.

Described as a trailblazer and trendsetter, Kadar has made original and creative contributions in such areas as auto|biography studies, Holocaust and trauma studies, Canadian ethnic studies, and archival research and methodologies. As several contributors to this volume note, she has pioneered new, exciting interdisciplinary approaches to the study of life writing in Canada and internationally, developing groundbreaking theories of the genre (Warley; Rak); introducing innovative methodologies such as tracing the auto|biographical fragment (Patrick Taylor; Mark Celinscak); drawing attention to gender in the archive (Morra; Elizabeth Podnieks); and advancing the rigorous and comprehensive work of editing and publishing personal narratives (Ozlem Ezer). In her role as editor of the Life Writing Series of Wilfrid Laurier University Press, Kadar has been tirelessly recovering and preserving the voices of women, immigrants, and marginalized "others," which would otherwise have been lost to us. In her research on World War II, Kadar ventures into territories explored by few scholars when she asks about the invisibility of the Roma Devouring, examines the lives of perpetrators, or probes the issue of representing the Holocaust to children. Her unprecedented investigation of the life journey of a former concentration camp guard has exposed the systemic loopholes in tracking down war criminals in Canada. In addition to boosting the concept of "life writing," her name has been welded to the idea of "autobiographical trace," an interpretive strategy allowing for reading lives preserved only fragmentarily, in ephemeral form (Rak). Often working collaboratively, Kadar remains faithful to her roots in feminist and leftist radicalism of the 1980s.

In thinking about the relationship between gender and genre discussed across the essays collected in this special issue, we are reminded of Kadar's precautionary statement in her treatise on life writing that "gender has determined genre in the past; in the future, we want to avoid any further 'gendrification'" (7). The abject feminization of certain genres, in a Butlerian sense, has historically served to undermine or diminish the worth of narratives constructed within said genre, thereby devaluating the life in the narrative. Genres that were traditionally undervalued—diaries, logbooks, journals, letters, nonverbal narratives, and others—have been aligned with marginalized peoples who did not have access to dominant discourses, a maneuver that affixes the nomenclature of worth-less to the authors as well as the texts. Kadar, however, warns us (readers, scholars, feminists) that, in our attempts to correct these systemic patterns, we can go too far by inadvertently emulating such destructive behavior. "It is difficult to *resist* continuing dualistic arguments that separate us," she argues ("Coming" 8). Our intent in this discourse on gender and genre in auto|biographical narratives, then, is not to ascribe gender to specific genres or to decide who performs gender in their chosen genre more successfully than another, but, rather, to explore the nuances of generic particulars in a manner that allows us to better grasp the means by which medium extends the potential for expressing gender in life narratives.

Kadar's departure from the limitations and constraints of the Aristotelian, paradigmatic model for approaching gender and genre, and her predilection for a Socratic mode of criticism that requires posing new questions and finding new ways of thinking and seeing, is also visible in her transitioning to a different voice in her latest writing, the voice that blends the autobiographical with the theoretical and the poetic. "Cultivating Gullibility," a triptych of Kadar's stories that opens this special issue, addresses itself precisely to the illusion of knowing—the epiphany coming from the body living with cancer. The title rings a cautionary note, confronting the reader directly with the voice from the world of the unwell, exposing the gullibility and illusions of certainty harbored by the well. All three parts pivot around the invisible chasm that separates the unwell from the well world in "Dross" and "The Shimmy of Limits," as much as the memory of trauma may be separated from its reality in "The Woman Who Sounded Like Zsa Zsa Gabor." Asking what kind of thinking is possible from within an unwell body, the body in crisis, Kadar's writing ponders the theme of the epistemic and aesthetic generativity of trauma and illness, where "renegade cells" become a somatic equivalent of renegade, unruly forms of writing and reading responses. Rather than raising expectations of scientific "fact" or rational pursuit of "objective" truth in life writing, her auto|biographical and scholarly texts opt instead for the truth of "what it feels like"—what it feels like to do this research, to witness trauma, to live in this body. The question concluding the last selection—"What do we choose to tell each other?"— might just be the most important self-reflexive question running through Kadar's writing, both academic and nonacademic.

Following this sample of her experimental prose, we present an interview with Kadar, conducted by Sidonie Smith, herself a well-respected scholar and the foundational figure in feminist auto|biography studies. As editors, we are grateful to both Marlene and Sid for graciously agreeing to stage this momentous event, the meeting of two generous minds and two great visions that in different ways have been instrumental in shaping the terrain of the field. At the opening of their conversation, Kadar is prompted to articulate what she calls "the defense of the fragment." While she identifies as inspirational for her own thinking Maurice Blanchot's theory of fragmentary writing and the New Historicist method of reading history *from* and *as* the fragment, she also acknowledges the political expediency of the fragment that can be utilized in the fight for more inclusive curricula, in Kadar's case in early women's studies classrooms, or against pro-Soviet censorship, as in 1970s Hungary, where she was involved in underground circulation of banned publications. For Kadar, "the fragment leaves many more opportunities for us to speak it, and write it, and narrate it," wherein lie both its possibilities and its limits. But in Kadar's practice, "the cocreativity between the fragment and the scholar" (Smith) transforms the limit into a space of possibility. Generically elusive, Kadar's new writing is driven by the autobiographical propulsion toward an interminable inquiry that takes place under death sentence, and she observes that the experience of illness and trauma, rather than producing some unequivocal truth, may necessitate what she calls "the semblance of the lie." In the remainder of their dialogue, Smith and Kadar—each with a huge record of engagement in feminist collaborative process—exchange comments on their similar experiences, with Smith admitting that in her writing partnership with Julia Watson, relationality emerges as a third voice. They conclude by revisiting Kadar's intellectual journeys and fascinations that have enticed her interest in life writing.

The ten Forum papers speak to Kadar's influence from several overlapping, reflexive angles: personalized biographical testimony (Warley; P. Taylor; Celinscak; Ezer); metacritical assessment (Rak; Julia Galbus); and applied critical praxis of reading the archive and the fragment (Morra; Buss; Podnieks; Rachel Dubrofsky). Warley's warm reminiscence in "Mar and Me: Following the Traces" underlines the humanity of Kadar's scholarship, its inclusiveness, ethics, empathy—what Warley calls "flexibility and generosity of mind." In shifting from "me" to "us," she eventually captures the collective spirit of "a community of scholars with a commitment to ethical, political, feminist, nuanced, flexible, open-minded approaches to the study of life writing texts in all media, genres, and subgenres" (Warley). Similarly, in "Marlene Kadar's Life Writing: Feminist Theory outside the Lines," Rak's rereading of Kadar's four best-known essays, an ethics of reading as "stand in" comes to the fore in Kadar's critical practice of approaching traces as testimonial evidence and treating the work of the critic itself as an act of witnessing, complicated by the fact that the critic is always a cocreator of meaning. Situating Kadar's contributions against the backdrop of Canadian and international developments in the field, Rak identifies Kadar's stance as "deeply feminist," indebted to standpoint theory's recognition of positionality and ordinary, everyday experience as integral to what knowledge and "truths" about life can be produced. A different set of ethical dilemmas informs Galbus's essay, "Working (with) History: Marlene Kadar and Louise DeSalvo," which focuses on repulsive, damaged, perhaps even morally objectionable subjects, asking implicitly whose lives are worthy of study. In taking up Kadar and Perreault's two-way concept of "working memory," a concept that simultaneously ascribes agency to and recognizes memory as a contested site, Galbus gestures at the interminable process of revision, (re)interpretation, and resistance to completion in every renewed engagement with history. She also acknowledges the emotional toll of doing such painful, ethically fraught archival research as the one performed by Kadar and DeSalvo.

The next group of Forum essays works the archive as an epitome of the fragment, offering four case studies that respectively embark on unleashing colonial silences while excavating the silenced family history (P. Taylor), analyzing maternal discourses in early popular culture (Podnieks), expanding the queer archive (Morra), and filling the gaps in Holocaust history (Celinscak). In "Escape from the Colonial Asylum," P. Taylor reconstructs parallel trajectories in his ancestral history from the records kept by mental health institutions in Barbados and Toronto. He meditates on power relations animating the colonial archive—whether in a settler colony like Canada or a plantation colony like Barbados—and finds buried in them the phantoms of ugly, dangerous collective memory of transatlantic slavery and the spoils of whiteness. In "Maternal Stars of the Silent Screen: Gender, Genre, and *Photoplay Magazine*," Podnieks immerses herself in a digital archive of the early-twentieth-century fan magazine to scan its representations of silent-film stars who became mothers. As she explains, her research on these celebrity auto|biographical profiles, by bringing together women's public (acting) and private (mothering) labor, inscribes itself in the feminist tradition of archival rescue and recovery from "historical anonymity" of women's ordinary lives. In Morra's "Inside the Cover, Outside the Archive: Reading the Dispersal of Jane Rule's Library and Modes of Female Sociability," a visit to a San Francisco bookstore and an accidental discovery of a book provoke a chain reaction that leads to the reevaluation of archival practices and calls into question how they serve the purpose of research on women writers. Following Kadar and Buss's methodological clues for expanding the meaning of what is collectible, Morra proposes to consider the book in question, and especially its inscriptions, dedication, and marginalia, as a paratextual fragment, a stand-in for the writer's larger intellectual formation and network of connections. Incompleteness, absence, deferral—a similar narrative of a frustrating encounter in the archive unfolds in Celinscak's account of military history in "Unlikely Documents, Unexpected Places: The Limits of Archive," which at times reads like a piece of investigative journalism. He begins by following fragments and traces that guide him to the discovery of the unrecognized role of Canadian military personnel in the liberation of the Bergen-Belsen concentration camp. In particular, fleshing out a biography of the Canadian pilot who was responsible for feeding the survivors, Celinscak restores visibility to one forgotten hero. He bemoans the losses in official state repositories whose acquisition politics doom to oblivion many documents and much artwork, especially those linked to ordinary participants in history.

The final cluster of Forum contributions provides examples of different applications of Kadar's theoretical and methodological insights in such diverse disciplinary contexts as communication studies, literary criticism, and research on refugees. Dubrofsky's "Frayed Edges: Selfies, Auschwitz, and a Blushing Emoticon" takes on the notorious case of the Auschwitz selfie in order to investigate how the popular press represents young women, and in the process she argues for the necessity of embracing "messiness." Refusing easy answers and resisting closure that precludes the possibility of telling "other stories," she problematizes the role of affect in reinforcing public stereotypes of gender and trauma. Her model of activist critical scholarship invested in paradoxes and contradictions resembles Kadar's "renegade" attitude in defiance of fixity and certainty of knowledge. Buss in "Kim Thuy's *Ru* and the Art of the Anecdote" looks at the work of Vietnamese French Canadian writer Thuy, who intertwines her family's experience as boat people with her own stories related to mothering an autistic son. When it manifests in flashbacks or anecdotes, traumatic memory feeds into the creative weave of Thuy's life writing, or—to use Perreault's term, which Buss prefers—her "autography." To Buss, such anecdotal life writing is a generic and gendered practice. However, according to her, the productivity of traumatic memory can also take other than creative or aesthetic form: Thuy's traumatic memory becomes her ethical "guide to loving" and to "new ways of being." The last piece in the Forum section, Ezer's "Drawing a Narrative Landscape with Women Refugees," heeds Kadar's call for finding innovative, unconventional approaches to addressing the lives of marginalized groups, in this case, those of Syrian refugee women whose narratives of successful integration confound the dominant media stereotypes of "victimized, vulnerable, and subordinate" others. Ezer recounts her book project of documenting the experiences of ten participants, whom she interviewed in Turkey, Germany, Sweden, Canada, and Greece. She shares her thoughts on the political urgency of collecting these stories of "postcrisis humans" against the onslaught of alt facts spread by the popular media.

When reading the essays in the next section of this special issue, we want to recall feminist visual artist Joanne Leonard's reflection on the introduction of digital media into art-making practices, in order to illustrate the need to consider more directly the attributes of genre and medium. Photoshop as a means of constructing visual life narratives, Leonard clarifies, cannot convey the same "physical layers" of her handcut-and-pasted photo collages (23). Collage, for her, is an art form that focuses on "textualizing" (21) one's life story through the compilation of individual photographs (or other materials). The genre of collage and the medium of hand-cut, pasted, and assembled photographs in her work afford Leonard a space to collapse and merge the layers and temporalities of her life, to narrate biographical as well as autobiographical stories. The physical layering—essential to her method of constructing her life story—becomes an extension of how she views the lives in the narrative: intertwined, relational. This example is meant to show how the materialities and possibilities of specific genres allow narrators to differently conceive, engage with, and represent gender in their lived experiences.

The first essay included in this segment, Manoela dos Anjos Afonso Rodrigues's "Translanguaging and Autobiogeography as Decolonial Strategies for Writing Life Narratives within Displacement," extends the discussion of finding the precise genre for narrating the self. Feeling linguistically muted by her move from Brazil to England, dos Anjos Alfonso Rodrigues describes wandering around London feeling insecure about her English-language abilities, looking for entry points into the new language and culture, considering what it means to be out of place and, conversely, to belong. Finding a street sign announcing a "Diversion" that had been graffitied with an accent mark to convert the word to the Spanish "Diversión"—deviation becomes enjoyment in this transformation—inspires dos Anjos Alfonso Rodrigues to use her skills as an artist to photograph words that she found and "collected in the city" and assembled "into artists books," thereby creating a series of language memoirs. In this way, she was "with|in silence but not silenced."

Positioned at the intersection of decolonial theory, diasporic studies, linguistics, photography, art therapy, and gender studies, dos Anjos Alfonso Rodrigues ultimately uses genre to undermine linguistic hierarchies and legacies of colonization through translanguaging and the practice she refers to as "turning": a process that she eventually taught as a means of voicing a silenced self to other Brazilian women who had also immigrated to London. Detailing her work with these women, the author concludes that her visual-verbal practices—"informed by a politics of location grounded in feminist geography and decoloniality"—are "way[s] to be epistemologically disobedient in-between languages and, thus, to move toward our decolonial selves." In other words, the relationship that emerged between dos Anjos Alfonso Rodrigues, the English language, her photography, and her art-making practice allowed her to subvert linguistic privileging and a systemic silencing that forced her and the other women in her community into subservient, colonial models of exclusion.

In her contribution to this special issue, "Sick Women, Sad Girls, and Selfie-Theory: Autotheory as Contemporary Feminist Practice," Lauren Fournier considers the ways in which the longstanding feminist practice of "theorizing from the first person" might be reimagined within the generic spaces of third and fourth-wave feminisms as autotheory. Considering "twenty-first-century examples of auto-theoretical feminist performative practices that span out across web-based social media platforms," Fournier argues that under the umbrella of auto|biography studies, there needs to be space for studying the self in the scholarship. Contemporary autotheorists, she posits, "take up the discourses of theory as artistic material to perform, iterate, reenact, and transform" the self. An impetus to view autotheory as a genre "more accessible to a wider public" and, therefore, more conversant with a reading or viewing audience, she suggests, may play a substantial part in driving contemporary autotheoretical practices. Focusing on performative aspects of "Sick Woman Theory" and "Sad Girl Theory," especially as they relate to digital platforms for self-expression, Fournier argues that autotheory "extend[s] the feminist practice of theorizing from one's subject positioning as a way of engendering insights into questions related to aesthetics, politics, ethics, and social and cultural theory. In autotheory, she explains, "one's embodied experiences become the material through which one theorizes, and, in a similar way, theory becomes the discourse through which one's lived experience is refracted."

Kathleen Venema continues this discussion on visual lives in her essay, "Remembering Forgetting: Graphic Lives at the End of the Line." She explores graphic memoirs that record struggles with parental dementia and Alzheimer's, focusing her study on what she names "remembering-forgetting" and "remembering to forget," theorizing that the unique "resources" of comix and other graphic media enable the telling of certain types of life stories. Considering both the ways in which typeface can be manipulated in graphic texts and the ability to manipulate perspective in visual narratives in order to emphasize specific aspects of the life story, among other points, Venema demonstrates that the texts she studies point to the idea that "work by female professional artists recording their extended engagements in care-giving—work that lands disproportionately on female shoulders ... deploy[s] the often startling resources of graphic form to help us look properly at their (and all) aging m/others." The graphic memoir, then, is in her estimation an ideal way in which to represent the ways "in which memory and forgetting mingle inextricably."

Applying the theme of "lives outside the lines" to the "children whose parents were forced to escape the repression of the Chilean and Argentinean dictatorships," Leonor Arfuch discusses "those who, as grownups, negotiate the traumatic past through artistic creation, without adjusting to the limits of genre." In her essay, "Childhood Exile: Memories and Returns," the author considers "women who narrate at the thresholds of the autobiographical," pushing the generic boundaries of autobiography, biography, and fiction on the page and screen. Studying the narrated lives of women who as children either immigrated with or were left behind when their parents were exiled, Arfuch discusses the ways in which they bend truths to explore the possibilities of imagined returns, longings to bridge realities that exist "here" and "there," and fantasies of being reunited. Of particular interest to the author "is the way in which the past comes to life from the present of enunciation and how new autobiographical and self-fictional forms give strength to memory work, outside the limits of canonical genres." Arfuch's analysis suggests that, in some cases, the impetus to remember an absent parent may be so great that the missing person must be imagined in order to fill the gap in a life story, moving the narrative outside of the confines of normative generic borders. This observation might offer great insight into future analyses of other lives constructed under the duress of forced migrations.

The final essay in this section, anthropologist Rose Mary Allen's "Women Making Freedom: Rethinking Gender in Intra-Caribbean Migration from a Curaçaoan Perspective," continues to theorize the genres that map women's migratory movements. "The scholarly research on migration," Allen asserts, "has long sidelined gender and made women nearly invisible." This indiscernibility in "official" documents, the author emphasizes, is a result of "coloniality in the production of information" that rests upon a patriarchal binary system of valuation. Interconnecting with Kadar's articulation of autobiographical traces, Allen extends her search for Curaçaoan women in transit to oral histories, logbooks, newspaper articles, folkloric materials, and song lyrics, among others, demonstrating that sometimes what is hidden may be revealed only by looking for and at things differently. As Allen concludes, "To engender migration studies, the selection and collection of different types of data is required … . This implies creative ways of managing documents that transcended the geographical and linguistic borders originally set by the colonial powers." Furthermore, "transcending the traditional male gaze and looking at the female experiences also requires expanding the idea of information archive to one that is intersectional."

Keila D. Taylor's methodological essay, "Rejecting Objectivity: Reflections of a Black Feminist Researcher Interviewing Black Women," is featured in The Process segment of this issue. Situating her self as subject in this reflexive piece, Taylor interrogates disciplinary demands to keep qualitative interviews impersonal by "illustrat[ing] that empathy is a powerful and vital component of collecting Black women's stories." Despite being taught as a social scientist "the scientific method and how imperative it is not to allow your personal biases and beliefs to influence your research practices," she attests that while her "identity as a sociologist allows [her to] step in and out of that role as necessary, [her] identification as a Black woman is not afforded that same flexibility." The connectivity between interviewer and subject in this instance demonstrates to Taylor that they "were uniquely bound by [their] shared experiences of iconoclastic Blackness and womanhood, and for roughly two hours, [her] participants and [she] no longer had to 'shift' [their] identities."

The concluding piece of this special issue is Rifkind's pedagogical essay, "The Work of Teaching Women's Auto|Bio Comics," featured in the How Would You Teach It? section of the journal. Rifkind connects the demographics, mission statement, and "long history of social justice in education" of her home institution, the University of Winnipeg—as well as the multiple courses in which she has "the luxury of … experiment[ing] with all kinds of alternate pedagogies and assignments"—to the development of her pedagogical strategies for teaching graphic lives. Her self-reflexivity in this essay affords readers a comprehensive foundation from which to build syllabi that include women's auto|bio comics in multiple classrooms. Focusing on visual literacy as an element necessary for reading graphic genres, Rifkind outlines several exercises that she has developed or adapted for her own courses, tying them particularly to the ways in which "female-identified cartoonists draw the taboo, unspoken, unrepresented, undocumented, ignored, overlooked, derided, repressed, and suppressed experiences of their lives." She cautions, however, that "Teachers of women's auto|bio comics need to understand that their students will often participate in this collective self-revelation as well," suggesting that the genre is utilized by women to reveal what is hidden in a way that promotes interconnectivity between comix and reader-viewers, fostering an impetus to in turn divulge. "Teaching auto|bio comics," Rifkind summates, "is about what they teach us, what new knowledge we gain from these life narratives themselves and from the homework they ask us to do, and what we learn from our students' affective and intellectual responses to them."

It is clear from the assembled contributions to this special issue that, as Rifkind states, "Many of us who work in the expansive field of life-writing studies are swimming in Marlene Kadar's wake." The contributions to our Forum on the work of Marlene Kadar demonstrate some of the ways in which a range of scholars are directly extending her scholarship, while the essays featured in this special issue—including The Process and How Would You Teach It? sections—trace the diffusion of her ideas across generic, geographic, linguistic, and disciplinary boundaries. The scope and breadth of Kadar's work has clearly impacted feminist scholars in multiple regions and fields of study.

Works Cited

Kadar, Marlene. "Coming to Terms: Life Writing—From Genre to Critical Practice." *Essays on Life Writing: From Genre to Critical Practice*. Ed. Kadar. Toronto: U Toronto P, 1992. 3–16. Print.

Leonard, Joanne. "Behind the Pictures: An Interview with Joanne Leonard." Interview by Sidonie Smith. *a/b: Auto/Biography Studies* 29.1 (2014): 11–25. Print.

Reflections

Cultivating Gullibility

By Marlene Kadar

Part One: Dross

I am looking for a less flappable way to inhabit an unwell body in a well world. I have an old red flashlight that I have used in the past when wounds would not heal and I could not see the forest for the trees.

Currently, the future is not clear to me. I almost don't know how to talk about it.

My words have escaped into some ether that hovers in and around renegade cells and I cannot seem to bring them back intact.

Their contours have altered; their attachment to good thinking and generosity has receded; their dressings have been stored away in a hope chest with other adverbs.

There rests my own mother's soul, tortured, laid out like a bride's linens. It has embezzled its own consciousness and escaped into a nether world where memory is edited; where killing machines are oiled in the basement and potions are disguised by rogues in white coats who say they are healers. Sometimes the job is done from on high and patients with impaired vision are pressed into columns by jealous muses. Shoved onto the roof. Pushed to their deaths below. This story is shocking but it was told with conviction.

Who, then, will care for this poor woman who, in her more cogent moments, can express with verve and excessive imagination the degree to which she distrusts her firstborn?

Sad and feeling alone, she talks forward and remembers backward, but cannot make the two directions meet in what is here. If today does not fulfill, why wait, she thinks.

It would be easier to narrow the focus of the beam on some made-up idea about profundity. I have heard things like: (incurable) cancer made me strong; or, leukemia is my teacher; or, migraine illumines superficial psychic flaw. I will belong to the world of the well again very soon if not next year, or maybe the year after.

All of these subjects in one story are almost too much for me. If we can meet before night falls, we can share a sofa on the main floor where the remainder of us are hidden in plain sight, where the unwell pretend they are normal, included, hopeful and well. Maybe then I won't have to think about this stuff any more.

Part Two: The Shimmy of Limits

When we have lots of money it is easier to sustain illusions about others and ourselves. When we have lots of good health, we are more likely to do the same.

Sometimes we come to rely on crutches that appear to sully the medical model of clean, socialized Canadian medicine, medicine that includes legal opiates for the ones who act normal, hide their anguish. Those of us fortunate enough to develop addictions in lieu of excessive wealth or death-dealing disease imagine the calming illusion of control over one's life. I would have preferred an addiction, or even wealth, but I got the disease part.

So I can join the crowd and whine about the flaws and the faults of the addict: the cost to society of incarceration, hospitalizations, employment insurance. Worse still those who believe they do not have addictions have the same psychic yearning: to feed the illusion that we are healthier or better adjusted than the ones we call addicted, or even so well adjusted, we don't get cancer. Heck no, I don't use crutches. I make money; I am healthy. I have accrued expertise. It is okay that I can't say that any more.

In our most righteous countenance we rail against the dreadful self-harm the addict performs. This fact of social life can create a kind of social nausea or a headache much like the one Joan Didion describes when she gets a migraine.[1]

We need to purge the addict from the neighborhood. We need to clean up the parks. We need to arrest the lonely bums who sleep on sidewalks. Otherwise, how will I walk on the thoroughfare here, or what about over there where the snow is falling in front of the theater? Or on my way home tonight?

In the silence, the quiet in which we can do little else but think, both striving and martyrdom evaporate. At dawn it has not been decided what is true and what is false.

So this is what Frank Seeburger (U Denver) said: "thinking is a sabbatical practice, the fruit of rest and not of restlessness. It begins only after we are set free to go home, to a place … of serenity rather than drivenness." The only good thing about being really ill is that you cannot easily continue to be driven. (But that doesn't mean that you think more: it mostly means you feel too much.) "Really," the philosopher continued, "to ask a question is to give up the illusion cf already knowing the answer, and to give up the sense of control that comes from such an illusion. It is to become, instead, open to learning, ready to be taught— already underway."[2]

Part Three: The Woman Who Sounded Like Zsa Zsa Gabor[3]

Okay, well, I think about this idea often, this idea that I have harbored the illusion of already knowing the answer when, of course, I could not have known it. But it was a woman whose voice was like my grandmother's that switched me over. Ever since I read the story about the inert or maybe just silent woman who had been transported on May 16, 1944 from Pécs—or maybe it was Pest—and who, likely one of the few tattooed,[4] worked the Kanada Kommando detail at Auschwitz-Birkenau. She told the story of the October 7 uprising gone wrong. She talked like Zsa Zsa Gabor.[5] She had witnessed the entire tragedy and had survived to tell the tale. The interviewer listened with attention, as would you.

The interviewer was not alone. Fellow historians at Yale, a scholarly panel had assembled to sniff out real history, something one might actually prove. They needed a true catalog of the events. We will add this person's story to our collection, they may have dreamed, and then we can document it, they might have judged. We can also then enlarge the picture, persuade the employer. But the interviewer, this historian about whom I speak in passing, had been deported from his home a young boy in Czernowitz, Romania in 1942: not that it mattered, or maybe it did?

I wonder: maybe Zsa Zsa was sixty-seven years old or so when this whole thing ignited. She proclaimed: what a scene when the *four* chimneys blew up, rubble everywhere, prisoners running, guards shooting, friends burning. But me, she said, I couldn't run; I was busy sorting clothes and jewels after my compatriots had been removed. I was not a martyr; I did not help collect the gunpowder like other women. You should remember that one of the Wajcblum sisters was not hanged on January 5, 1945: Hana Wajcblum. She died in Ottawa in 2011 as Anna Heilman.[6] (In between she had other names, such as Hanka or Chana Weissman, or Weissblum.)[7] She had a good job, too, in what she called the "shit Kommando."[8]

Sorting was a good job. Other peoples' children had relinquished their satin yarmulkes and their shawls and clips: the adults, they wore silks. The silks were torn but had hems. I found rubies and laces in a red taffeta hem, she said.

I stole things from the suitcases for my comrades. I saved lives, yes, I did. Yes, four chimneys blew up; it was such a thing that day. Irina was punished for stealing, in the courtyard of Block 11 where the hanging post had been planted in cement warm enough to spread in December in Poland. Anna watched. There were two performances: one for the day shift; one for the night.[9]

Maybe *S. S. Aufseherin* Alice Orlowski did it but she died in 1976 anyways. Alice worked hard. She hated the Jews, she despised the Gypsies, as required. They say she softened in January 1945. But they said that about Hermine Braunsteiner, too, the one I knew best.

The woman who testified against Alice had worked in the Kanada Kommando. She edited as she relived the day. But she could not edit the memory of how it felt. She refused in her mild way the warrant for her death. It did not matter that we were not there then to hear her.

Dori Laub did not trespass that chasm between what the sorter-woman knew and what she did not know, could not know.[10] He said: how could it be otherwise? How do I know what I do not know? Only she was there to witness the explosion. It must have sounded like four chimneys. It would be better if it were four and not one, wouldn't it?

For her, there were four chimneys. That is the truth at the limits of the woman's knowledge, truth at a slant. The woman offered the Yale interviewers a backstory—what it truly "felt like" to be among others during the explosion, not all of what "really" happened. The historians dismissed her version of the story as inaccurate because what we know from the history books is that only Crematorium IV blew up, at the deft hands of prisoners, men and women both, after which the brave were tortured, hanged, shot in the treed courtyard of Block 11. Crude bombs they say.

We are scrupulous but rarely accurate, neither the survivors who remembered that it was only one chimney nor the witness who remembered four. Neither is Dori Laub, whose limits of knowledge had to shimmy in order to tell about a different truth. The historians must evade the memory of four chimneys. The historians had other interests. They wanted the truth; they did not want to know how the woman broke the frame of the memory of the truth of the rebellion. They had to foreclose on the deal and delete her story from the true one.

Between the worlds of the well and the unwell is the same irrevocable gap wherein the story lives and breathes with the fact of life. Between the well and the unwell is a huge chasm, an almost necessary silence, where the limits of knowledge shimmy. The unwell can never adopt the rules of behavior prepared for healthy, sane people, even if they wear crutches. They cannot hurry to the office. They cannot eat the meals on tap. They can't go to the library when their skin bleeds, or their red blood cells cry.

They can't even run a half marathon or jump a rope. What if their feet don't work? They may have a hard time satisfying the highest ethical standards established by the nonfiction police because the story of illness is not romantic or essentially happy and so they may lie or write about something that resembles a lie. They want to be happy and have every reason to be.

There were indeed four chimneys, says the sick woman with lymphoma. I was there, I think. Yes, my memory is now flawed. I remember four bags of poisons that took seven hours to decant. That was on day one and there were many endless days, if I do remember correctly now. Although I was guarded, I did not have to steal jewels.

What do we choose to tell each other? Sometimes we err on the side of historical and scientific "fact." Sometimes we don't. Who among us gets to go home? I do not always listen either, I guess, and yet I often think I do.

Notes

1. Didion, Joan. "In Bed." *The White Album*. New York: Farrar, Strauss and Giroux, 1979. 168–72.
2. Seeburger, Frank. "Thinking Time, Drinking Time: A Beginner's Thought (3)." *Trauma and Philosophy*. Web. 28 May 2018.
3. There are many women who sound like Zsa Zsa Gabor, some of whose names we will not know, and some of whom found respite in Canada at some point after the war.
4. Getting a tattoo can be seen as a good sign in the camps. If I were to be killed upon arrival at Auschwitz-Birkenau, I would not be processed first for tattooing. Thus, the tattooed person lived beyond arrival.
5. Although I do not have a physical body in mind when I refer to the Zsa Zsa person, I do have two such persons in mind: Ibolya Szalai Grossman (author of *An Ordinary Woman in Extraordinary Times*. Toronto: Multicultural History Society of Ontario: 1990 and author with her son, Andy Réti, of *Stronger Together*. Toronto: Azrieli Foundation, 2016); the second person is Elisabeth M. Raab, author of *And Peace Never Came*, Waterloo: Wilfrid Laurier UP, 1997.
6. Her obituary reads: "Heilman, Anna, Jewish Resistance Fighter (December 1, 1928–May 1, 2011) Anna Heilman (nee Wajcblum) died peacefully in Ottawa, Canada on May 1, 2011 after a short illness. Born in Warsaw, Poland, Anna participated in the 1943 Warsaw Ghetto Uprising and as an inmate in Auschwitz helped smuggle gunpowder with her older sister Ester for the October 1944 Sonderkommando uprising. Anna was predeceased by her mother Rebecca and father Jacob, both murdered in the Majdanek concentration camp (1943); by Ester (executed as a Jewish resistance fighter in Auschwitz [1945]); by her oldest sister Sabine (1995); and, by Anna's husband of 58 years Joshua Heilman (2005)." "Anna Heilman Obituary." *Ottawa Citizen*. Postmedia Network, 3 May 2011. Web. 29 May 2018.

7. See "Witness statement from Marta Bindiger Cige," Nov. 19, 1945, by Susan Katz. Library and Archives of Canada R 11520. Anna Wajcblum Heilman's Diary. File 1–2. Marta worked in the Kommando Weissköpfchen (Whitehead—the sorting room 1).

8. R 11520, vol. 2 File 2–23. Publications and Articles.

9. "Witness Statement from Marta Bindiger Cige" 4.

10. Laub, Dori. "Bearing Witness, or the Vicissitudes of Listening." *Testimony: Crises of Witnessing in Literature, Psychoanalysis, and History*. By Shoshana Felman and Daub. London: Routledge, 1992. 57–74.

Marlene Kadar interview with Sidonie Smith – May 15, 2017

Figure 1. Sidonie Smith interviews Marlene Kadar at the 2017 International Auto/Biography Association Americas Chapter Conference at York University, Toronto.

Sidonie Smith: Thank you so much, Marlene, for launching this conference with a reading from your powerful memoir. We are honored to be your audience, awed by your courage, and moved by your struggle to live with renegade cells. What we witness is the urgency of writing a life story, composing a struggle, communicating words, and persistence, in the face of a future that is not clear to you. I for one am called back to what you wrote in your essay "What Is Life Writing?" about "getting us a heart of wisdom." That too, is what we need today … . I want to start the conversation about what is so distinctive about your piece, and that is you read fragments, you write in fragments, and as a scholar of life writing, you invoked the fragments of archives that you have mined over three decades. So I thought it might be interesting for people to hear you talk about what makes this practice of the fragment so compelling for you at this moment. And just some other questions related to this; what does the fragment do for you, and what might it set up as an obstacle for you as you're writing now?

Marlene Kadar: Thank you, Sid, for agreeing to come here and be with me at the front of this room where we are going to have a conversation. The fragment became important to me many years ago when teaching Introduction to Women's Studies with Susan Ehrlich. We asked how and why women had been excluded or misrepresented in the literary and historical canons. Our subject was the reclamation of women's voices, but sometimes there weren't enough women's voices to teach, and the majority of those were published by elite white women, when what we wanted was a fuller representation of the scope of voices. I probably at first thought about fragments and ordinary persons who were figuring in fragments in the context of the syllabus for that course.

Later I thought about Maurice Blanchot's essay "Writing the Disaster," first published in French in 1980. He wrote that the fragment is an unfinished separation, or we might say, it behaves like an unfinished separation. For me, two glorious opportunities were imbedded in this formulation. First: if the fragment is an unfinished separation, then within it is harbored a longing to reinhabit that which it may have belonged to once upon a time when the proposition was intact, or unabridged. Second: this separation, then, is not necessarily a real event, although the life-writing scholar is obliged to imagine its performance in various contexts and its unspoken connectedness to other separations. In other words, the fragment stands alone and yet holds within its boundaries a language that allows us to speak about it separately, and also to imagine a longing that it represents. Along these lines, Stephen Greenblatt and others have further argued that histories are not coherent stories. A history that is "a glorious fragment," to use his words, attracted me further.

The third and final defense of the fragment has to do with the genre of samizdat, or underground literature that was circulated in Central and Eastern Europe during the Soviet period. Leon Trotsky's *The Permanent Revolution & Results and Prospects* explained that the law of uneven and combined development is the basis of the political strategy of permanent revolution; in other words, all countries develop disproportionately according to their own and differing social and economic factors, and political and social change develops variously according to need and opportunity. In the Hungary of the 1970s, for example, censorship prevented the dissident movement from either circulating Trotsky's books or publishing their own political analyses and commentaries. Samizdat was made up of fragments of political texts that were less complicated to reproduce and exchange. When I was an exchange fellow living in Budapest in 1978–79, I helped collect, translate, and smuggle samizdat in and out of the country and thereby support the Hungarian movement and its free university while under Soviet control. In this context, fragments were more practical, easier to hide. So when Sid asked me this question, I thought about these three instances of fragments.

Sidonie Smith: To follow up on that, do you think that, for the person who holds the fragment, say from an archive, the fragment has to give up its desire, or is there something in the fact that the fragment opens up the imagination of the one who holds the fragment, or the one who views the fragment? It's very different, let's say in terms of thinking about life writing, very different than holding Augustine in your hand. It's not that Augustine isn't a totally compelling narrative, but it draws you in so that you are contained by it, more than you're contained by the fragment. Or is that too much of imagining the cocreativity of the fragment and the scholar?

Marlene Kadar: Well, I guess we could go either way, but I certainly don't think it's too much. And certainly as I have begun a different kind of writing, I think it's pertinent. Yes, the fragment leaves many more opportunities for us to speak it, and write it, and narrate it. But it also holds a danger. And the danger is that we will repeat the story of the fragment over and over and over again until the fragment and the memory of it become ossified. Primo Levi warns, for example, that repeating the story of the memory ["of the offense"] too often without giving it some breath and release can lead to its "installing itself in the place of raw memory and growing at its expense."[1] Although the fragment aids the project of textual representation, it is also a limit, a boundary that must be crossed.

Sidonie Smith: This is going to tie into my next question. Do you think that the spaces between the fragments are always spaces of possibility? Have you thought as you've been working of constantly repositioning the fragments vis-à-vis one another, and where the reference to the mother comes in the first one?[2]

Marlene Kadar: I'm not sure. Maybe I can't answer your question as gracefully as you have asked it. One can eventually use the journey as a scholar to somehow organically change those fragments or enhance the historical record. So for example, lists are important sources in Holocaust research, or research about the *Porrajmos* or "the Devouring" [the Roma Holocaust]. I discovered the extermination or death lists from the segregated so-called "gypsy camp" in the archives at Auschwitz[-Birkenau]. I treated a list as if it were a primary text in order to amplify uneven features of a Roma lament—so it performed the work of standing in for conventional finished forms of life writing, such as memoirs, as did the lament.

The singer of the lament "Oshwitsate" mourns the fact that her husband is inside Auschwitz-Birkenau and she's outside. The [singer of the] verse begs the guard to let her in to see him or to release him. When I discovered her name—Ruzena Danielova—I was able to go to the archive at Auschwitz and find the death list on which her name appeared. What I learned from that was that there were many other relatives who were taken with her and to whom she had referred obliquely in the song. I thought that might be an answer to your question. In other words, there was a way for the fragments to build on each other and to provide me with historical variants that I needed in order to proceed with the question, how are we going to represent the Roma devouring if we don't have published or translated texts? The answer appeared to be: use stand-ins for memoirs and other autobiographical texts, such as fragments.

Sidonie Smith: This turns to your practice of writing now. Can you tell us something about what things you have around you as you write? What's the feeling of writing now as you're working on, what do you call it, do you call it memoir?

Marlene Kadar: What I'm doing?

Sidonie Smith: Yes.

Marlene Kadar: I don't call it a memoir. I call the various pieces individual stories. There is a lot of autobiographical impetus, but I do manipulate the facts to make each story interesting. The overwhelming feeling I have is that now that I've crossed over, it's effortless for me to—explore is too boring a word—to go down there and under. Witnessing my own mother's aging process has offered me some guidelines about both the limits and the promise of memory. Within her speech and her sentences, her stories often don't make sense, like the one she told with conviction about the nurses and doctors taking the blind patients to the roof of the hospital and pushing them off. She was convinced that this had happened. I wanted very much to try and imitate the way she was thinking and feeling so I could fulfill my role as daughter more fully. I thought it was much more like Deborah Britzman said, it's more about how it feels than how I remember it: "the time of belatedness, when learning is made from loss" and discontinuity rather than a disavowal to engage what might be a traumatic memory of both.[3]

Sidonie Smith: Yes. So what has surprised you about writing autobiographically now? Has it unfolded the way you thought it would? Has it offered up the kinds of, and I'm going to put this in quotes now, the kind of "truths" you're after? You were talking about how it's coming, it's coming easily, the feel of it is pulling you. Are there other things that you've learned about or have found in it that would have surprised you if somebody had said this is what it's like, say ten or twenty years ago?

Marlene Kadar: I guess I would have been surprised. Could you give me a hint about how I could face this? What direction should I go to answer this question? What surprised me? What really surprised me was that when supposedly writing autobiographically I wanted to pervert "the truth," the facts even more than I should have because the truth did not satisfy; I could not avoid "a painful encounter."[4] What the facts revealed isn't really the same as what I learned in the last five years from my experience, learning that comprises my present.

Sidonie Smith: I think there's a kind of renegade response to play with—to recognize the need to play with—what truth-telling is, or is defined as being. Even more than your theoretical analysis would allow you. To learn even more about the sliminess, or the shimmeriness, of the autobiographical.

Marlene Kadar: It's true. I have a noble teacher in Patrick Modiano, also consumed by literature's representation of memory and trauma, especially in *Dora Bruder*, a novel that tells the story of the disappearance of young Dora during the Nazi occupation of Paris in 1941. Why did his protagonist urgently need to search for the fifteen-year-old Jewish Dora Bruder after the war? The writing makes me think about the unsettling spaces [of loss and forgetting] that need to be imagined when the memoir form is fictionalized in order to memorialize a life. Magda Szabó uses the genre also to explore a writer's disconcerting relationship with her housekeeper in *The Door*. Contemporary memoirs of illness, such as Paul Kalanithi's *When Breath Becomes Air* or Susannah Cahalan's *Brain on Fire*, document medical delays and terrifying misdiagnoses and diagnoses that are equally disconcerting but do not purport to be fictional.

Sidonie Smith: You write in the piece that the unwell may have a hard time satisfying the highest ethical standards established by the nonfiction police because the story of illness is not romantic or happy. And so they may lie or write about something that resembles a lie.

Marlene Kadar: That's me.

Sidonie Smith: When you say lie or the resemblance of a lie, that's a really interesting parsing of it, not to land just on the lie, but to land on the resemblance of the lie. But I'm going to change …

Marlene Kadar: … the subject.

Sidonie Smith: Talking about your practice, or your professional life over the last several decades. As Eva said in the introduction, and everybody remarks, you've been a consistently collaborative scholar … . Indeed, you are a part of the cabal of Canadian scholars, the majority of them from the province of Alberta.

Marlene Kadar: And who knows why?

Sidonie Smith: Right, I asked, why all these scholars of life writing who've radically transformed the field, who've opened up all these avenues, come out of Alberta. There's something so exciting about that, as I think of you in the center of this cabal, but also this collaborative ensemble of scholars. And I wonder if there was some discussion this morning with graduate students about the importance of collaboration. I wonder if you could talk, especially to the younger scholars, about what collaboration has meant to you, and what it is that it has allowed you to do that has become defining of your contributions in so many areas?

Marlene Kadar: Thank you very much for the question. The women with whom I've collaborated are distinguished scholars in the field. I'd like to tell you that the reason we collaborated in the first instance is because we can cross-fertilize each other's ideas, or working in a group is better than working alone. It is true that collaborative work can better suit the academic requirements of an interdisciplinary project. Apart from this, women scholars working in the life-writing genres in the early days were wary of the ways their work in the autobiographical could be excluded from discussions and literary planning ventures. Working together improves courage over time.

Sidonie Smith: I've done a lot of collaborative work and it's the same for me. I could do my own work—but I never could have done the projects I did without collaborating. That is how I became a better thinker. And also that sense of having partners, they aren't necessarily there with you, or on your own campus, but they're partners with whom you're going through your career. I think your experience was like mine. Sometimes you talk to people who have done a lot of collaboration and they've had terrible experiences. But I never had any of those terrible experiences.

Marlene Kadar: Me neither.

Sidonie Smith: Or falling outs. Or projects that didn't get done. You know.

Marlene Kadar: That's right.

Sidonie Smith: I think in part it was because of the friendships that became so deep that there was always a place to go when you were angry at one another, or when you were at an impasse. Or where one person was exhausted and another person wasn't.

Marlene Kadar: Or when one person knew how to hook up an iPad and you didn't.

Sidonie Smith: Exactly.

Marlene Kadar: I wanted to say one more thing. Yes, one hopes collaborative thinking makes one a better thinker; such claims have been made by feminist scholars such as Geraldine Pratt, and its suitability for interdisciplinary projects has been lauded by Linda Hutcheon. Moreover, collaborative research has the potential to make one a more generous thinker because you have to learn how to speak in a way that makes a quandary pliable and generative in spite of disagreements.

Sidonie Smith: Right. I wonder if you've had any sense of this. Julia Watson, with whom I've written a lot, said, "We have a third voice, it's neither your voice or my voice, it's a third voice." It took me a while to understand that this was probably right. That you gain, that there's something about a voice of people who work together, that can have qualities that aren't there in the writing that you do on your own.

Marlene Kadar: Right, I agree.

Sidonie Smith: I was just going to ask a devious question—do you still believe that there's a woman in women's writing? But we're not going to go there. So this is kind of a practical question, especially for someone who's done so much thinking about interdisciplinarity. It's a question that looks to the next generation of scholars. What do you see as the skills and capacities that emergent scholars of life writing now require, in addition to deep reading?

Marlene Kadar: I really want to answer this question. The first thing that I want to say is that three languages aren't enough. This doesn't mean that you have to be entirely fluent in the languages that you learn. But learning other languages provides a context that is just not replaceable in any other way. Besides which it makes you capable of following "the drinking gourd" [1928 American folksong]. In my own case: how could I follow the life of a Vienna-born concentration camp guard whose journey included disembarking in Halifax, Canada, and eventual immigration to the United States of America on the basis of documentation in which she declared she was "a hotel worker" in the German concentration camp system [at Ravensbrück near Fürstenberg/Havel, Germany] and Majdanek [Lublin, Poland]?

The next thing I thought about was my doctoral examining committee, a cabal of learned white European men who insisted on many languages in their PhD students as well. My external examiner was Jean van Heijenoort, who was Leon Trotsky's secretary during the difficult times—during Trotsky's exile abroad and eventually in Coyacan, Mexico City with Frida Kahlo and Diego Rivera. When Trotsky feared his life was going to come to an end earlier than he would wish, he arranged for his archival materials to be sold to the Houghten Library at Harvard University in 1940, not to be opened again until January 1, 1980. Van Heijenoort celebrated the opening by uncrating the papers he had forty years earlier crated. "Van," as he is known in the archives, delivered a welcome speech to visiting scholars, including a brief history of the papers in the previously closed section of Trotsky's exile papers. There is nothing that can replace that kind of intimate space where you work with a subject and have the opportunity to ask questions as clues and hints are slowly uncovered. Without Van's assistance, I would not have learned that Earl Brownstone was really Earl Birney, one of Canada's poet laureates, about whom I wrote an article in *Canadian Dimension*. Birney read the article and then sent me a postcard and he said, that's not me, I didn't write that piece you describe. It was an analysis about the Ukrainian farmers' movement in Alberta and Saskatchewan. He said, no no, I didn't do that. And then he invited me to meet him at U of T [University of Toronto], where I showed him the documents with the signature Earle Brownstone. I also showed him copies of his letters to Trotsky, and he, like Van Heijenoort years later, had to hold back his tears. He said, yes, that's me—it was his handwriting and his pseudonym. I now have a large two-way collection of letters between Earl Birney and Leon Trotsky.

There's one more thing. There is this need, this fearlessness that young scholars are much more capable of honing—a fearlessness to reach into the root, that is, into the *radical* idea that might be in the germ, might be part of the germ of the idea. And so the significance of the fearlessness of the young scholar cannot be underestimated.

Sidonie Smith: Hear, hear. So I think it's our final question. I want you to take us back to the 1980s and to tell us the story of your intellectual journey at the time you claimed life writing and feminist autobiography studies as your field. What were the passions, or the incentives, the struggles that motivated you and constrained you at the time?

Marlene Kadar: I've already touched on a few of those issues, but I've had the opportunity in the last five years to think about what I might have done that was useful or interesting or scary or dangerous or exciting. And in the first instance I needed a PhD dissertation topic and knew that it had to be of a certain type. I was committed to a notion of world revolution at that moment and wanted somehow for my writing to represent that wish, that desire, that need to improve social conditions for my brothers and sisters in Hungary and elsewhere. I took my doctoral project from a prodigious biography of Trotsky by Isaac Deutscher—a trilogy, the third volume of which is titled *The Prophet Outcast: Trotsky: 1929–1940*. And in that book and two short footnotes—barely legible because footnotes in those old Vintage books are so tiny—were two pieces of information that gave me the project that I wanted to pursue. One was that Trotsky's papers were in the closed section of the archives at Houghton Library. This section is described in detail in the bibliography under the heading *The Trotsky Archives*.[5] I learned that the archives had been closed on Trotsky's orders until January 1, 1980 in order to protect the correspondents. The other was, among the correspondence were letters exchanged between Trotsky and various artists, such as the editors of *Partisan Review* in New York and the Surrealists in Paris. Deutscher was given access to the closed section by Trotsky's widow, Natalya; he wrote brief explanatory notes about Dwight Macdonald and Philip Rahv[6] and about Andre Breton,[7] who, I later learned, wrote all of his letters to Trotsky in turquoise ink. In any case, these notes gave me the incentive I needed to propose a theory of cultural politics dominated by Trotsky and his literary and political ideas, which I developed in my PhD dissertation, titled "Cultural Politics in the 1930s: *Partisan Review*, the Surrealists and Leon Trotsky."

Apart from numerous political works, Trotsky had written a diary, an autobiography, and two books about literature and art. His theory of literature and art challenged the value of "proletarian art" because, for him, it represented a proletarian regime that is meant to be "temporary and transient." This regime, he argued in 1924, lays the foundation of a culture that is above classes. Thus, various cultural schools or groups, such as the Surrealists or the Mexican muralists, or the writers and editors at *Partisan Review*, he reasoned, must be allowed "complete freedom of self-determination in the field of art."[8] I wanted to explore this identity further in the archives, which led me to many other places, like the passionate correspondence between Frida Kahlo and Ella Woolf. My research was guided by Van Heijenoort and by Ella Woolf, both of whom were working at Stanford University or in its archives in the Hoover Institution Library and Archives. It was only days after meeting with Van that he was called to his estranged fourth wife's home in Mexico City. His wife, Ana Maria Zamora, the daughter of Trotsky's Mexican lawyer, shot him in his sleep before taking her own life. It is this mixture of influences—of lives found in the archives, of the autobiographical and the biographical, of persistent political and human longings—that got me hooked on life writing.

Sidonie Smith: That is such a high point to leave on. Please join me in thanking Marlene for this wonderful conversation.

Notes

1. Levi, Primo. *The Drowned and the Saved*. Trans. Raymond Rosenthal. New York: Vintage. 24.
2. The reference here is to Kadar's story "Dross," published in this issue.
3. Britzman, Deborah. *Lost Subjects, Contested Objects: Toward a Psychoanalytic Inquiry of Learning*. SUNY P, 1998 118–19.
4. Britzman 119.
5. Deutscher 530.
6. Deutscher 430–33.
7. Deutscher 30, 431–32.
8. Trotsky, Leon. *Literature and Revolution*. Ann Arbor: U of Michigan P. 14. Ann Arbor Paperbacks for the Study of Communism and Marxism.

Forum: The Work of Marlene Kadar

A|B

In Brief: The Work of Marlene Kadar

By Eva C. Karpinski

The ten essays gathered in the Forum section were originally presented as plenary sessions at the 2017 International Auto|Biography Association Chapter of the Americas conference. The authors approach the question of Marlene Kadar's influence on their own work and on the field of life writing at large from a variety of perspectives, offering personal testimonials, metacritical assessment, and applied critical analyses. While Linda Warley and Julie Rak emphasize the feminist roots of Kadar's ethics of criticism, evidenced in her respect for collaborative process and for understanding reading as an act of witnessing, Julia Galbus situates Kadar's research alongside Louise DeSalvo's work to draw attention to the ethical challenges of working on morally compromised or objectionable subjects of archival memory. Focusing on the archive as an epitome of the fragment, Patrick Taylor's essay excavates the silenced family history linking colonial Barbados to Toronto. Elizabeth Podnieks scans a digital archive of an early twentieth-century fan magazine for its representations of silent-film stars who became mothers. Linda Morra calls for expanding the queer archive of Jane Rule to include paratextual elements preserved in the writer's dispersed library. Similarly, Mark Celinscak reports on his archival discovery of the unrecognized role of Canadian military personnel in the liberation of the Bergen-Belsen concentration camp. The final three essays offer case studies applying Kadar's theoretical and methodological insights. Rachel Dubrofsky discusses the notorious case of the Auschwitz selfie in order to investigate the role of affect and gender stereotypes in popular-press depictions of young women. Helen Buss reflects on the efficacy of anecdotal life writing in the work of Vietnamese French Canadian writer Kim Thuy. Finally, Ozlem Ezer addresses the lives of Syrian refugee women whose narratives of successful integration confound dominant media stereotypes. Altogether, the Forum essays constitute a fitting tribute to Kadar, supporting the argument that her work deserves more visibility.

Mar and Me: Following the Traces

By Linda Warley

It is truly my privilege to reflect on the influence that Marlene Kadar's scholarship has had on my own thinking, for she has had a hand in shaping not just the work I have done (and continue to do), but also the way in which I do my work.

For more than twenty years, I have been following and learning from Marlene Kadar. It all began when I read her edited collection *Essays on Life Writing* while I was a doctoral student working on my own research on situated subjectivities in contemporary Canadian and Australian life writing. Here was a book that brought together *Canadian* scholars, mostly *women* scholars, to theorize what life writing can be and what life writing does. Here was a book that included an essay by my then professor, Shirley Neuman, whose graduate seminar on autobiography changed my whole relationship to the poststructuralist cultural theories prevalent at the time. Here was a book that modeled that deeply thoughtful, respectably theoretical scholarship about life writing did *not* have to deny the person-in-the-world who had a personal story to tell.

Neuman's course and Kadar's book, along with Sidonie Smith and Julia Watson's *De/colonizing the Subject*, which was published in the same year as Kadar's, came at the right time for me. The late 1980s and 1990s, when I was a graduate student doing my doctoral work at the University of Alberta, were the days of "the subject," not the person. The author was "dead"; identity was not inherent but a social construct; experience was not, well, experienced but discursively constructed as something that we recognized as experience; subjects might believe they had agency, but agency too was part of the ideological systems that shape us all; truth claims were under suspicion. I read all the big theorists of the day, including Paul de Man, whose essay "Autobiography as De-facement" argued that the "I" of autobiography is nothing more than a trope, a metaphor. But I was troubled. I was troubled not because I was so naïve as to think that ideology and discourse have nothing to do with shaping how we understand ourselves to be selves—or subjects (I use the term too)—but because I was studying life narratives written by Indigenous and Aboriginal people in Canada and Australia whose lands, histories, truths, and identities had been stolen, distorted, discounted, and denied. It felt politically and ethically wrong to me to analyze their autobiographical narratives through the lenses of then-dominant Eurocentric continental theories associated with post-structuralism. But I was also not prepared to go down the dead-end path of cultural relativism. I was searching for a methodology that would permit me as a reader and critic to listen to the stories of these Indigenous and Aboriginal authors and to understand how they used language—English, a non-Indigenous language—to shape their identities and tell of their personal and communal experiences.

What I found in the chapters gathered in *Essays on Life Writing* was a way of conceiving of autobiographical telling as a critical practice, rather than a thing—autobiography as an act, not a genre or a set of genres around which certain kinds of scholars would wish to put borders. In that book, Kadar legitimized the term "life writing" (even though not all autobiographical texts are either written or narrated), which to my mind demonstrates a flexibility and generosity of mind that honors both what people do when they tell, sing, dance, perform, paint, or write their lives and how we might understand the significance of those acts. Life writing matters, not only to those who tell their personal stories, but also to those who engage with them.

What I have termed Kadar's flexibility and generosity of mind extends to her personal and professional relationships as well, including with those just entering the field. In 2000, at the International Auto|Biography Association world conference at the University of British Columbia, a woman sat down beside me at Philippe Lejeune's keynote address on "How Do Diaries End?" "Hi. I'm Marlene Kadar," she said, and turned to me with a smile on her face. I believe I audibly gasped. She behaved as if she were pleased to meet me, whereas I was gobsmacked that she was even talking to me. I had been invited to the University of British Columbia to be part of a collaborative research group that was planning to apply for a large, multi-institution research grant (a Social Sciences and Humanities Research Council Major Collaborative Research Initiative grant, or SSHRC MCRI, as they were called), with the ultimate aim of establishing an auto|biography research center in Canada (among other projects). Our late and much-missed colleague Gabriele Helms and I were definitely the most junior members of that group. Ultimately, we did not win the grant, but collaborative projects ensued anyway. There were meetings and conferences at York University and at the University of

Calgary. Eventually, Kadar and I, along with Jeanne Perreault and, for the first project, Susanna Egan, went on to coedit two books and a special issue of a journal together. To my mind, the research meetings at the University of British Columbia began something important in life-writing studies in Canada. They affirmed collaboration as a desirable model of scholarship. And not just pairs of scholars—like the publishing power-house duo of Smith and Watson—but collaboration among groups of individuals. I will return to the issue of collaboration later, but I have more to say about Kadar's scholarship.

It was when I read her essay for our first book, *Tracing the Autobiographical*, that I saw how much Kadar could stretch the idea of life writing even further and find even more lives, vulnerable lives, in the most unexpected places. In that essay, Kadar considers the case of the Roma people who were exterminated in the Nazi death camps. She finds the survivors who did not write their stories as memoirs but, instead, relied on the recording of personal experience and collective memory through oral story and song. She goes further: she argues that even when no self-narrated text is extant, the witnessing of others can stand in for the autobiographical act, becoming a biography of a person—a life, a self—who is more than a name on, for instance, a deportation list. She states in that essay that she "want[s] to propose the fragment and the trace as member-genres in the taxonomy of auto/biographical practices" ("Devouring" 223). These traces and fragments represent lives; they contain stories; they honor particular people. They preserve histories. And note again that she puts the emphasis on auto|biographical practices— what people do when they tell their life stories and what we do with those stories when we receive them.

I told Marlene at the time that I thought this was the best thing she had ever written. I still think so, for it still stands as a model of an ethical critical practice, a way of reading life stories that do not actually seem to be there. Not to recognize and affirm these traces and fragments would be to consign the Roma people who perished in what they call "the Devouring" to the recesses of history—a kind of history that calculates numbers and talks about communities but is seemingly incapable of recognizing the individuals who had particular lives and particular stories to tell. Nor is such a history capable of empathy; one of the other great things that Marlene has taught me is that autobiographical practices are not just about what happened, but how what happened is felt. She draws on Deborah Britzman's discussion of "difficult knowledges" and reminds us that "Memory registers what it felt like, not exactly what it was like" (223). I have never forgotten that comment and quote it often in my own work. To experience the lives of others, expressed in whatever medium, is to enter into a relationship that is at once intellectual and emotional. Why else do people read memoirs if not to discover something of the people who wrote them? Why care about those people unless the shape of a self constructed in a text somehow touches the reader—a touch that can scale the emotional continuum from love and identification to horror and rejection?

Kadar's life-writing scholarship opens up the possibility of finding lives in unexpected places. It also shows us how a careful analysis of those lives (represented in whatever genre—letters, personal documents, songs, self-portraits, memoirs, etc.) can tell us much not just about the particular human subjects who created the texts (or are named by the text), but also about the historical and political contexts of their times. Kadar's scholarship is always carefully theorized and historicized. She conducts extensive research but also conducts fieldwork. Of course, all scholars travel to conferences and archives, but how often do we do research *in situ*, conducting our research as some kind of life-writing anthropologists? Certainly Kadar travels to archives, as she did when she explored the "epistolary constellation" between Leon Trotsky, Frida Kahlo, and Earle Birney (among others) during the anti-Stalinist leftist political climate of the 1930s and 1940s. But sometimes she also travels in order to be in a particular place, to feel the place, to experience the stories that places themselves have to tell, as she did when she traveled to Germany and the Nazi concentration camp for women and girls called Ravensbrück. That was also a trip to an archive. As she explains in "Ambivalent Image: Twisted Use" (which was published in our second book, *Photographs, Histories, and Meanings*), the Ravensbrück Concentration Camp Archives had opened in 1994, and there she viewed an album of propaganda photographs that were intended to be part of "National Socialist Concentration Camp quality control history" (73). Kadar unpacks the status of one so-called "Inspection photograph" that documents a visit to the camp by SS Reichsführer Heinrich Himmler. These photographs were staged. Their purpose was to present a "sanitized … picture of the camp to international visitors and agencies, such as the Red Cross" (75). Kadar rightly insists that it is our duty as critics to "lift the veil" of such seemingly "documentary" photographs. But I know, because I was with her at a conference at the University of Athens, where she first presented this work, that she also took her own photographs of the camp and its surroundings, showing, for instance, a lovely lake just adjacent to the Ravensbrück camp. Only through fieldwork would the critic be able to experience that particular tension between beauty and horror. In that essay, Kadar makes her reader feel, as well as look at, a concentration camp and its particular surroundings.

Kadar's scholarship always has a political edge to it. That is an understatement. It is thoroughly feminist—another understatement. It is informed by a deep sense of social justice. Her scholarship takes the shape of an ethical critical practice. She is not interested in the narcissist or the famous person (well, except for Kahlo, perhaps); she is interested in the almost lost, the wounded or murdered, the women and girls whose stories have been silenced, submerged, or distorted. Kadar's scholarship is a practice of care.

Marlene extended her practice of care to me when she invited me to take part in an editing collective, first with Perreault and Egan and later with just her and Jeanne. To be honest, I was nervous, terrified even (and not just because of the usual imposter syndrome so many academic women live with every day). I was nervous because although I had some previous coediting experience, I had never worked on what I considered to be such important projects. Books! In life-writing studies! In photography and cultural studies! Furthermore, I would be editing papers written by academics who were much more established and accomplished than I was at that time. Who was I to tell Helen Buss how to improve her paper?

We embarked on a wonderful collaboration, producing the two books I have already mentioned and *Life Writing in International Contexts*, a special issue of the journal *ARIEL*. Thousands of emails passed among us. Marlene's voice was pretty much my daily companion. I missed her if she did not send me an email every day. Her voice was so supportive, thoughtful, generous, wise, encouraging—and funny! I loved her wit and her insight. I still do. I still miss those almost daily emails.

I worked harder with and for those women than I ever would have for myself. Collaborative research and authorship are common aspects of many disciplines, particularly in STEM (science, technology, engineering, and mathematics) and the social sciences. But not in my discipline. Not in English. Coauthorship is undervalued in my discipline (though I think this is slowly changing). My discipline continues to valorize the single-authored paper or, even better, a single-authored monograph as the highest academic achievement. By choice, I have been working collaboratively for most of my career, beginning with a couple of coauthored articles and book chapters with Renée Hulan, whom I first met in graduate school when we were both doing our Master's degrees at the University of Guelph. That too was a joy, and I am proud of the work we produced together. But when I came up for tenure and promotion in 2000, my coauthored papers counted as half a paper, even though anyone who has written with others knows that it takes considerably longer to produce the finished work, and the work is better because you have your best reader by your side. It is also worth noting that unlike in the STEM disciplines, where the order of names establishes who is the "first" (i.e. the main) author, in the coauthored and coediting work I have done, names (except on one occasion) have been listed alphabetically. As a "W," I am almost always last. But I do not care. I do my best work when I am thinking and writing with other people. And I certainly have more fun.

Jeanne and Marlene and I did most of our work over email, sending documents and drafts as digital attachments, "talking" by computer sometimes several times a day. Yet long-distance relationships need some face-to-face time, and these scholarly working relationships needed that too. So, at some point during these projects, we would gather. The first such meeting took place at Marlene's house in Toronto: that was *Tracing the Autobiographical* work. When we were working on the special issue of *ARIEL*, we met at my house in Kitchener. Once we went to Santorini, Greece, following a conference in Athens. While walking and overlooking the beautiful sea, we dreamed up the *Photographs, Histories, and Meanings* book. We worked on that book in Mexico. In Mexico, I remember Jeanne and Marlene taking draft chapters down to the beach to read and edit them. I could not do that; I was not so self-disciplined. I worked in the coffee shop and met up with them later for beach and margaritas. I remember Marlene and Jeanne splashing about in the waves like children. I am not a strong swimmer and was afraid of the big waves and strong current. Memorably, astonishingly, one day Jeanne went parasailing. I loved the fierce intelligence and courage of these women. I loved working with them. We worked hard during those gatherings, but we also had tremendous fun and built up a cache of glorious memories. Our friendships, as well as our professional connections, deepened.

I also learned an awful lot from Jeanne and Marlene not just about the scholarly contexts of the books we were shaping, but also about the editing process. I learned how to read with more care than I would for a peer review—more care because this was our book. Our names would be on the title page. And we wanted to present to our communities the very best work we could pull together. I learned how to help the authors whose papers I worked on see where there were gaps or redundancies; I learned how to ask questions that would prompt the author to go deeper; I learned how to be provocative but kind. I tried to be a good feminist editor, as my collaborators were and are.

I have modeled my more recent collaborative scholarly endeavors on the ways in which I learned to work with Marlene and Jeanne. Last year, Candida Rifkind and I coedited and published *Canadian Graphic: Picturing Life Narratives*. In that volume, Candida and I coauthored the introduction. I also coauthored a chapter of the book with my life collaborator—my husband, Alan Filewod. Collaboration continues in my career. Most recently, Eva C. Karpinski and I have coauthored a chapter for a volume being edited by the Romanian scholar Simona Mitroiu on wom-en's memories of Central and Eastern Europe. This latest chapter was also the result of fieldwork. In conducting research into my German maternal family's history as refugees during World War II, I felt I had to do more than library research. I had to be in the place that was my mother's Pomeranian home. I needed to see and feel the place where she was born and from which she escaped as a refugee with her mother and grand-mother in the final months of the war in advance of the Russian army that was about to overrun them. And I needed to be there with Eva, who herself was born in Poland, in a city that was once German: Wrocław|Breslau.

So, in 2015, Eva and I traveled to what is now the Polish village of Kępice, and began the work of trying to understand the intertwined per-sonal stories of Germans and Poles who had both lived in that part of Eastern Europe at different moments in history. We alighted on the same train-station platform from which the women in my family were trans-ported west in cattle cars. We looked at the German style of architecture that characterized some of the buildings. And we talked to some of the Polish residents who were surely descendants of the Poles who themselves had been forced out of the east and relocated. We found fragments of German headstones in a graveyard. We read the place as a palimpsest. We too experienced the complicated stories that places themselves have to tell.

This essay is titled "Mar and Me: Following the Traces," but it is really about "Mar and us," a community of scholars with a commitment to eth-ical, political, feminist, nuanced, flexible, open-minded approaches to the study of life-writing texts in all media, genres, and subgenres, the literary and the "nonliterary"—those works that are recognized as being part of "high culture," but perhaps more urgently those that are associated with "low" or "popular" culture. Even those life stories that are found only in fragments.

Mar and us. I now draw attention to the hugely important role that Marlene Kadar has played in the field of life writing through her work as general editor of Wilfrid Laurier University Press's Life Writing Series. This series has put life-writing scholarship in Canada on the map. It does not publish solely Canadian texts or Canadian authors, but there sure are a lot of us in that series. And what a wonderful series it is to be part of. I quote from the Press's own description: "In the Life Writing series, Wilfrid Laurier University Press publishes life writing and new life-writing criticism and theory in order to promote autobiographical accounts, dia-ries, letters, memoirs and testimonials written and/or told by women and men whose political, literary, or philosophical purposes are central to their lives" ("Life Writing").

This description contains the touchstones of Kadar's view of the field—life writing as a capacious term that is inclusive of many genres; life writing by women and men (women first); life writing that foregrounds the political, the literary, and the philosophical aspects of personal lives; life writing that invites new ways of theorizing and interpreting what it means to construct a self in that place, in that context, in that time; life writing as practice; life-writing scholarship as ethical critical practice. That is a scholarly world that I am honored to be part of. That is the world I found when I first encountered Marlene Kadar as scholar and woman. And that is the kind of scholarship I have tried to pass on to those who will follow me.

Works Cited

Kadar, Marlene. "Ambivalent Image: Twisted Use." *Fhotographs, Histories, and Meanings*. Ed. Kadar, Jeanne Perreault, and Linda Warley. New York: Palgrave, 2009. 73–89. Print.

—. "The Devouring: Traces of the Roma in the Holocaust: No Tattoo, Sterilized Body, Gypsy Girl." *Tracing the Autobiographical*. Ed. Kadar Marlene, et al. Waterloo: Wilfrid Laurier UP, 2005. 223–46. Print.

—. "An Epistolary Constellation: Trotsky, Kahlo, Birney." *Working in Women's Archives: Researching Women's Private Literature and Archival Documents*. Ed. Helen M. Buss and Kadar Marlene. Waterloo: Wilfrid Laurier UP, 2001. 103–13. Print.

"Life Writing." *Wilfrid Laurier University Press*. WLU Press, n.d. Web. 21 Apr. 2018.

Marlene Kadar's Life Writing: Feminist Theory Outside the Lines

By Julie Rak

In 1989, as part of her landmark collection *Essays on Life Writing: From Genre to Critical Practice*, Marlene Kadar wrote an introduction called "Coming to Terms: Life Writing—from Genre to Critical Practice" and included another essay, "Whose Life Is It Anyway? Out of the Bathtub and into the Narrative." With these two essays, Kadar created what should be a touchstone for everyone working in the field of life writing today, one that is as intimately concerned with the ethics of reading as much as it is with writing by ordinary people, in extraordinary forms, when writers and forms appear as testimony. Life writing, as Kadar conceives it, is meant to be a way to see what has been overlooked and to bear witness to that, to understand the activity of bringing a life into view through a text. In Kadar's work, the act of criticism itself is deeply socially responsible, and responsive, to the other who writes or is written about.

But what should be a touchstone isn't, or at least it isn't yet. Kadar was the first critic to frame life writing as a way to name a genre and a critical practice together, but major works in life writing criticism focus only on life writing as a more capacious term for autobiographical and biographical representation, neglecting the ethics of criticism Kadar sought to bring to the study of the area and not crediting Kadar for the first feminist use of the term. I propose to remedy this gap in the critical literature about life writing by reading Kadar's two early essays alongside two more she wrote: "The Discourse of Ordinariness and 'Multicultural History'" and a later, beautiful essay called "The Devouring: Traces of Roma in the Holocaust: No Tattoo, Sterilized Body, Gypsy Girl." Over time in these essays, Kadar thinks about life writing as a method that is deeply socially responsible to the texts and to the traces of life that can be found in ephemeral documents.

In order to get at the argument Kadar makes in this part of her work from the late 1980s and early 1990s, I think some context is necessary. When I first read Kadar's essay collection *Essays on Life Writing: From Genre to Critical Practice*, I was blown away by it because of what the critical landscape looked like in Canada at the time. As Shirley Neuman also observed in an issue of *Essays on Canadian Writing* devoted to autobiography, theory, and criticism of life writing, the "theory wars" were played out in autobiographical poetics too (4–6). As was the case elsewhere in the humanities, approaches in autobiography studies using critical theory paradigms were on the rise in the 1980s, along with a backlash against theory, broadly conceived. Internationally, in 1987 Sidonie Smith published *A Poetics of Women's Autobiography*, one of the first books of feminist autobiography theory that took on androcentrism as a discourse. It was joined by Carolyn Heilbrun's *Writing a Woman's Life* and important feminist collections by Shari Benstock and Bella Brodzki featuring other feminist theorists and critics.[1] Essay collections by James Olney were expressing tensions between liberal humanist and phenomenological approaches to autobiography, and there were debates too about poststructuralism's premature announcement of the death of the autobiographical subject.[2] Structuralists Philippe Lejeune (1983) and Elizabeth Bruss (1976) were writing about what made autobiography a genre. Critics of African American literature were rethinking what the slave narrative meant as autobiography.[3]

Feminist interventions at the time were concerned with questions of agency and representation during the poststructural and psychoanalytic turns. Almost none of this work appears in the first collection about Canadian autobiography, K. P. Stich's *Reflections* of 1988, a collection that Neuman later wrote explicitly did not feature "theory" essays and that did not have much reference to the developing international field of auto/biography scholarship. Neuman said that in Canada, only she and Susannah Egan were producing work about autobiography and questions of theory in the 1980s (5–6). Enter the work of Kadar in 1989 and her connecting of poststructuralism, international autobiography theory, and feminist critique in and through life writing. In her introduction, Kadar lays out three possible ways in which autobiography taxonomy has developed, and she makes the case for understanding "life writing as an inclusive term for biography and autobiography which predates the latter by centuries" ("Coming" 4). Today, the term "life writing" is mostly used in this way—for example, Margaretta Jolly's summary description of the *Encyclopedia of Life Writing* presents the term as a convenient way to understand all autobiographical and biographical production, within which subgenres of self-representation exist. Life writing includes not only autobiography and biography but also "letters, diaries, memoirs, family histories, case histories, and other ways in which individual lives have been recorded and structured" (Jolly). Sidonie Smith and Julia Watson in *Reading Autobiography* discuss life writing as a more heterogeneous and inclusive term for self-representational practices not part of the

Western canonical tradition of autobiography (4). In the past decade, "life writing" has become the term for the critical field devoted to studying many kinds of texts and even nontextual objects.

It's important to see here that Kadar was less interested in the term as an expression of "pure" inclusivity, however. She warns that there are androcentric assumptions in that term as there are in autobiography, and she is at any rate not all that interested in its origin ("Coming" 4–5). What she is interested in is thinking of life writing as what she calls a "genre" that includes ephemera, and most specifically, ephemera that are unpublished, by people without privilege, including many women, people of color and Indigenous people. Ephemera, she argues, again without much precedent, do not have to be narrative (10–12). In other words, it does not have to be something that can be paraphrased in order for it to be about a life or constructive of subjectivity.

Although the capacious use of such a term inevitably activates Derrida's law of genre, which sets a limit that must be exceeded in order for the limit to exist, a possibility Kadar raises herself (6), Kadar does see potential for the quotidian to be a response to the critique of autobiography through the poststructuralist work of Michael Sprinkler and Paul de Man as an impossible gesture, an address to the dead, in the latter's words (8–9). Kadar says that it is right to critique the truth claims and referentiality of autobiography as a genre, but it is also important to assess the *jouissance* of life writing that exceeds such terms, connecting it to the body, the world, and to politics (10–12). To do that work is to move away from the tendency to abstraction in genre theory and to think about what the details of a life add up to. Moving from the abstraction of "I" to an understanding of the history of enunciation creates for Kadar a feminist space within life writing for a "whatever singularity"—in Giorgio Agamben's words (1)—and a space for the critic to be a co-constructor of meaning. To pay fine-grained attention to what life writing can bring into being, Kadar ends the essay with a meditation about life writing not just as genre but as critical practice. Life writing "encourages the reader to develop and foster his/her own self-consciousness in order to humanize and make less abstract … the self-in-the-writing" ("Coming" 12). For Kadar, humanism does not seek here to restore grand narratives of humanity and recenter the "I," as some feminist critiques of poststructuralism in the social sciences were trying to claim, but to understand enunciation as grounded in what she sees as a deeply feminist and ethical response to any text about a life. Life writing is also life reading, and the standpoint of the critic should be brought into view as a kind of co-creation. This way of thinking about life writing is much rarer, and it renders the making of criticism about life writing texts more difficult, and rewarding.

This is the subject of Kadar's essay "Whose Life Is It Anyway?," a joyful piece about the problem of genre as an evaporating formation. If we think of genre as water in a jar and then we empty the jar to better see what is inside, we are tricked, Kadar writes, for the water will pour away and there will be nothing to see: "like water, the shape of genres does not really exist, and their essence cannot be captured" ("Whose" 153). Better, she suggests, to take up the example of Gail Scott in her novel *Heroine* and sit within the vessel itself, the multiplicity of life writing forms and narrative possibilities, to let the subject of a narrative be decentered, to be in the narrative and submerged within it, rather than tip the tub and pour out what is essential to subjectivity and the story (153–54). The world and writing of women, she says, has been treated as if it is a fiction in any case. To respond to such a charge is to sit squarely in genre, the place of *jouissance*, and connect *écriture au feminin*[4] to the critical act of self-life reading as well as writing (156). Such a method is interdisciplinary and it does not respect genre boundaries, but it respects the written and the speaking voice.

In 1996, Kadar developed the critical practice of life writing to bring into view how an unlikely source, the ethnographic story produced within and through discourses of multiculturalism in Canada, can contribute to poststructuralist and feminist debates about ethnicity and subjectivity. This essay, called "The Discourse of Ordinariness and 'Multicultural History,'" is for me a key intervention, and it has deeply influenced my own thinking. Kadar argues that feminist critics had recently used the narratives of ordinary writers who are not literary professionals as "evidence" of diversity and as a corrective to poststructuralist readings of the subject. Not so fast, Kadar says. Such "multicultural" texts do challenge the implicit values of the literary and of privileged forms of reading. They do facilitate the project of reclaiming and paying attention to the voices of women. But the act of reclaiming for feminism also brings into view the limits of official, government-sponsored multiculturalism and its valorization of depoliticized representations of difference that do not address questions of systemic racism and colonialism in Canada ("Discourse"). Kadar's text here is Ibolya Grossman's *An Ordinary Woman in Extraordinary Times*, a Holocaust narrative of survival by a Hungarian woman. Grossman's characterization of her ethnographic identity as that of survivor, Kadar argues, works as testimony to the survival of more than one event: the Shoah itself and the ordeal of displacement and xenophobia in Canada. Her home is taken from her. Now her home will be in the future, a time and not a place. This is not what multicultural discourse would have such an author say, because that discourse tends to emphasizes a place, Canada, as the place where ethnic conflict from the "old country" can be resolved. What Kadar calls "the life genres including self-portraits, letters, and testimonios—are better suited than is multicultural history to conveying, without pretence, the ordinary woman's experiences of how power is meted out" ("Discourse"). Grossman's story conveys what it felt like to survive, challenging multiculturalism's narrative of the happy ending through its evocation of particulars, not abstractions or types, of identification. This is one of the first critiques I ever read of the limits of multicultural discourse. Kadar's work showed me the possibilities of testimony when it constructs its own agency, apart from discourses of truth, value, and celebrity that can inform the work of other kinds of better-known texts.

Kadar's essay in *Tracing the Autobiographical* about the fate of the Roma in the Holocaust is another working-out of her earlier thoughts about the importance of ephemera, interdisciplinary and theoretically informed analysis, and the ethics of witnessing. By 2005, when it was published, Kadar had become interested in the developing fields of trauma theory and memory studies. "The Devouring: Traces of Roma in the Holocaust: No Tattoo, Sterilized Body, Gypsy Girl" brings together aspects of those fields with a sensitive and astute attention to detail that can break a heart: the three figures (or hauntings, or fragments) Kadar investigates are a way to argue that when narratives of survival are lost or could not ever be produced, what is left must be made central to any investigation: autobiographical ephemera, fragments, names, oral stories, songs. These, Kadar says, stand in for other kinds of historical and autobiographical works of testimony ("Devouring" 223). They *are* testimony, and the work of the critic is to stand with and beside them and say what they are as an act of witnessing in the present because there were no witnesses in the past. In this sense, "The Devouring" is a companion to Philippe Lejeune's essay "The Autobiography of Those Who Do Not Write" and its model of collaboration as a creative process involving an internalization of a story by another so that the story can be told (190–91).

I would like to consider what it might mean to "stand in" as a critical practice. Kadar references Dori Laub's discussion of witnessing as an important aspect of what can be given to testimonials when an event such as a genocide unfolds without anyone to recall it or give it context ("Devouring" 225). Fragments and traces here do the work of a complete story of an event "where no other finished, polished, printed, or published autobiographical or life-writing texts exist" (223). The fragment and the trace are "member-genres in the taxonomy of auto/biographical practices" (223) because they record what an event felt like but without the context of what happened (224). That context, like a witness, was denied to those who made the fragments. Working from Blanchot's formulation of knowledge as "an unfinished separation that is always reaching out for further interpretation" (224), Kadar understands the fragment as part of "necessarily unfinished genres that call out to us to *attempt* to finish them. I say attempt because the job can really never be accomplished" (226). In the case of the Roma, whom the Nazis tried to wipe out, there are few full narrative sources that record their experiences during the genocide, called by them "the Devouring" (223). What remains, Kadar says, are fragments and traces of what they went through. The role of the critic here is to have those traces stand in where completed autobiographies never will, an act of finishing something that does not close off the representational possibilities of the fragment.

I do not understand Kadar's "standing in" as an act of finishing someone's sentences or interrupting something that is happening already. Rather, Kadar's method gives place to the fragment as a nub or kernel of a story and provides context so that something of the kernel can be grasped in its own fullness and on its terms. She discusses the story "Traces" by Ida Fink as difficult knowledge in Deborah Britzman's sense, a being inside of an event that the speaker and the interlocutor record but without an independent frame of reference ("Devouring" 224). Kadar also reads the deportation list of Roma, with its names instead of narratives, as a story that stands in for those whose voices were taken from them. Kadar's research on tattooing in the camps brings into view tattoos as a marking and numbering designed to dehumanize the Roma (among others), a sign of what they were marked for. But at the same, tattoos were a sign of life, because Kadar discovers that Roma who were not tattooed were probably sent directly to be gassed. The heterogeneity of the tattooing practice, and the folk practices of Roma in the camps who had tattoos of their own, brings into view tattoos as a kind of life writing in themselves, what Kadar calls "an autobiographical symbol both of an erasure of identity and evidence of a life" (234).

Kadar ends this essay with a discussion of a Roma song about Auschwitz that exists in different oral versions. The song itself is by a woman whose husband is incarcerated. It is a song of mourning and of sorrow as well as anger at what is happening. Each time it is sung, it is taken up autobiographically by the new singer, who stands in for the body of the composer and the beloved. Kadar's role here, when she reproduces the lyrics of the song, translated into English, is to be another person who stands in for those who cannot continue to represent what it means. As she says, to stand in is to further the work of witnessing. It is an act of love and respect to do this, and it is a way to learn as well: "even as we love the numerous autobiographers who have stood in for that first historical witness in this song" (244).

What, then, can Kadar's version of life writing give to the field of life-writing studies as it shoots off in new directions? I think that the importance of the work lies in its continued insistence on so-called minor genres of life writing: the unpublished diary, the letter, ethnographic documents, the list, the song as central to questions of value. Kadar understood that we would need to use different kinds of methods to understand what these minor genres are doing, and she understood that the work of ordinary people has dignity and gravity and deserves critical respect and attention. She focused in these essays on the small details as a way to work through the problems of theoretical abstraction, without letting the details obscure larger ethical issues inherent in memory practices. And she brings the role of the theorist into view not as another autobiographer but as a witness. I think that this last emphasis is vital as Indigenous life writing texts and other stories are considered within colonial frameworks (which they often critique) and within other kinds of genres that are culturally specific. In life writing studies, so often we use the term "life writing" as a catch-all, a vessel, but we don't climb inside it and make part of our work the work of standing in. It is time to pay attention to this way of doing the work of life writing. Whose life is it anyway, Marlene Kadar has asked us. That question, I hope, can form the basis for more work in life writing studies on the politics and ethics of paying critical attention.

Notes

1. See Smith 3–20 on androcentrism. Important feminist scholarship from the late 1980s includes Heilbrun's *Writing a Woman's Life*, Benstock's collection *The Private Self*, and Brodzki's collection *Life/Lines*. Also see Breé's key essay, "Autogynography," of 1986.
2. Olney edited two essay collections that were important for the development of life writing studies, particularly in the United States: *Autobiography: Essays Theoretical and Critical* of 1980 and *Studies in Autobiography* of 1988.
3. Smith's *Where I'm Bound* of 1974 is an early study of slave narrative as life writing. See also Olney's article for *Callaloo* and Andrews's *To Tell a Free Story* for arguments that slave narratives are autobiographical.
4. The critical term *écriture au feminine* describes the work of avant-garde Québec feminist writers (notably Nicole Brossard, Madeleine Gagnon, and Louky Bersianik) and anglophone Canadian feminist writers of the 1980s in experimental genres and forms of rhetoric that were meant to work against and beyond androcentric traditions. Such writing was informed by continental poststructuralist and psychoanalytic approaches to language but was also understood to have immediate political application. For critical background, see Carrière's introduction to *Writing in the Feminine*, 12–13.

Works Cited

Agamben, Georgio. *The Coming Community*. Trans. Michael Hardt. Minneapolis: U of Minnesota P, 1993. Print.

Andrews, William L. *To Tell a Free Story: The First Century of Afro-American Autobiography, 1760–1865*. 1988. Champagne: U of Illinois P, 2010. Print.

Benstock, Shari, ed. *The Private Self: Theory and Practice of Women's Autobiographical Writings*. Chapel Hill: U of North Carolina P, 1988. Print.

Breé, Germaine. "Autogynography." *Southern Review* Spring 1986: 223–45. Print.

Brodzki, Bella, ed. *Life/Lines: Theorizing Women's Autobiography*. Ithaca: Cornell UP, 1988. Print.

Bruss, Elizabeth. *Autobiographical Acts: The Changing Situation of a Literary Genre*. Baltimore: Johns Hopkins UP, 1976. Print.

Carrière, Marie. *Writing in the Feminine in French and English Canada: A Question of Ethics*. Toronto: U of Toronto P, 2002. Print.

Heilbrun, Carolyn. *Writing a Woman's Life*. New York: Ballantine, 1988. Print.

Jolly, Margaretta. *Encyclopedia of Life Writing*. 2 Vols. Chicago: Fitzroy Dearborn, 2001. Print.

Kadar, Marlene. "Coming to Terms: Life Writing From Genre to Critical Practice." *Essays on Life Writing: From Genre to Critical Practice*. Ed. Kadar. 1989. Toronto: U of Toronto P, 1992. 3–20. Print.

—. "The Devouring: Traces of Roma in the Holocaust: No Tattoo, Sterilized Body, Gypsy Girl." *Tracing the Autobiographical*. Ed. Kadar et al. Waterloo, ON: Wilfrid Laurier UP, 2005. 223–46. Print.

—. "The Discourse of Ordinariness and 'Multicultural History.'" *Essays on Canadian Writing* 60 (1996): 119–38. *Academic Search Complete*. Web. 13 May 2018.

—. "Whose Life Is It Anyway? Out of the Bathtub and Into the Narrative." *Essays on Life Writing: From Genre to Critical Practice*. Ed. Kadar. 1989. Toronto: U of Toronto P, 1992. 152–61. Print.

Lejeune, Philippe. "The Autobiography of Those Who Do Not Write." *On Autobiography*. Ed. Paul John Eakin. Trans. Katherine Leary. Minneapolis: U of Minnesota P, 1989. 185–215. Print.

—. "Le Pacte autobiographique (bis)." *Poetique: Revue de Theorie et d'Analyse Litteraires* 14 (1983): 416–34. Print.

Neuman, Shirley. "Introduction: Reading Canadian Autobiography." *Essays on Canadian Writing* 60 (1996): 1–13. Print.

Olney, James, ed. *Autobiography: Essays Theoretical and Critical*. Princeton: Princeton UP, 1980. Print.

—. "'I Was Born': Slave Narratives, Their Status as Autobiography and as Literature." *Callaloo* 20 (1984): 46–73. Print.

—. *Studies in Autobiography*. Oxford: Oxford UP, 1988. Print.

Smith, Sidonie. *A Poetics of Women's Autobiography: Marginality and the Fictions of Self-Representation*. Bloomington: Indiana UP, 1987. Print.

—. *Where I'm Bound: Patterns of Slavery and Freedom in Black American Autobiography*. Santa Barbara: Praeger, 1974. Print.

Smith, Sidonie, and Julia Watson. *Reading Autobiography: A Guide for Interpreting Life Narratives*. 2nd ed. Minneapolis: U of Minnesota P, 2010. Print.

Stich, K. P., ed. *Reflections: Autobiography and Canadian Literature*. Ottawa: U of Ottawa P, 1988. Print.

Working (with) History: Marlene Kadar and Louise DeSalvo

By Julia A. Galbus

Marlene Kadar and Louise DeSalvo ventured into their life-writing projects on World War II from starkly different perspectives. What connects them is their willingness to ask difficult questions about seemingly ordinary people, to engage in painful archival work, and to position themselves as self-conscious, deliberate participants in the transformative life writing each undertakes. In the introduction to the collection *Working Memory: Women and Work in World War II*, editors Kadar and Jeanne Perreault acknowledge the extensive and time-consuming patience necessary in archival research. Their volume's cumulative yield intertwines personal and national histories from World War II. They suggest that archival documents and photographs can lead to a writer's ability to "change things in the present by *working* memory" (3; emphasis added). Rather than treating historical facts and documents as static fragments of the past, the practice of excavating new details and piecing them together in the present allows Kadar to revise and correct what is remembered about her subject. Her truth-seeking creates the potential to turn the archives into an ethical space because Kadar restores the account of a singular life. The archives invite a moral query by allowing room for the interpretation of new artifacts in the present. At the same time, the repair is a reminder that we can never recover a complete story of anyone. We amend what is known to augment and revise our understanding and perception.

The pursuit of archival research implies an underlying desire not only to get the details right, to find evidence, solve puzzles, interpret in context, and notice what has been preserved, but also to forge new correlations actively. Always necessarily inexact and incomplete, one can only work with what is found. Not wanting to miss something, a researcher aims for thoroughness but realizes that much may be irresolvable. At the start of *Working Memory*, Kadar and Perreault emphasize the *creative* aspects of archival work and research, the pleasure of searching and recreating, especially because available information is always partial, leaving gaps of knowledge. They assert that we make sense of the past to change things, both in our understanding and in the public record. What we learn from the work we do is rooted in the specific details of a person's life, rather than fully representative of "some national or geopolitical agenda" (3). In the process, authors are intentionally disruptive, cracking open or stirring up, becoming "agents of creative responses to necessity" (3). Research deepens our understanding and contributes to the complexity of the emotional wake while facing historically laden details that can be intimate, daunting, and provocative.

Kadar's work potentially yields a transformative present understanding. Her essay "Resisting Holocaust Memory: Recuperating a Compromised Life" is introduced as a "meditation in progress" that begins with the "unsavoury life of Hermine Braunsteiner," a former concentration camp guard whose biographical details are constructed from archival fragments (111). Kadar explores the states of both resisting and following Braunsteiner, which has "helped [her] tolerate the incommensurable aspects of traumatic subjects and the unfinished work of remembering Hermine B" (111). In so doing, Kadar opts to preserve the tension. She has inquired about Braunsteiner's life and the governmental institutions that masked her identity and her migrations, without condoning her choices and without having a "last word." Telling this kind of story necessitates an open, irresolute end.

In her quest for information about her subject, Kadar pursues the biographical details that permitted Braunsteiner to live in Halifax, Nova Scotia, and Queens, New York, *after* she was convicted of war crimes. As Kadar explains: "I do not in any way want to suggest that the events of the Holocaust deserve forgiveness. What I want to explore is the possibility that the tender, poignant ambiguities of life writing (life writing writ large) 'complicate and dissemble the victim/perpetrator dichotomy in ways that encourage us to think through alternatives' to what Jill Scott calls 'blame and hatred,' even while it is clear where culpability lies" (112). Claiming we must *uncover* before we *overcome*, Kadar argues that "there is repressed material in the stories we tell ourselves about evildoers and 'the enemy among us,' about their difference from us, about our national purity and/or safe borders, and about humanity" (112). She has struggled against the myth of the moral superiority of women, knowing that Braunsteiner was a cog in the wheel of matrons staffing concentration camps. Kadar resists the urge to "find … a lesson" and therefore ameliorate the history of violent harm committed by Braunsteiner and others who worked in concentration camps. Deciphering more of Hermine's past is a way of seeking social justice; tracking Hermine makes her visible and accountable in the present. Even though her life has ended, her history has not. Kadar builds on the work of previous scholars who elucidate the moral quagmire of such an inquiry and refuses to sum up her findings into a tidy, less realistic, less complicated knot.

The peculiar and particular story of Hermine Braunsteiner involves incredulity, indignation, curiosity, and missing information. She worked at concentration camps in Germany and German-occupied Poland. Kadar discovered that Hermine was one of at least 3,950 matrons working in the Ravensbrück camp between 1939 and 1945. One hundred and thirty-two thousand women and children were incarcerated there. Prisoners were forbidden to call their supervisors by name, but they created nicknames as a way to bear witness. Braunsteiner was referred to as the "old mare." There is evidence that she was particularly brutal.

The available information about what happened after the war is piecemeal. Hermine fled Austria and headed to the US via Canada. Taking cover under a newly married name, she might have felt she was sheltered from her past. However, she became the first person to be denaturalized in the US for lying on her visa application. Many of the Canadian documents that might have aided Kadar's research had been destroyed, hidden, or lost. Hermine's husband had disappeared. A frustrated Kadar explains, "I had no interest in Hermine's life until it became impossible to ask questions about her life" (116). Fortunately, a Kansas storage facility had copies of identity papers later used for her hearing and deportation. Hermine was arrested in New York City in 1973 and extradited to West Germany, where she was convicted of war crimes a second time and received two consecutive life sentences. Yet in 1996, three years before she died, she was released from prison and lived in a German seniors residence supported by a pro-Nazi group with nonprofit status. Someone had intervened against justice again. Knowing that the long reach of the Holocaust is current and deeply entrenched in contemporary issues of immigration and various forms of prejudice, Kadar persisted. She found herself an "incredulous researcher who longs to know how it could happen" (122). "It" was the story of Hermine's life, as well as the lack of preserved evidence. Kadar explains the significance of Hermine's life and the complexity of the search: errors in the archives, assumptions about gender and brutality, multiple languages, and the passage of history all converge to yield a disturbing, fragmented portrait of a life.

Kadar employs carefully nuanced ethical judgment and historical correction not only to explain, but also to manage, emotionally and ethically, her pursuit of Hermine. She is appalled by the lack of careful documentation by government offices when it came to archiving the evidence of a war criminal. She is moved by the sheer number of matrons and female prisoners, and the cultural assumption that ordinary women would not become brutal. The details unsettle her as they unsettle the past and our understanding of the present.

In parallel to Kadar's self-reflexive performance of academic life writing, DeSalvo's *Chasing Ghosts: A Memoir of a Father, Gone to War* offers a more traditional personal memoir that also mines archival sources to come to grips with the effects of World War II not only on her life, but also on her Italian American neighborhood in New Jersey. Since she was a young child when her father fought in the navy, DeSalvo both researched and imagined her father's service alongside a generation of working-class soldiers. The archives she sought helped her map the location of the ships where he was deployed and understand his life as an airplane mechanic. Her father returned home after two tours deeply changed, but his wife, Mildred, and daughter, Louise, also experienced trauma in his absence and after his return. The title refers not only to her father's mistaken recognition of soldiers' faces when he walked the streets in New Jersey, but also to the longing for people the way they used to be, or the way they are remembered once they have changed.

DeSalvo also published *The Art of Slow Writing* a year earlier, which draws not only on how particular scenes in *Chasing Ghosts* were written, but also on the lives of dozens of writers who accumulate pages slowly and in complicated circumstances. Throughout both of DeSalvo's books, and in reading them together, one finds guidelines for flourishing in spite of the sometimes painful work of writing memoir. Both Kadar and DeSalvo use precisely selected, necessarily fragmented constructions of selves to direct their compassion not only toward their subjects, but also toward their audiences and, indirectly, themselves, thereby providing models of research for life writing that cultivate empathy without dismissing a subject's cruelty.

Sections of *Chasing Ghosts* are separated not only by titles, but also by the years when an incident occurs. Like Kadar, DeSalvo works memory by splicing periods of time, skipping between the past and the relative present. She starts with an uneasy truce between her and her father in his old age, after her mother has died and he has remarried. During the last two years of his life, he began talking to her and to her sons about the war. Learning his perspective, DeSalvo balances what she desired in terms of attention and affection from her father against what her father might have expected from his young family and from the navy. Her willingness to imagine his point of view creates gradual space for acceptance, and partial forgiveness, while acknowledging his physical and psychological abuse. Like Kadar, DeSalvo realizes that time and information have helped her come to terms with the family's past: 'As I begin to fill in the blanks of my father's early life in the navy, as I try to understand what it was like for him to be a sailor who would witness, first hand, his country's preparation for participation in a war that many civilians felt sure wouldn't happen, I begin to sense how those years must have affected him. But I don't begin to understand this until long after he's gone. And this, I believe, is the human condition: that we learn what we need to know about our parents after they've vanished from our lives" (61).

DeSalvo's father is not a hero, not "important" in the traditional historical sense. Initially, he enlists in the navy in order to leave his abusive and crowded home, and because he needs the work and the skills that he will acquire in the military. He also believes he has talent to offer the navy; his aptitude with automobile engines is valuable. He harbors a desire to become a pilot, but he is ineligible because he never graduated from high school. When he asks an officer whether he might be given the chance to be trained, the man replies, "when pigs can fly, son, then you can fly" (84). In the war, he served primarily as an airplane mechanic on an aircraft carrier. Although there are scenes of tension concerning how "direct" his combat experience is in contrast to pilots, DeSalvo learns that he was in danger every day he served, from enemy fire, from accidents related to doing dangerous work, and from orders that failed to put the safety of men ahead of the progress of the war.

Archival work allows writers to document infamous, damaged, and fierce people whose lives are worthy of examination. Kadar worked with civil documents of immigration and marriage, as well as news stories; DeSalvo used news clippings, history books, television programs, and maps to comprehend as much as she could about the specific details of US sailors' lives during World War II. Her immersion is so thorough that her husband warns, "I think you are trying to stop the war" (178). DeSalvo seeks tangible evidence of her father's work after reading about it. She tracks down a tool that her father helped to manufacture. A "transit theodolite," based on one taken from the Germans, "measures horizontal angles and elevations, to understand terrain, to map and direct artillery fire, to track weather balloons, to measure high altitude winds" (148). One of these tools functioned well during ten campaigns on her father's ship without being destroyed. Louise purchased one for $700 in 2005, and told her father. He considered her treasure "a terrible waste of money"; Louise was proud of the instrument, its beauty and heft, its wooden carrying case (149). It manifested his contributions to the war. Perhaps it also offset his mean temper.

The most difficult passage in *Chasing Ghosts* is the section called "Rage," where DeSalvo details her father's unpredictable temper. As she visited her father in a nursing home, she recalled the times she was told that her father was charming. He was never charming to her, only to other people, sometimes in front of her. One day, she watched him play checkers with an aide, whom he helped to win, and she thought, "nothing I can do will elicit such a smile" (201). When Louise and her father were alone in his room, he attacked her, and it took three people to pry him off and wrestle him into his bed. The nurses chalked it up to dementia. But, to her, "it's more the rest of my life" (202). The reader senses how much energy the visits cost Louise. When she returned from the nursing home, her husband suggested that she looked "like a beaten dog that's sidled up to its master trying to win his love" (201). Accommodating an often vicious man because he is family takes a toll on her psyche. He had not changed enough in his old age.

Louise recalls that when she was younger, her father beat her body (but never her face). He took all the locks off the doors inside the house so she could not lock him out. After each of his outbursts, though, she felt free to do as she pleased for a while. She refused to help her mother and grandmother clean up the messes he had made smashing plates and furniture. The women in the household kept silent, hoping not to provoke him again. But often, Louise's mother would lapse into a depression. The household was troubled. While things seemed normal from the outside, there was not enough food and she recalls few moments of nurturing parenting. "During the best of times, it felt like trying to balance on an ice flow that was racing toward a waterfall" (205). After the war, her father worked as a fireman. Louise remembers wishing he would die when he left to fight a fire. She trudges forward, a dutiful adult daughter, but becomes a prolific author with a tenacious work ethic that she credited to him. In 2009, Louise dreams that she is destroying her written pages to keep her father away, holding them up to him in defense. She tells him that no matter what he does, he will not stop her. She vows to herself, "I will write beyond him. I will not take what I write and offer it up to him in peace, protection, rage or honor" (206–07). Writing the book becomes not only protest and personal salvation, but also a contribution to working-class sailors and naval history. It is published in Fordham University Press's series on World War II: The Global, Human and Ethical Dimension.

Chasing Ghosts affords DeSalvo a way to come to grips with the complexity of her father's life. He was not a "war hero" in any typical sense, but he deserved a stalwart respect for the stress of serving in the US Navy and the aftermath of surviving, including the toll it cost his family. DeSalvo's resistance to making the book a peace offering demonstrates a resilience and a willingness to forestall a permanent resolution. As a form of testimony of her father's life, but also that of many World War II veterans, it echoes Kadar's dogged search and nuanced compassion toward her complicated subject. Both writers contextualize the circumstances of relatively ordinary people who deserve to be considered because they are emblematic of larger sociopolitical concerns related to World War II and the way it continues to affect families generations later.

For both authors, death is omnipresent. Theoretically, Kadar draws on Jacques Derrida's *Archive Fever: A Freudian Impression*, where Derrida uses Freudian concepts to argue that the archive yearns toward that moment of death and dying, a moment that we think about, regardless of our emotional response (*Working* 7). DeSalvo finishes her memoir after her father dies, but death haunts them both. She recalls what her father said about losing fellow soldiers: "'Every death is like that first death,' my father says. 'You're supposed to get over it. You pretend you're over it. You go about your business, you do what you have to do. There's always something to do, and work takes your mind off it. But you never get used to it, no matter what anyone says'" (*Chasing* 66). DeSalvo gradually realizes that all of her father's stories are elegies for what he has lost (96). As she neared the end of her formal writing career, the elegy for her father and his generation was the memory she chose to rework.

Archives are a major source of evidence; however, they also trigger the need to get the feeling and the tone of a text right. In the introduction to *Tracing the Autobiographical*, the editors (including Kadar) suggest that their book requires the reader to listen for the memory and the ethics of a text (3). Sometimes the details found in archives give an author pause. DeSalvo notes that her early drafts are often "constrained and safe" (*Art* 113). Pushing past that benign version requires courage as well as a willingness to tap into the "darker self" as a source of authentic work (265). Although it is possible to rely on memories or ideas of the past, of people, events, and situations, without seeking, knowing, or consulting the specificities that informed the past, its yield is skeletal. What we create, when we omit that context, is a shell, a sketch rather than a detailed schematic. Photographs, tools, newspaper clippings, and visits to neighborhoods and buildings provide clues and context for interpretation. That is something scholars of life writing intuit and experience—a fact that many of us emphasize in our classrooms but that can be strangely difficult to communicate, because there is never enough detail preserved and never a sense that the researcher has found everything. Although many human experiences are common, it is only through details that we can distinguish lives. Specifics revive the individual and collective communal past.

DeSalvo and Kadar both imagine the difficulty of being, or seeking to be, ordinary when the subject has had a complicated past. They address an implicit question about whose lives are worthy of study. Their archival work helps each of them to consider the implications of allowing a subject to remain ordinary, anonymous, unexamined. By bringing relevant details to light, and by allowing the unanswered questions to be articulated even without answers, they raise the historical value of seemingly ordinary people, insisting on their relevance.

In the most general terms, Kadar and DeSalvo write about gender and World War II history, using archival evidence to demonstrate how particular individuals were affected by the war and how their choices influenced others' lives. With compassion, empathy, and patience, both scholars demonstrate a keen ethical resistance, a refusal to simplify, reduce, or dilute their discoveries. Their insistence on preserving the complicated circumstances helps to create a healthier, measured distance from their volatile subjects. Works that maintain the complexity of a person's life and circumstances are ultimately truer to their source because they resist an easier, reductive formula or a judgment that a person's life was wholly "good" or "bad." Each author's emotional strength supports a deliberate lack of resolution. In doing so, they provide a model of scholarly discourse that resists an impossible completion by design.

Works Cited

Derrida, Jacques. *Archive Fever: A Freudian Impression*. Trans. Eric Prenowitz. Chicago: U of Chicago P, 1998. Print.

DeSalvo, Louise. *The Art of Slow Writing: Reflections on Time, Craft and Creativity*. New York: St. Martin's Griffin, 2014. Print.

—. *Chasing Ghosts: A Memoir of a Father, Gone to War*. New York: Fordham UP, 2015. Print.

Kadar, Marlene. "Resisting Holocaust Memory: Recuperating a Compromised Life." Kadar and Perreault 111–28. Print.

Kadar, Marlene, and Jeanne Perreault, eds. *Working Memory: Women and Work in World War II*. Waterloo: Wilfrid Laurier UP, 2015. ProQuest. Web. 1 May 2017.

Kadar, Marlene, et al., eds. *Tracing the Autobiographical*. Waterloo: Wilfrid Laurier UP, 2009. Print.

Scott, Jill. *A Poetics of Forgiveness: Cultural Responses to Loss and Wrongdoing*. New York: Palgrave, 2010. Print.

Escape from the Colonial Asylum

By Patrick Taylor

David Taylor was a white Barbadian, a member of my immediate family, who died in 1963 at age 46 in the Barbados Mental Hospital, as the island's psychiatric hospital was then known. Although making sense of his story is meaningful to me for personal reasons, I have wondered what interest, if any, other people might have in the story of this obscure witness to the march of history. Marlene Kadar has been my friend and colleague in the Department of Humanities at York University over many years, and in solidarity together we have engaged in various collegial and personal struggles. I have listened to presentations by her, read some of her writings, and worked with a few of her many students, but I remained an ambivalent outsider to the field of life writing. True, she invited me to write a contribution for *Working Memory: Women and Work in World War II*, the volume she coedited with Jeanne Perreault, and I had done so, but I was still questioning the value of doing research on David's life and writings. "Well, you are doing it," she replied, "so you must need to do it!" I entered the archives cautiously, anxiously, for Ranjana Khanna's words in *Dark Continents: Psychoanalysis and Colonialism* remained fixed in my mind: "If the archive appears by some to be a national monument and thus a collective memory, it can also be a home for the unhomely and unbeautiful: the phantoms from *limbo patrum*" (268).

My contribution to *Working Memory* consisted of a study of a short unpublished memoir written by an aunt of mine, Doreen Allen, about her life in the British Army's Auxiliary Territorial Service during World War II. My approach to the memoir was to try to understand the ways in which a white, middle-class woman, the daughter of a plantation manager in Barbados, represented her experience of leaving Barbados and traveling to the US and Canada for "basic training" in the Auxiliary Territorial Service, followed by employment in the British Army's Ordnance Division in Washington, DC. What I found, however, was a trace, to use a term Marlene has invoked (e.g. see "Devouring" 223–24), which echoed back historically to the race relations of the colonial plantation system in Barbados and forward to contemporary North America. Two photographs of St. John's Ambulance trainees in Barbados seemed to reveal a story that was also a history: one, with a black face among the many white faces; the other, with that black face absented, as if that person had to be there but could not be there, as if this person both present and absent in my aunt's memoir represented some ancestral haunting or, perhaps, an unrequited longing in my family. I was concerned that I might be betraying my aunt by revealing her secrets. But these were also family secrets, and perhaps it was the fact that these were my secrets, too, that gave me cause for concern (Taylor 87–88, 104–05).

Silencing, as Michel-Rolph Trouillot has so adroitly argued in his discussion of the misrepresentations of Haitian history, is a product of the power through which the past is produced. Presences and absences in historical sources and archives are generated by the power relations governing historical actors and the researchers studying them. Trouillot notes that the inequalities experienced by historical actors result in the privileging of particular inscriptions of the traces out of which sources are generated and history constructed: "Mentions and silences are thus active, dialectical counterparts of which history is the synthesis" (48). He emphasizes that silencing is an active practice, that "one 'silences' a fact or an individual as a silencer silences a gun" (48). The task of the researcher, therefore, is to understand this process, unpack the sources, and find the traces that have been silenced. If, for Trouillot, the distortions of Haitian history are multifaceted and run deep, colonialism and plantation slavery in Barbados have left a similar legacy. In *White Skin, Black Kin: Speaking the Unspeakable*, Barbadian Canadian artist Joscelyn Gardner comments that her own visual art "suggests that slavery is both a white issue as well as a black issue ... and that the white subject must be accountable to this history in order to accomplish healing" (55). Silenced in my aunt's narrative, the lingering history of plantation slavery emerged in a trace that haunted her text, a black figure at once close and distant, included and excluded, a phantom from *limbo patrum*, in pursuit of redemptive justice.

David was the same generation as Doreen Allen and from a similar background, though only related to her through marriage. Without an actual memoir by him to guide or, perhaps, lead me astray, I wanted to see where those traces of his life to which I had access might lead me, to listen for the silences that might start to reveal themselves, and to confront the ghosts from his colonial past. I am working with a set of documents dealing with aspects of David's life in Barbados and Trinidad from the 1930s through to his death in the early 1960s. These documents include various items, from pay statements, postcards, letters, recipes, and newspaper clippings to David's notebooks and poems, a family tree he had researched, and a book manuscript and related articles he had written on Trinidad and its quest for nationhood in a federation of British West Indian territories. Somehow, these documents had ended up in my hands, in a file box in my home office in Toronto. From time to time, I would dip into this small family archive, and though I had always emerged surprised at what I found, there was really nothing more there than fragments of an ordinary life. Nevertheless, David was attempting to manage the challenges of major social and political upheaval leading up to national independence in the British West Indies while facing a debilitating personal illness that would end in premature death. In "Things Gone Astray: The Work of the Archive," her prologue to *Working Memory*, Kadar calls our attention to the "place of belonging, where life's longings interpenetrate with death's desire." "There is always something missing," she writes, "always a lack in remembering family stories. Yet there is more of a desperation to know when blood is at stake, or when the continuity of life is threatened and we desire to know its roots" (9). I wanted to know more about these documents, to be able to find some meaning in them.

When I was a high-school student in Barbados, I had a history teacher who informed us one day that she would no longer be teaching because she had been hired by the Barbados National Archives. She said she hoped that she would see us there in the future doing research. I never forgot her words, but it was not until I began further investigations into David's background a few years ago that I found myself in the Barbados Archives. In David's files there was mention of a seemingly illustrious ancestor, George Nelson Taylor, a lawyer, elected politician, and former speaker of the island's parliamentary assembly. Historian Robert Schomburgk, a contemporary of George Nelson and apologist for the Barbadian plantocracy, depicted George Nelson as a benevolent, enlightened, and progressive legislator. George Nelson had drafted the colony's emancipation law in 1833. As speaker, he presented the assembly's address to the new governor, Sir Charles Grey, in 1842, stating that the Barbadian legislature was influenced by "a consideration for that portion of the population which had so recently emerged from a state of absolute dependence, and whose ignorance and inexperience gave them an especial claim to protection from those entrusted with the care of the public weal" (Schomburgk 496). Schomburgk reported that George Nelson stood up for the rights of parliamentary assembly in opposition to the governor's political intervention (468), and had promoted the steam engine in sugar production and the railway for transportation (528). It seemed to me that George Nelson might be an interesting person to research and that I might be able to find useful information relating to him in the archives.

Among other things, the Barbados National Archives hold George Nelson's last will and testament, probated in 1861. On reading it, I was startled to find a reference to a son, George, living in "Toronto Upper Canada under care of Richard Taylor." The will continued: "The unfortunate speculation I made on the purchase of Walker's Plantation having greatly reduced my circumstances has compelled me to confine the disposition of my property to my unmarried daughters and to provide for my son George, who are the most helpless of my children." Not only was Toronto my own city of residence, by some strange coincidence, but there had been no mention whatsoever of this person in David's personal files, even though there was mention of his brothers and sisters. Reference to this son had been excised from his family's history in Barbados.

The strange reference in the Barbados Archives to "Toronto Upper Canada" haunted me, and I kept wondering what its significance could be. However, it was only when the Ontario Archives held a special open house, encouraging passers-by to visit, that I thought to follow up on the lead. As it happens, the Ontario Archives are housed in the same building as my own office at York University. A helpful archivist suggested I check various sources, including, to my surprise, psychiatric hospital records. Scrolling through the extensive microfiche of the Casebook Male General Register, Volume 1 (21 January 1841–23 July 1853) of the Provincial Lunatic Asylum, Toronto, known today as the Centre for Addiction and Mental Health, I experienced what I can only describe as a Marlene Kadar moment. I was startled once more to find the name George Taylor, identified as a native of Barbados, West Indies, under the care of a certain Richard Taylor. Though few documents remain in George's file, he is identified as being male, single, with tawny hair and gray eyes, and is described as being a "planter," but the word is crossed out and replaced with the word "gentleman." He was admitted to the asylum on 6 May 1851, when he was thirty years old, suffering from "insane attacks" of "unknown" cause, diagnosed as "mania." He died in the asylum on 14 June 1868 of phthisis—that is, consumption, presumably what we now call pulmonary tuberculosis or TB. According to the asylum register, he had remained confined for seventeen years, one month, and eight days ("Provincial" 70).

By virtue of his position as speaker of the assembly, George's father, George Nelson, was one of the commissioners of the Barbados Lunatic Asylum, as it was formally known when it was first established in 1846.

The facility adjoined the police station near the main prison, Glendairy. Writing at the time, Schomburgk painted a positive picture of the new buildings and praised the legislature for its charitable work, commenting, "The appearance of the Asylum does not bespeak the melancholy object for which it is erected, and, except for the high walls, it would scarcely be conjectured that it is intended for those bereft of reason" (130). Writing from today's perspective, historian Leonard Smith provides a more critical viewpoint: "Having its own high boundary walls," the asylum "visibly formed a part of the island's custodial framework" (108). Jamaican psychiatrist Fred Hickling has argued that the lunatic asylum in the Caribbean can be seen as "a sophisticated extension of slavery" (qtd. in Smith 3). In Barbados, the majority of the asylum admissions between 1875 and 1880 were identified as black (46%) and mixed (35%), although there were also a significant number of whites (19%). There were more men (134) than women (101), but whereas among the women 55.1% were identified as black and only 11.2% as white, among the men only 39% were black while 24.6% were white. Smith suggests that while these figures reflect the adversity faced by the black and mixed population, they also indicate the relative adversity faced by black women and poor white men (130–31).

As early as 1874, the medical superintendent complained that the accommodation was defective and insufficient, and in 1887 a government commission reported that consumption, diarrhea, and dysentery were prevalent. A new psychiatric hospital was eventually opened in 1893 on the old Jenkinsville Plantation in Black Rock, with access to the ocean, where patients could bathe. As opposed to the older custodial institution, it was intended to be a modern "curative hospital based on moral management principles, with an extensive program of patient employment" (Smith 114; see Lloyd-Still). Smith attributes the delay in building the new hospital "to the vagaries of Barbadian elite politics and the social perspectives of legislators constrained by indecision, parsimony and narrow, racially bound class attitudes" (113). Not surprisingly, conditions in the new hospital remained less than optimal: patients suffered from dysentery, diarrhea, tuberculosis, pellagra, psilosis, and other diseases, and the mortality rate was high (115).

In his psychoanalytic essay on Bartolomé de Las Casas, Antonio Benítez-Rojo writes that "whenever an uncanny fiction erupts within a chronicle intended to inform us, it should be seen as surrounded by violence" (94). George Nelson's will is hardly a chronicle, but it is an uncanny expression of the "proliferating character of the Plantation" as described by Benítez-Rojo (34). To say that his son George was under the care of Richard Taylor was the fiction that belied the violence. It is possible that George Nelson foresaw the problems that his son George would have faced had he been committed to Barbados's custodial asylum in 1851. It is also possible that he simply wanted to rid himself of the problem his son was deemed to represent by sending him away to Toronto. As ethnographer Lawrence Fisher writes, the "Barbadian views the madman as the embodiment of all that is stigmatized" in the society (251). In late-nineteenth-century Toronto, those patients who could pay their way had somewhat better accommodation and treatment than other patients, the majority of whom were admitted to the public wards, but all of the patients were stigmatized by the wider community. In *Remembrance of Patients Past*, historian Geoffrey Reaume observes that some families "showed concern in the early stages of confinement and then nothing more is heard as the years go by, whereupon it becomes evident that the patient has been abandoned by what seemed to be interested relatives" (196).

Although the details of his case are not available, it is apparent that George was abandoned by his family after he was sent from Barbados to the newly constructed Provincial Lunatic Asylum, Toronto. The asylum was built in what was then countryside, just west of Toronto, and like much of the city and surrounding area was located on the ancestral lands of the Mississaugas of New Credit First Nation.[1] Despite the promise of George Nelson's will and notwithstanding Richard Taylor's signed bond agreeing to be financially responsible for George's maintenance costs of fifteen shillings per week, the hospital records indicate that the province had assumed responsibility for supporting George. Ironically, although George may have avoided one colonial asylum plagued with consumption, he would nevertheless die of that very same condition in another asylum that was itself essentially colonial, notwithstanding the birth of the new Dominion of Canada one year earlier in 1867.

Kadar and Perreault comment on the painful awareness of "the fragmentary nature" of life writing in "The Lives and the Archives," their introduction to *Working Memory*. Yet there is a pleasure, they state, in "the searching and the recreating—the making of a narrative about and with those fragments." According to them, the working of memory may be personal and even intimate, for "the layering of narrative fragments that recovery requires or involves brings us within touching distance of ourselves" (2). The new psychiatric hospital in Black Rock adjoined the property at Brighton where David had lived as a child, and he had explored the land behind the hospital, including the so-called "Indian cave" that the hospital had used subsequently for sewage disposal, Indigenous peoples having been driven off the island centuries earlier. The main road into town from his house ran along the front of the hospital, and passers-by could see patients behind the hospital's extensive green fence returning their curious gazes (Figure 1).[2]

David left Barbados as a young adult during World War II to join the Trinidad Royal Navy Volunteer Reserves, subsequently obtaining work as a unionized shipping clerk in the Trinidad oilfields. He returned to Barbados after the war, married, and settled down in a family property located across the road from where he had grown up. While working as an editor for a local newspaper, he found time to draft a manuscript entitled "Trinidad: Our Federal Capital." Based on his experience working and traveling in Trinidad and the few secondary sources that were available to him, the short book was intended to introduce visitors to the history, geography, culture, and politics of the island. What is notable about the manuscript is that it was witness to the negotiation of national independence that would take place under a federation of British West Indian territories. Although he was a descendant of the white colonial-planter elite, he advocated federation and self-government for the West Indies, which, like Canada, he and others hoped would nevertheless remain within the British constitutional order.

The West Indies Federation came into being in 1958 with Trinidad as the new capital and a Barbadian as prime minister. Yet David's manuscript remained unpublished, despite several revisions, with the exception of two sections published as separate articles in a local West Indian journal. The revisions to the manuscript during the 1950s were responses to the changing political, social, and cultural history leading up to the creation of the federation. They also demonstrate David's personal contradictions as he attempted to grasp a political reality from which his own elite education,

Figure 1. The metal fence enclosing the Barbados Psychiatric Hospital, formerly known as the Barbados Mental Hospital, painted silver in an attempt to defuse negative stereotypes associated with its former green color.

social status, and cultural formation excluded him. The idea of a federation of the British Caribbean territories was fraught with its own contradictions, and the West Indies Federation itself would fail just as David's publication efforts would fail. But whereas the independence of individual territories such as Jamaica, Trinidad, and Barbados provided a possible way forward at a national level, albeit leading to problematic postcolonial futures, David's personal journey was becoming more and more impossible.

One of David's Trinidad poems was written during a strike of oil workers in 1947. Entitled "In Depression" and signed Anonymous, the poem expressed the plight of the striking workers, beginning with the lines, "In fields of oil, O Lord, we dwell: | How can we see another Hell?" Although the poem ends with a redemptive moral imperative, "But yet there's joy and pleasure too, | And joy you'll find if good you do," the overwhelming feeling of the poem is one of desperation: "No blame can Thou to us attach | If we with spirits our sorrows dispatch" (David Taylor Archive). Whether his problems with depression started in Trinidad or whether depression was a deeper condition related to a sequence of illnesses, firings, and publication failures, David had developed a growing dependency on alcohol that would lead to Alcoholics Anonymous, periodical voluntary admissions to the Barbados Mental Hospital, and treatment with barbiturates. Finally, in 1963, there was the call from the hospital: a cerebral hemorrhage, presumed to be related to excessive alcohol use, had taken his life.

In an extensive analysis of the formation of white creole culture and identity in Barbados, David Lambert shows that white Barbadians were eager to express their loyalty to England and their Englishness (Barbados was represented as being "Little England") while also asserting their difference as Barbadians with their own local customs and rights (12–18). In David's life and writings, this ambivalent white creole romance of Englishness sat uneasily with a utopian embrace of West Indian decolonization. David was a melancholic, his life prefiguring aspects of postcolonial melancholia. Postcolonial theorists have used the term "melancholia" to describe the affect associated with the loss of empire (Gilroy) and the failure of independence with the emergence of the postcolony (Khanna). Following Freud and Derrida, among others, Khanna argues that melancholia "is not simply a crippling attachment to a past that acts like a drain of energy on the present, even though it is indeed an impoverishment of ego. Rather, the melancholic's critical agency, and the peculiar temporality that drags it back and forth at the same time, acts toward the future" ("Post-Palliative"). According to Khanna, this critical agency can be released by reading the silences haunting the postcolonial nation, the phantoms in *limbo patrum* (*Dark* 271–72).

"And limbo stick is the silence in front of me," offers Barbadian Edward (Kamau) Brathwaite in his rich, poetic reading of the popular Caribbean limbo dance; "stick is the whip / and the dark deck is slavery" (194). Unknowable to David was a silenced past, an ancestor hidden away in the fragments of the archive: this son of a colonial legislator and former owner of enslaved persons had been diagnosed with mania and committed by his own father to a so-called lunatic asylum in a distant land, where he would die, his memory lost to his family. "[N]arratives are made of silences," writes Trouillot, "not all of which are deliberate or even perceptible as such within the time of their production" (152–53). Plantation slavery and its legacy perpetuated a social order in which the humanity and the human rights of persons could be granted or denied based on skin color and ethnicity. But this denial also turned in on itself, and George Nelson's son George suffered the consequences.

White Barbadian masculinity constructed itself historically as noble, immutable, and free, as codified in a charter in 1652, when Barbadian colonists won the right to self-government as overseas Englishmen (Lambert 162–63). Trapped in itself, however, Barbadian masculinity returned to haunt its descendants in what Aimé Césaire has called, in a different but related context, the "boomerang effect of colonization" (20). The modern sugar plantation was born in Barbados in the seventeenth

Figure 2. The high walls that once enclosed the grounds of the Asylum for the Insane, Toronto—formerly known as the Toronto Lunatic Asylum—now preserved on the open grounds of the Centre for Addiction and Mental Health as memorials to the patients who built them.

century, and with it came a new alcoholic beverage: rum, sugar's nemesis. David loved Barbados and the wider Caribbean, struggled to find his place in a changing world, and worked to share his experiences with others. Depressed, an alcoholic, his goals unrealized, his life ended behind the metal fence and stone walls of a psychiatric institution that his illustrious ancestor had helped to establish.

The notion of fragmentation reverberates through Caribbean history. Renowned Saint Lucian poet and artist Derek Walcott reminds us in his 1992 Nobel speech, "The Antilles: Fragments of Epic Memory," that the region was traditionally perceived as a place with "No people," containing only "Fragments and echoes of real people, unoriginal and broken." He continues, "Break a vase, and the love that reassembles the fragments is stronger than that love which took its symmetry for granted when it was whole. … This gathering of broken pieces is the care and pain of the Antilles, and if the pieces are disparate, ill-fitting, they contain more pain than their original sculpture. … Antillean art is this restoration of our shattered histories" (505–06).

If art brings us back to our shattered histories, however fragmentary they might be, history, as Trouillot reminds us, is written from the perspective of the present, and "the focus on The Past often diverts us from the present injustices for which previous generations only set the foundations" (150). My excursus into life writing started with Doreen Allen's memoir of World War II and her journey as a woman of privilege from Barbados to Canada and the US, a journey haunted by the silence of her family's plantation past. That spectral past emerged again as a neglected family archive drew my attention and led me in a search for David Taylor's forebears. British colonialism linked the Caribbean plantation colonies to the North American settler colonies, and if many of the stories of that linkage are lost to memory and buried in public and private archives, the fragments that are unearthed and reassembled can still speak to us today. As Kadar and Perreault have noted, the work of memory as life writing must address the ethical impulse to "change things in the present" ("Lives" 3). The institution of the asylum is in flux, and psychiatric patients are advocating for themselves, calling for the removal of the physical and mental walls with which they have been constrained. A lingering history of colonialism is also being challenged as Indigenous peoples work toward a viable reconciliation and Caribbean peoples seek meaningful reparations for transatlantic slavery. My home today is not far from the Centre for Addiction and Mental Health, and my street runs directly along the hospital's eastern boundary (Figure 2). There, segments of the old colonial asylum walls stand as melancholic monuments in remembrance of patients past (Reaume 9).

Notes

1. Given the inequities of the Toronto Purchase of 1787 and 1805, a more definitive land-claims settlement between Canada and the Mississaugas of New Credit First Nation was reached in 2010.
2. The fence was painted silver following the advice of Lawrence Fischer, who informed hospital authorities that in his interviews with Barbadians, the color green was associated with grief (Fisher 63–64). Indeed, the hospital was known colloquially as the "Green Gate Hotel," a term that stereotyped and ridiculed patients. Additional fencing was also added on the inside of the old fence to further separate patients from passersby.

Works Cited

Archives of Ontario, RG 10-271, Queen Street Mental Health Centre Patient Registers, MS-640, Reel 1. Toronto, Canada: Provincial Lunatic Asylum Casebook Male General Register Volume I (21 Jan. 1841–23 July 1853).

Barbados National Archives, Original Proved Wills. Black Rock, Barbados: Will of George Nelson Taylor, Proved 2 Aug. 1861.

Benítez-Rojo, Antonio. *The Repeating Island: The Caribbean and the Postmodern Perspective. Translated James Maraniss.* Durham: Duke UP, 1992. Print.

Brathwaite, Edward. *The Arrivants: A New World Trilogy.* Oxford: Oxford UP, 1973.

Césaire, Aimé. *Discourse on Colonialism. Translated Joan Pinkham.* New York: Monthly Review, 1972.

David Taylor Archive (author's personal collection). Print.

Fisher, Lawrence E. *Colonial Madness: Mental Health in the Barbadian Social Order.* New Brunswick: Rutgers UP, 1985

Gardner, Joscelyn. "Postcolonial Portraits: 'Speaking the Unspeakable.'" *White Skin, Black Kin: "Speaking the Unspeakable."* Ed. Gardner. St. Ann's Garrison, St. Michael: The Barbados Museum and Historical Society, 2004. 52–57.

Gilroy, Paul. *Postcolonial Melancholia.* New York: Columbia UP, 2005.

Kadar, Marlene. The Devouring: Traces of Roma in the Holocaust: No Tattoo, Sterilized Body, Gypsy Girl. *Tracing the Autobiographical.* Ed. Kadar et al. Waterloo: Wilfrid Laurier UP, 2005. 223–46.

—. "'Things Gone Astray': The Work of the Archive." *Working Memory: Women and Work in World War II.* Ed. Kadar and Jeanne Perreault. Waterloo: Wilfrid Laurier UP, 2015. 7–9.

Kadar, Marlene, and Jeanne Perreault. "The Lives and the Archives." *Working Memory: Women and Work in World War II.* Ed. Kadar and Perreault. Waterloo: Wilfrid Laurier UP, 2015. 1–6.

Khanna, Ranjana. *Dark Continents: Psychoanalysis and Colonialism.* Durham: Duke UP, 2003.

—. "Post-Palliative: Coloniality's Affective Dissonance." *Postcolonial Text* 2.1 (2006). Web. Postcolonial.org. 23 June 2017.

Lambert, David. *White Creole Culture, Politics and Identity During the Age of Abolition.* Cambridge: Cambridge UP, 2005.

Lloyd-Still, R. M. "The Mental Hospital." *Caribbean Medical Journal* 17 3–4 (1955): 135–38.

Reaume, Geoffrey. *Remembrance of Patients Past: Patient Life at the Toronto Hospital for the Insane, 1870–1940.* Toronto: U of Toronto P, 2009.

Schomburgk, Robert H. *The History of Barbados*. Harlow, UK: Longman, 1848. Google Books. Web. 11 May 2017.

Smith, Leonard. *Insanity, Race and Colonialism: Managing Mental Disorder in the Post-Emancipation British Caribbean*, 1838–1914. Basingstoke: Palgrave Macmillan, 2014.

Taylor, Patrick. "From Planter's Daughter to Imperial Soldier and Servant in Britain's War." *Working Memory: Women and Work in World War II*. Ed. Marlene Kadar and Jeanne Perreault. Waterloo: Wilfrid Laurier UP, 2015. 85–110.

Trouillot, Michel-Rolph. *Silencing the Past: Power and the Production of History*. Boston: Beacon, 1995.

Walcott, Derek. "The Antilles: Fragments of Epic Memory." *Routledge Reader in Caribbean Literature*. Ed. Alison Donnell and Sarah Lawson Welsh. London: Routledge, 1996. 503–07.

Inside the Cover, Outside the Archive: Reading the Dispersal of Jane Rule's Library and Modes of Female Sociability

By Linda M. Morra

Over the course of several years now, I have been steadily grappling with the approximately seventy boxes that make up the Jane Rule fonds housed at the University of British Columbia's Rare Books and Special Collections. Since that research began, I have studied and theorized more generally about how women's archives have been consciously deployed to shape and extend their life narratives, in ways that respond to Marlene Kadar and Helen Buss's injunction in *Working in Women's Archives* to expand the conceptual framework of autobiography, to open up the strict boundaries by which autobiography was once governed, and to make room for genres that were more readily accessed by women. Taking Kadar and Buss's work as my cue, I argue in my book *Unarrested Archives* and elsewhere how archival research for women writers necessitates moving radically beyond a standard comprehension of what constitutes archival materials and formal repositories. The reasons are related to the fact that state-sanctioned institutions typically endorsed male subjects and erased traces of women's citizenship (to which they were largely not entitled) and their sociopolitical investments. In addition, I have suggested reading in, around, and against archival caches preserved by women writers as unique expressions of their agency and of the conditions of the period.

Although I have elsewhere demonstrated how to approach and read the archives of Jane Rule and other women writers in Canada as a means of laying bare new models of archival research about women's lives,[1] I argue here about revisiting Kadar and Buss's injunction to expand the generic boundaries of autobiography—and its specific incarnation in terms of the archive—by specifically evaluating the importance of a woman writer's personal library, which is not often (indeed rarely) safeguarded as part of an archival fonds.[2] The idea was prompted by a visit to the Rare Books and Special Collections at UBC in Vancouver in early 2016, when I perused the letters exchanged during the late 1960s through the 1970s between American writer Faith Baldwin and Rule herself (Jane Box 20). Comprising several hundred letters, the correspondence bears witness to a respectful and affectionate friendship that unfolds between writers of vastly different ilk: Baldwin primarily wrote mainstream fiction about heteronormative relationships and pandered to the masses, whereas Rule endeavoured to make available what was considerably less popular material at the time—queer subject matter—to a much wider readership.

I evidently know considerably more about Rule. Born in 1931 in California, she was to become a pivotal figure in—a veritable icon for—mainstream queer fiction and deeply involved in queer activism. She was a contributor to *The Body Politic*, for which she wrote a regular column titled "So's Your Grandmother," and she also published several novels and short-story collections. I knew comparatively little about Baldwin, but I came to discover that she was a prolific writer whose career spanned almost fifty years and spawned close to one hundred books. Born in New York in 1893, she initially contributed to women's magazines, after which she published approximately sixty novels, many of which focused on the social obligations of American women in the mid-twentieth century (*Time* 38). *Time* magazine characterized her as one of the most highly paid women romance writers, such that, by 1936, notably during the Depression, she earned well over $300,000 per annum. By the time she and Rule were exchanging letters, she was earning well over two million dollars a year, and her books were being adapted for the Hollywood screen. She also began to host a weekly Saturday afternoon anthology series, *Faith Baldwin Romance Theater*, on the ABC network in the United States. However conventional Baldwin may have been in terms of romantic literary tropes, her wild success as a writer offered Rule one possible template for what an author could accomplish in a lifetime and how to go about doing so.

In making this preliminary search about Baldwin, however, I also made a strange discovery—a copy of one of her books, *Take What You Want*, was available for purchase at a bookstore in San Francisco called Bolerium. Established in 1981 and a member of the Antiquarian Booksellers' Association of America, Bolerium Books represents itself as "purveyors of rare and out-of-print books, posters, and ephemera on social movements" (Bolerium). These social movements encompass the history of labor, the struggles of the Black and Chicano communities, the gay liberation movement, feminism, and Asian American activism. In view of how prolific Baldwin was, the fact that one of her books could be purchased at Bolerium was not in itself so striking—except that Bolerium, which focuses almost exclusively on activist movements and issues, seemed an odd context for one of Baldwin's novels. The context was less strange, however, when I discovered the fact that the novel had been dedicated to Rule herself, in addition to Helen Sonthoff (Rule's partner) and George (George Garden, their house in Vancouver). Indeed, I realized, much to my great surprise, that the book had once belonged to Rule, as the handwritten inscription made evident, and moreover, that it had somehow migrated from Rule's home on Galiano Island, from her very own library, to California, where Rule had been born and raised. As it happened, I was going to California to do research about Rule in archives across the state, so Bolerium held this book for me in advance of a visit I made in February 2016 (Morra, "Item").

Three central questions arose to inform the several tacks I make in this paper: first, why are books from the libraries of women authors, when considered rare objects and sold by antiquarian book sellers, not afforded the same status in an archive?[3] Second, when those books are considered commodities rather than research objects, what are the repercussions? What, if anything, do we lose from the perspective of research and from the perspective of documenting women's lives when we consider books as commodities rather than as research objects, and when they are thus removed from consideration as part of the fonds of an author? Third, what recuperative acts can we engage in to compensate for the said losses to research when we view books as commodities rather than as research objects? In attempting to answer these questions, I began to assess the decisions by which this book from Rule's library had arrived at Bolerium and, as a corollary, what other of Rule's books I could find.

Bolerium itself had once held forty-five other books from Rule's library, although at the time of my inquiry, only thirty-two remained. The store had been thorough in its records and retained the complete list of its original holdings. The owners graciously furnished me with this list, in which each entry contained pertinent details about inscriptions (usually to Rule, sometimes to both Rule and Sonthoff), about the category and genre of the book, and, in some instances, about the sociohistorical importance of the book itself. I comment briefly on these details at a later point in this paper.[4] I thus turned to one of the executors of the Jane Rule estate to ask her about how she dispensed with the books from Rule's library—and why these books were not retained as part of the archive.

The executor explained that she did not believe the books belonged with the other archival materials, an impression the head archivist at the University of British Columbia's Rare Books and Special Collections later corroborated—and which, in fact, has largely a sound basis in both theory and practice. There are exceptions, as Lisa Sloniowski demonstrates in her intriguing essay about setting up an archive for Barbara Godard's "sprawling, delightfully textually promiscuous collection" of books alongside her papers, but even Sloniowski observes that archivists "tend to distinguish between books and papers in libraries and archives" and that all of Godard's library could not be preserved (328; 326). As books were increasingly mass produced in the twentieth century, the reasons to preserve or see books as rare or unique objects diminished. Typically, therefore, personal collections of books are no longer included as part of an archive, in spite of the fact that they are, generally speaking, "central to the intellectual, cultural, political, economic and domestic history of the world" (Carr 114). Peter A. Hoare notes that rare books may still "form the core of many special collections" (57) and that these collections may be developed because of their own inherent uniqueness, their own history, especially if they carry "local or national importance" (58). University libraries in particular, he adds, tend to focus on fulfilling the "needs (within practical limits)" and supporting "the teaching and research of its members," even though the needs of programs are variable and "unpredictable and cannot be anticipated fully" (59). Reg Carr confirms that "library accommodation" has taken on "much greater complexity as the academic world [has become] ever more cost-conscious" and as the "academic research library is to a large extent dominated by the financial interests of what has become an increasingly lucrative commercial activity" (2; 122). The issue of acquiring or preserving such collections has thus become complicated by locating appropriate resources to support them: one must "gauge the cost and be realistic about the benefits" and bypass concerns about the collection becoming "a drain on resources" (Hoare 62). These resources may be financial (the money to acquire and sustain such collections, to pay archivists to manage them), physical (the environment, air quality, and storage space), and temporal (time invested by archivists).

I confirmed that this was the case for Rule's library. When I asked the executor about a comprehensive list of books that formed part of Rule's archive, she replied that she did not have one, nor was one ever made. She added that the "local library on Galiano could not take them as they did not have a need for most of the titles in Jane's collection"; thereafter, the executor and a few others selected titles in which they were personally invested, and "finally, a small book seller on Vancouver Island took the rest" (Walker). These considerations did not mitigate the fact that thirty-two books were what remained of the sixty-six boxes of books to which the executor of the estate referred. I mulled over where and how the rest had been dispersed. At my promptings, the executor of the Rule estate also suggested I get in touch with Odean Long. Long is the owner of the Haunted Bookshop, which was established in 1947 on Vancouver Island and stocks both out-of-print materials and rare books (Long). Four items related to Rule's library had found their way to Long's store, one of which she had already sold: a first edition of *Desert of the Heart*, which had been inscribed from Rule to her grandmother. Undoubtedly, that book had been returned to Rule after her grandmother had passed away. Another two consisted of a copy of Christina Strobel's article with a holograph postcard tucked in it and a first United Kingdom edition of *After the Fire*. The remaining book was *The House of Love*, which I purchased. A collection of poems written by her uncle Lucien Rule and published by the Bobbs-Merrill Company in 1910, *The House of Love* was inscribed with this dedication: "To Jane Rule, With fond affection and hope for her future, from her Uncle Lucien, May, 1947." As indicated by her grandfather in Rule's memoir, *Taking My Life*, this uncle was an ordained Presbyterian minister, a source of family pride, although not everyone felt such admiration for her uncle's literary work. Apparently, Rule's paternal grandmother "promptly burned" some of his "erotic poems," which she discovered after he died (44). The inscription makes evident that her uncle saw himself as a literary progenitor, that he wanted to encourage Rule in her own aspirations, and that there was a family history of striving for such literary accomplishment, which offered a context from which Rule herself worked.

This book, however, is one of many to have been inscribed to Rule—indeed, if the list that Bolerium provided about the surviving books is any indication, many of those that had once been part of the original collection of books had such inscriptions and suggest a cultural context from which she worked. The next question to be raised, then, is why these books or, at the very least, a list of the books from a woman writer's library should be preserved? What value do they carry? My initial response is related to the fact that, if women were busy trying to create a room or space of their own, that space might be seen as encompassing their own libraries, an extension of their literary and autobiographical lives—and the books as suggesting the kinds of values and parameters that informed these lives. Perhaps as importantly, the book inscriptions, dedications, and marginalia reveal the kinds of networks in which women played a significant part.

I should note that much has been written about the phenomena of dedications and book inscriptions and marginalia (Marshall and Brush; Redgrave); about the materiality of the text as a collectible item and as offering material pleasure (Borgerson and Schroeder); about the "ways marginalia affect subsequent readers" (Jackson); about the social experience of reading (Dickinson); about how inscriptions induct books into "an economy of sentiment" (Dickinson 57); and about how "marginalia is a means of communication from reader to reader" (Fajkovic and Björneborn). David Brewer notes that book dedications were historically "either bids for patronage or public acknowledgements of patronage" and could sometimes express "a strong partisan slant" (Brewer). Dedications could also express the relationship between the dedicatee and the author, usually in economic or promotional terms (Beyer).[5] A quick glance at the list of the books that remain from Rule's library and the dedications and inscriptions therein express something about the relationship between the dedicatee (Rule herself) and the author, who often adds an inscription to the book being gifted to the recipient. The inscription to Rule from her uncle demonstrates, for example, how a literary torch might be passed through generations—even though Rule was to occupy a far more significant and public literary place than her uncle.

More particularly, I am suggesting that researchers may approach personal dedications and inscriptions comprehensively within the context of an author's personal library as a way of reconstituting and understanding the sociopolitical networks and modes of sociability that informed and undergirded a queer female writer's life, literary ambitions, and role within certain spheres. In particular, the inscriptions of the books that survive from Rule's library (and as a result of Bolerim's catalogue) offer rich details about the community around Rule, the key players in her life, the audiences and admirers of her work, and the extent and range of her reading patterns—she and Sonthoff would have undoubtedly retained books by those about whom they cared or with whom they shared similar interests.

The books and their inscriptions—as provided by Bolerium's descriptive catalogue—offer some such details. One example is Sheila Ortiz Taylor's *Slow Dancing at Miss Polly's*, often considered to be "the first lesbian novel with a Chicana hero" (Enszer 298–99); a Los Angeles-based writer, Taylor wrote a "warm, lengthy inscription to Jane Rule expressing the poet's admiration of the Canadian author and the wish to meet her someday." Rule had also apparently reviewed her book *Faultline* in terms that were supportive and effusive; the gifting of the book confirms their mutual approbation. Eloise Healey, a West Coast poet who corresponded with Rule between 1981 and 1986, had apparently sent a copy of *Artemis in Echo Park* in 1991, *Passing* in 2002, and *The Islands Project: Poems for Sappho* in 2007—this example suggests that Rule sustained literary relationships across decades. Two of David Watmough's books also found their way to Bolerium's shelves: *No More into the Garden* (his sixth book, published in 1978) and *The Year of Fears* (his twelfth, published in 1988).

The latter is signed in the following manner: "To Canada's Elder Gay Stateswoman from her Elder Gay Statesman! Love David." What also becomes readily apparent from this quick list is the kind of intellectual sociocultural community, primarily forming along the West Coast, of which Rule was a part, the kind of stature she occupied within various networks, and the level of intimacy she shared with many of these writers.

If there were yet another reason, however, to have properly documented this library for its contents, that reason is made more apparent by three books that were listed in the catalogue, two of which had already been sold by the time I contacted Bolerium: the Canadian poet D. G. Jones's *Under the Thunder the Flowers Light up the Earth* and Kate Millett's *Going to Iran*. Tucked within the pages of the former was a two-page letter by Jones and within the latter a note by Millett—these letters, which would have been retained as part of the archival record, are now lost. The book that had not sold, and which I now have in my possession, is a collection of poems by award-winning Canadian poet Phyllis Webb, *Wilson's Bowl*, which has an inscription to both Rule and Sonthoff—and a postcard with a note to Rule and Helen: "The final *Wilson's Bowl* for you. More later. Thank you again for loving care & good company. Nothing settled here but the feeling is better. The cover came out paler than in original—but I think the book is beautiful. Hope you enjoy it. Happy '81. Love P. XX." The book is inscribed "To Jane and Helen, faithful friends." Webb was referring to how the book was overlooked for a Governor General's Award nomination in 1980.[6] *Wilson's Bowl* was later "awarded a prize of CA$2,300 by fellow Canadian poets; the letter accompanying the prize money stated that 'this gesture is a response to your whole body of work as well as to your presence as a touchstone of true good writing in Canada, which we all know is beyond awards and prizes'" ("Phyllis Webb"). The "gesture" to which the collective referred also speaks to the sheer number of writers, many of whom were women, who were becoming involved in protesting the lack of attention to female authors, a fact that is more striking when one considers that, in the 1970s, only one female poet won the Governor General's Award: Miriam Waddington. *Wilson's Bowl* highlights the politics of sex and gender to which women writers were subjected, the conversations in which they engaged, and the tangible and intangible means of support they offered each other. As Sloniowski notes, a book "full of papers" may operate "like a miniature archive in and of itself," and, at times, "an almost incomprehensible 'inter-text'" (332).

At this point, the preservation of Rule's library is, if not entirely lost, certainly a more challenging endeavor. I have had scholars suggest setting up a website or generating a digital humanities project, whereby I am able to track and record books as they surface. I hope to pursue both avenues.[7] For the moment, I use these examples to demonstrate, however cursorily, that the value of a woman writer's personal library is not necessarily the contents of the books themselves; that is, I am not arguing for the preservation of entire libraries of women writers within the archive, although, in an ideal world, that would happen. Digitization, I appreciate, may allow for broader scope for the preservation of materials—including books—even as we recognize that digitization is *another form* of materiality that is also vulnerable to the ravages of time.[8] I recognize the value of such libraries in terms of learning about women's patterns of reading and their sources of intellectual engagement; even so, a list of books or a detailed and comprehensive catalogue would be extremely useful—even as the production of the latter would imply the destruction of the library proper. However, inscriptions—and, of course, marginalia—alter the way we approach or categorize books. Books are no longer necessarily secondary sources but rather primary ones when they are treated as material objects, as significant in terms of material history. In this instance, Jane Rule's library, whatever remains, highlights the communities and supportive networks in place made up largely of women as writers and as intellectuals (in this case, largely a West Coast one that crosses the American-Canadian border); in its dispersal, the archive has, as Sloniowski would suggest, been implicated "in erasing communities and collectivity while rationalizing the subject" (335). Documenting these holdings, at the very least, showcases modes of sociability related particularly to women and to the queer community and offers a rich resource for further study. Approaching personal libraries by women writers thus has implications for archival practice and what we value in terms of documenting the lives of women beyond conventional, mainstream institutions and structures.

Notes

1. See Morra, *Unarrested*; *Basements*; "Beyond"; "Sheila"; and "Autobiographical."
2. Gender does not always make a difference in whether or not a library is preserved. See Sloniowski for an excellent example of how archivists grapple with the legacy of a woman's library.
3. See Sloniowski as an exception to this generality.
4. Though I followed up several times to find out how or from whom they received their stock, I received no answer.
5. See also Griffin; Speck; and Rogers.
6. The award eventually went to Stephen Scobie.
7. I am extremely grateful to Julie Rak, who made these suggestions at IABA-Americas.

8.   See Mak; and Darnton, who argues that one "solution" to the problem of overwhelming information and archival materials is "a library without books" (44). Carr observes, however, that our enthusiasm for digitization, while understandable, should not allow us to ignore, bypass, or forget "the responsibility of providing for the acquisition, use, and ongoing care of the massive quantities of material in traditional printed form which exist" (125).

Acknowledgements

I gratefully acknowledge Ricia A. Chansky and Eva C. Karpinski for organizing IABA-Americas, "Lives outside the Lines: Gender and Genre in the Americas," in 2017, at which I presented a version of this paper, and for their advice that I consult Lisa Sloniowski's article.

Funding

This work was supported by a Bishop's University Senate Research Committee Grant and by a Social Sciences and Humanities Research Council Grant [435-2017-0533].

Works Cited

Correspondence with Faith Baldwin. Box 20, files 1–4. Jane Rule fonds, University of British Columbia Archives, Vancouver, British Columbia.

Baldwin, Faith. *Take What You Want*. London: Robert Hale, 1971.

Beyer, Jürgen. "Re: [SHARP-L] book dedications." Web. 9 Feb. 2017.

Bolerium Books. Home page. Bolerium, 2018. Web. 29 May 2018.

Borgerson, Janet, and Jonathan Schroeder. "Reading Others' Texts: Marginalia and the Inscription of Meaning in Collectible Books." *Advances in Consumer Research* 36 (2009): 188–89. Association for Consumer Research, 2018. Web. 29 May 2018.

Brewer, David. "Re: [SHARP-L] book dedications." Web. 9 Feb. 2017.

Carr, Reg. *The Academic Research Library in a Decade of Change*. Oxford: Chandos, 2007.

Darnton, Robert. *The Case for Books: Past, Present, and Future*. New York: PublicAffairs, 2009. Print.

Dickinson, Cindy. "Creating a World of Books, Friends, and Flowers: Gift Books and Inscriptions, 1825–1960." *Winterthur Portfolio* 31.1 (1996): 53–66. Print.

Enszer, Julie. "Eloise Healey." *Contemporary LGBTQ Literature of the United States*. 2 vols. Ed. Emmanuel S. Nelson. Westport, CT: Greenwood, 2009. 298–99. Print.

Executor. "Re: Jane Rule, her library, and more." Message to Linda Morra. 29 Dec. 2016. E-mail.

"Faith Baldwin, Author of 85 Books and Many Stories, Is Dead at 84." *The New York Times*. The New York Times Company, 19 Mar. 1978. Web. 14 Apr. 2018.

Fajkovic, Muhamed, and Lennart Björneborn. "Marginalia as Message: Affordances for Reader-to-Reader Communication." *Journal of Documentation* 70.5 (2014): 902–26. *Emerald Insight*. Web. 29 May 2018.

Griffin, Dustin. *Literary Patronage in England, 1650–1800*. Cambridge: Cambridge UP, 1996. Print.

Hoare, Peter A. "Loads of Learned Timber: Special Collections in the Smaller University Library." *The Modern Academic Library: Essays in Memory of Philip Larkin*. Ed. Brian Dyson. Chicago: Library Association, 1989. 58–66. Print.

Jackson, H. J. *Marginalia: Readers Writing in Books*. New Haven: Yale UP, 2001. Print.

Jane Rule Fonds. *Rare Books and Special Collections*, University of British Columbia.

Kadar, Marlene, and Helen Buss. *Working in Women's Archives: Researching Women's Private Literature and Archival Documents*. Waterloo: Wilfrid Laurier UP, 2001. Print.

Long, Odean. "Re: With thanks." Message to Linda Morra. 25 Jan. 2017. E-mail.

Mak, Bonnie. *How the Page Matters*. Toronto: U of Toronto P, 2011. Print.

Marshall, Catherine C., and A. J. Bernheim Brush. "Exploring the Relationship between Personal and Public Annotations." *Proceedings of the 4th ACM/IEEE CS Joint Conference on Digital Libraries*. New York: ACM. 349–57. Print.

Morra, Linda. "Item number 195628." Message to Bolerium Books, 22 Feb. 2016. E-mail.

—. *Unarrested Archives: Case Studies in Twentieth-Century Canadian Women's Authorship*. Toronto: U of Toronto P, 2014. Print.

—. "Autobiographical Texts, Archives, and Activism: The Jane Rule Fonds and Her Unpublished Memoir, *Taking My Life*." *Out of the Closet, Into the Archive: Researching Sexual Histories*. Ed. Jaime Cantrell and Amy Stone. New York: SUNY P, 2015. Print.

—. *Basements and Attics, Closets and Cyberspace: Explorations in Canadian Women's Archives*. Ed. Morra Jessica Schagerl. Waterloo: Wilfrid Laurier UP, 2012. Print.

—. "Beyond the Limits of Canadian Women's Literary Archives and Biography." *Companion to Literary Biography*. Ed. Richard Bradford. Hoboken, NJ: Wiley, 2018.

—. "Sheila Watson's Paris Journals and the 'Imminent Narrative.'" *Translocated Modernisms*. Ed. Emily Ballantyne, Dean Irvine, and Marta Dvorak. Toronto: U of Toronto P, 2016. 179–96. Print.

"Phyllis Webb." *Canadian Women Poets*. Ed. Marilyn Rose and Erica Kelly. St. Catharines: Brock University, 12 Apr. 2011. Web. 15 Apr. 2018.

Redgrave, Gilbert R. "Inscriptions in Books." *The Library TBS* 4.1 (1898): 37–46. *Oxford Academic*. Oxford University Press, 2018. Web. 13 May 2018.

Rogers, Pat. "Book Dedications in Britain 1700–1799: A Preliminary Survey." British *Journal for Eighteenth-Century Studies* 16 (1993): 213–33. Print.

Rule, Jane. *Taking My Life*. Vancouver: Talon, 2011. Print.

Rule, Lucien. *The House of Love*. Indianapolis: Bobbs-Merrill, 1910. Print.

Sloniowski, Lisa. "In the Stacks of Barbara Godard, or Do Not Confuse the Complexity of This Moment with Chaos." *Transacting Culture, Writing, and Memory: Essays in Honour of Barbara Godard*. Ed. Barbara Godard and Eva C. Karpinski. Waterloo: Wilfred Laurier UP, 2013. 355–68. Print.

Speck. W. A. "Politicians, Peers, and Publication by Subscription, 1700–50." *Books and Their Readers in Eighteenth-Century England*. Ed. Isabel Rivers. Leicester: Leicester UP, 1982. 47–68. Print.

Walker, Alison, to Linda Morra. Subject: "Re: Jane Rule, her library, and more." 29 Dec. 2016. E-mail.

Maternal Stars of the Silent Screen: Gender, Genre, and *Photoplay Magazine*

By Elizabeth Podnieks

My ongoing research, driven by archival praxis, has been grounded in life writing, women's studies, modernism, and popular culture. After becoming a mother in the late 1990s, I was increasingly invigorated by and eager to contribute to the bourgeoning field of motherhood studies, and I began to filter my scholarship through a maternal lens. My most recent project is a monograph about modernist mothers, and in one of the chapters I examine celebrity journalism—specifically, the fan magazine *Photoplay* of the early twentieth century. In surveying how silent-film stars who were also mothers are profiled, I aim to enhance our understanding of the ways women straddle the boundaries of public and private spheres at the nexus of gender and genre. In my essay here, I touch on some of the key facets of this longer work. One of the first two periodicals devoted to followers of American cinema, the monthly *Photoplay Magazine* was launched in August 1911.[1] Asserting that the movie or fan magazine "was very much a magazine genre in its own right," Anthony Slide defines it as "fundamentally a film- and entertainment-related periodical aimed at a general fan, an average member of the moviegoing public who more often than not was female" (11). The genre is part of the broader field of celebrity journalism developing in the 1880s and 1890s, which Charles L. Ponce de Leon calls "a new form of reportage that expressly focused on public figures, evoking interest in them as 'personalities'"(43). Within a decade of its appearance, *Photoplay* was recognized as the leading publication for celebrity profiles. These auto|biographical pieces are a salient resource for investigating how popular periodicals constructed and responded to maternal ideologies of the day.

Before exploring these ideologies, I want to touch on the implications for scholarship of *Photoplay* as an archive and, more pointedly, as a digitally archived trove. *Photoplay* spans the twentieth century, with its final issue appearing in April 1980, at which point it was folded into the weekly *Us* magazine (Slide 71). My research is limited to the era of silent film—that is, up to the release of the first talking movie, *The Jazz Singer*, in October 1927. This temporal boundary serves both theoretical and practical purposes. Focusing on reportage of silent-film stars allows me to trace the inscription of maternal themes as they emerge in a post-World War I period informed by dramatic changes to (largely white, middle-class) women's lives consequent to suffrage, access to birth control, and entrance into public spheres of higher education and labor, for instance, but contextualized by the same cinematic medium of nonsynchronized sound technology. Moreover, given that each issue of the monthly magazine ranges in length from approximately 180 pages in the early 1910s to around 140 pages in the late 1910s and 1920s, it was essential that I limit my research sample to a manageable number of installments. Even so, my ability to locate these hundred-year-old magazines and efficiently search thousands of pages is enabled by the *Media History Digital Library*, launched in 2011 by David Pierce and Eric Hoyt, which contains a full run of *Photoplay* from 1914 to 1943 in its Fan Magazine Collection.

Reflecting on my position as a scholar immersed in this digital library, I am inspired by Helen M. Buss and Marlene Kadar's collection *Working in Women's Archives: Researching Women's Private Literature and Archival Documents*. Kadar emphasizes that "researching women's archival writing yields new insights into the study of women's lives in significant political, historical and cultural ways" (Afterword 115); such insights are provided in this essay by a study of celebrity mothers whose autobiographical voices are showcased in *Photoplay* profiles. Kadar goes on to explain that "women's archival research documents the multiple goals produced by the recovery and deconstruction of archival texts by women," and that the goals include, among others, "The reclamation of women's lives" and "The reclamation of women's ordinary, everyday (or 'trivial') experiences as valuable" (116). While female celebrities are certainly conspicuously displayed within the magazine, my research contributes to reclaiming for them a subjective (rather than objective) identity by way of feminist scholarly inquiry into constructions of gender and maternity. Additionally, by placing their professional jobs as actors alongside their personal ones as mothers—labor that is domestic, everyday, and inherently "trivialized" within private and thus devalued spheres—my study participates in what Kadar calls the "rescuing" of "women's lives and cultures" (specifically maternal ones) from historical anonymity (116).

In like spirit, my work contributes to the project advanced by Jennifer A. Bean and Diane Negra in *A Feminist Reader in Early Cinema*. Bean acknowledges how factors such as the digitization of archival materials and a new attentiveness to the gendering of silent film have "made visible the remarkable number of roles played by early women producers, directors, stars, and writers in the formation of the young industry" (1). The book also recognizes the whiteness of the industry, paying attention to "Hollywood's tendency to embrace white American girls while expunging ethnic others" as both performers and spectators (20). This "tendency" is a racializing feature of magazines like *Photoplay* as well. In the period of my study from 1914 to 1927, every cover spotlights a white celebrity, and almost all of the figures profiled within are white. Comprehensively, Bean and Negra's collection is predicated on our era's "age of discovery in which the inaugural phases of cinematic novelty and narrative development … increasingly appear as rich terrain for assessing women's participation in the aesthetic, industrial, and cultural shape of the cinema," and as such it "lays the ground, in both theoretical and historical terms, for a feminist account of early cinema" (2–3). Bean identifies a number of crucial archival sites constitutive of and integral to film-culture study, including memoirs, screenplays, advertisements, and, of importance here, fan magazines (3).

Kadar's collaborative work, along with Bean and Negra's, further resonates with my engagement with the "new modernist studies," which Douglas Mao and Rebecca L. Walkowitz trace to the 1990s, and includes an "expansionist" agenda for who contributes to, and what constitutes, literary modernism (737). By gendering modernism (738), we can ascribe cultural and aesthetic significance to women's texts too long neglected or excluded by scholars, and here I include not only fan magazines in general, but also auto|biographical profiles of female celebrities in particular. In this light, I heed Kadar's claim that "the distinction between literary and nonliterary texts should be made less absolute," a move facilitated, she posits, by our reading within and across women's archives in the service of privileging diverse voices and accounts ("Epistolary" 107–08). Further, new modernism attends to developments in "novel technologies for transmitting information: telegraph, radio, cinema, and new forms of journalism" (Mao and Walkowitz 742). As a text about film, and a "new form of journalism" in and of itself, *Photoplay* is an exemplary "novel technology." Its position as such extends to the twenty-first-century digital shift in the humanities, which has made hard-to-access archives like the *Photoplay* collection instantly available. The "novel technologies" that communicated and represented modernism in the early twentieth century are now in turn preserved and disseminated by the "novel technologies" of the next century.

Within these contexts, I focus on how maternal ideologies within *Photoplay* reflect the Victorian *fin-de-siècle* debates about the so-called

Woman Question relating to women's legal rights, status, and selfhoods within the public and private spheres. Lyn Pykett's notion of the "proper" and "improper" feminine speaks to how white, middle-class mothers were either idealized as self-sacrificing angels in the house, valued for tending to the hearth and for reproducing—and being morally responsible for the purity of—not only their children but also the race, or they were Othered as deviant, denigrated as animalistic, sexually voracious, self-assertive, and independent (12–17). For Ellen Bayuk Rosenman and Claudia C. Klaver, so-called "maternal aberrations" (i.e. the sexualized, working-class, absent, or demonic mother) became "fraught sites of instability" that generated "both anxieties and discursive possibility" (9). Such "fraught sites" were racially inflected as well. Citing the 1906 "Sixth Annual Message" by President Theodore Roosevelt, Allison Berg explains that his "warning that the falling birthrate among native-born white women would lead to 'race death'" is reflective of "his own fear that college-educated, middle-class women might choose vocations other than marriage and mother-hood and a more widespread cultural anxiety." This fear was registered in the 1920 *The Rising Tide of Color against White World-Supremacy*, which articulated "the common white perception that immigrants and African Americans would soon overwhelm the white, native population through unchecked reproduction" (1–2).

The emergence of the (white) New Woman—my focus here—contributed to these "fraught sites." Martha H. Patterson describes her broadly as a "suffragist, prohibitionist, clubwoman, college girl, American girl, social-ist, capitalist, anarchist, pickpocket, bicyclist, barren spinster, mannish woman, outdoor girl, birth-control advocate, modern girl, eugenicist, flap-per, blues woman, lesbian, and vamp" (1–2). Sally Ledger underscores that the New Woman was "construed (or constructed) as a threat" to Britain's imperial supremacy in her potential rejection of maternity (18), while calling her "an unmistakably 'modern' figure … committed to change and to the values of a projected future" (5). *Photoplay* is a "fraught site" in which such values of white modern womanhood and motherhood are played out. Indeed, while Berg and Ledger make it clear that the politics of race was a component of the broader cultural arena within which the magazine would have circulated, race is never men-tioned in the maternal profiles. In its promotion of the New Woman, then, the magazine reifies "the values of a projected future" as being white.

My study reveals that *Photoplay* is a kaleidoscopic space of fluid and shifting resistance to and privileging of middle-class, "proper" feminine maternity, as contextualized by Pykett and Ledger. Images of stereotypical femininity associated with nurturing, moral fortitude, domesticity, romance, fashion, and home decor dominate the pages. Yet they overlap with *fin-de-siècle* discourses of the New Woman and new mother, signaled by celebrities who experienced historically unprecedented feminist gains, including the recognition and valuation of their professional work in the public sphere, and independently earned economic wealth through their demanding and adventurous careers, which further granted them physical freedoms to cross gender lines as they traveled to set locations, performed feats of derring-do for the camera, and purchased their own homes and automobiles. Significantly, many of these women challenged traditional maternity as they continued working outside the home after becoming a mother, flaunted their sexualized screen personae, valued adoption over biological birthing, and parented as single mothers after divorcing their husbands or becoming widowed. As such, *Photoplay* is a montage offering multiple points of view, wherein "mother" is not only one of many possible identities for women, but also itself a multivalent role.

Fan magazines like *Photoplay* have been gendered female and feminine from early on. Kathryn H. Fuller explains that while men had responded to the genre's initial broad treatment of acceptably "masculine" topics related to film production and technology (116), by around 1915—with the end of the nickelodeon era and the entry of the US into World War I—content related to women expanded, and male fans, feeling marginalized, shifted their attention to "sporting events, wireless radio, and war news" (118). In light of new modernism, we can appreciate that fan magazines have been neglected critically because of this gendering of genre. Andreas Huyssen posits, "Modernism constituted itself through a conscious strategy of exclusion, an anxiety of contamination by its other: an increasingly consuming and engulfing mass culture" (vii). This mass culture, which includes popular and family periodicals, was equated with women: "In the age of nascent socialism *and* the first major women's movement in Europe, the masses knocking at the gate were also women, knocking at the gate of a male-dominated culture. It is indeed striking to observe how the political, psychological, and aesthetic discourse around the turn of the century consistently and obsessively genders mass culture and the masses as feminine, while high culture, whether traditional or modern, clearly remains the privileged realm of male activities" (47). Huyssen's reference to first-wave feminism invokes the New Woman as a threat to the status quo. Gayln Studlar contends that "virtually all fan magazines of the 1920s textually inscribed a female reader in their address: in their fiction stories, talent searches, editorials, star interviews, and advice to readers columns," and while fan magazines promoted white, middle-class femininity associated with "marriage, romance, and consumerism," they did so "within a broader ideological framework marked by women's growing economic and sexual emancipation and the widespread belief that changes in women's behavior were contributing to a radical subversion of American gender ideals" (268).

More pointedly, *Photoplay* and its featured celebrities negotiate conventional and unconventional maternity. Age-old imperatives of nurturing, femininity, and domesticity, as mentioned earlier, are consistently reinforced. Actors Alice Joyce, Billie Burke, and Florence Vidor, for instance, are angels in the house who revel in their motherhood. Joyce is described in one photograph as "bending over her [baby] with such ill-concealed admiration," and in another as "sewing something for the child" ("Alice"); Burke inspires her interviewer to muse, "We could think only of the 'Madonna and the child' as she might have been painted by Titian" (Underhill 55–56). And shortly after giving birth, Vidor is preoccupied with "being Mrs. King Vidor, her husband's wife and her daughter Suzanne's devoted mother" (York, "Plays" Apr. 1920). Simultaneously, though, *Photoplay* champions Joyce, Burke, and Vidor as mothers eager to return to the screen. Within and against the many at-home tableaux, Joyce's assertion that "I must earn my own money" (Smith 77) is echoed by Burke's insistence—"Please tell *Photoplay* readers how important it is for a woman who has ever had a career to keep right on loving her work though she's married" (Johnson 105)—and by Vidor's: "Today I believe absolutely that a woman who has a definite talent, a real, deep undeniable craving for a certain form of self-expression does more for her family by answering that call and working out her happiness, than by denying it" (Jordan 46).

The magazine further depicts mothers in nonconventional terms by addressing topics like divorce, single motherhood, adoption, and sex. Joyce and Vidor are variously profiled as both married and then divorced, as are Irene Rich and Gloria Swanson. Rich had two failed marriages, the second to a US Army colonel; because divorce "is not looked upon with favor in the army, it goes without saying that she went through some deep waters" (Winship 32). And yet *Photoplay* hails her for overcoming economic and social stigma: "It is always heroic—the fight that a woman makes single-handed against the world for her little ones" (113). Swanson embraced her second divorce by privileging her career and child over a husband: "I have my beautiful little baby daughter to love and make a home for and she and my work will completely absorb me" (York, "Plays" Dec. 1921). Single professional mothers like her are portrayed as resilient, dedicated, and capable of raising their children without a partner. The heteronormative romance script is also rewritten by narratives of adoption. Swanson adopted a son on her own, following her separation from husband number two. Similarly, Barbara La Marr adopted a baby when she was unattached, having already had four husbands, scoffing, "Men—bah! I am sick of men." In contrast, "the only thing I've found in this world that it's at all satisfactory to love is a baby" (La Marr 31). Stories like these may reinscribe motherhood as the imperative of "proper" femininity—even suggesting that motherhood supersedes marriage as the arbiter of ideal womanhood—but they also normalize alternative maternal practices and liberate women from a specifically biological destiny.

Swanson and La Marr are additionally compelling because of their reputations for sex and scandal. We are told that "for a long time" Swanson "suggested somehow a naughty lady—or rather, she never at any time suggested a lady at all. She was the glorified chorus girl, the Parisian coquette of the Longchamps race track, the ultra-vamp" (St. Johns, "How" 113). However, Swanson is elsewhere described as "an ideal mother" (St. Johns, "Gloria!" 105). La Marr equally acknowledges of herself, "They call me a vampire on the screen. Sometimes, in my life, I have been called something very like that off the screen"; however, she refuses to allow sexuality to impinge on her maternal competencies: "you can't tell where you will find mother love, in this world. It doesn't belong exclusively to any little circle of women who look blonde and spiritual and perfect. You can't put a fence around mother love and say—this kind of women shall have it, and this shan't" (31). Moreover, La Marr asserts, "But I'm not willing to admit that because I've got black hair and green eyes and what they call beauty, I'm not going to make a good mother to my son" (31), illuminating how *Photoplay* upends long-held assumptions of "good" and "bad" mothering.

Perhaps the greatest role played by celebrities like these is that of role model. To be sure, "Few actresses had or have the personal following of Alice Joyce," readers are reminded, and "it can be readily seen Alice Joyce has achieved the maximum of what every woman wants" (Durling 73). Likewise, "with an unwonted unanimity of opinion all of the women worship at the shrine" of Billie Burke (Underhill 55), while Swanson has "exceptional talent and drawing power," and every element of her style is "copied by women and girls in every civilized country" (Quirk 32). In this capacity, the women are exemplars of modernity, with notions of Victorian propriety and femininity confronted and overrun by modernist sensibilities. Vidor is "interesting" because she signals "a vital and definite development of Twentieth Century woman"; she is "a supreme example of the struggle between the old and the new woman," and as such she "demonstrates that the New Woman may do justice to both a home and a career" (Jordan 45). Vidor is the paradigmatic figure of modern motherhood as registered by *Photoplay*, with the rhetoric of her coverage contextualizing her within the shifting grounds of public and private spheres.

My brief overview showcases *Photoplay* as a specifically female space affording historically unprecedented auto|biographical inscriptions of women as professional as well as domestic beings. The digitization of archives has been invaluable to the recovery of women's texts and voices such as these. Given that fans, then as now, regard famous figures as role models and seek to emulate their lifestyles and accomplishments, we gain much by examining how *Photoplay* packaged and unpacked maternity. With our own contemporary obsessions with celebrity baby bumps, the "mommy wars" pitting mothers in the home against those in the labor force, and debates about work-life balance, *Photoplay* reveals some of the ways maternal discourses can be shaped by the media—and by celebrities in the service of that media—across the lines of gender and genre for ordinary women in the early twentieth as well as the early twenty-first century.

Note

1. The first, the *Motion Picture Story Magazine* (renamed *Motion Picture Magazine* in 1914), was launched from New York in February 1911.

Works Cited

"Alice Joyce and Her Baby." *Photoplay* June 1916: 38–39. Web. 12 Feb. 2017.

Bean, Jennifer A. "Introduction: Toward a Feminist Historiography of Early Cinema." *A Feminist Reader in Early Cinema*. Ed. Jennifer M. Bean and Diane Negra. Durham: Duke UP, 2002. 1–26. Print.

Berg, Allison. *Mothering the Race: Women's Narratives of Reproduction, 1890–1930*. Champaign: U of Illinois P, 2002. Print.

Buss, Helen M., and Marlene Kadar. *Working in Women's Archives: Researching Women's Private Literature and Archival Documents*. Waterloo: Wilfrid Laurier UP, 1995. Print.

Durling, E. V. "Alice Where Have You Been?" *Photoplay* May 1924: 72+. Web. 12 Feb. 2017.

Fuller, Kathryn H. *At the Picture Show: Small-Town Audiences and the Creation of Movie Fan Culture*. Charlottesville: UP of Virginia, 1996. Print.

Huyssen, Andreas. *After the Great Divide: Modernism, Mass Culture, Postmodernism*. Bloomington: Indiana UP, 1986. Print.

Johnson, Julian. "Lending Enchantment to Distance." *Photoplay* May 1919: 43+. Web. 6 Jan. 2017.

Jordan, Joan. "Old Lives for New." *Photoplay* Apr. 1921: 45–46. Web. 6 Jan. 2017.

Kadar, Marlene. Afterword. Buss and Kadar 115–17. Print.

—. "An Epistolary Constellation: Trotsky, Kahlo, Birney." Buss and Kadar 103–13. Print.

La Marr, Barbara. "Why I Adopted a Baby." *Photoplay* May 1923: 30+. Web. 19 Jan. 2017.

Ledger, Sally. *The New Woman: Fiction and Feminism at the Fin de Siècle.* Manchester: Manchester UP, 1997. Print.

Mao, Douglas, and Rebecca L. Walkowitz. "The New Modernist Studies." *PMLA* 123.3 (2008): 737–48. Web. 16 Feb. 2015.

Patterson, Martha H. Introduction. *The American New Woman Revisited: A Reader, 1894–1930.* Ed. Patterson. New Brunswick: Rutgers UP, 2008. 1–25. Print.

Photoplay (1914–43). *Media History Digital Library,* mediahistoryproject.org.

Ponce de Leon, Charles L. Self-Exposure: Human-Interest Journalism and the Emergence of Celebrity in America, 1890–1940. Chapel Hill: U of North Carolina P, 2002. Print.

Pykett, Lyn. *The "Improper Feminine": The Women's Sensation Novel and the New Woman Writing.* London: Routledge, 1992. Print.

Quirk, James R. Editor's Note. "There Is No Formula for Success," by Gloria Swanson. *Photoplay* Apr. 1926: 32+. Web. 7 Jan. 2017.

Rosenman, Ellen Bayuk, and Claudia C. Klaver. Introduction. *Other Mothers: Beyond the Maternal Ideal.* Ed. Rosenman and Klaver. Columbus: Ohio State UP, 2008. 1–22. Print.

Slide, Anthony. *Inside the Hollywood Fan Magazine.* Jackson: UP of Mississippi, 2010. Print.

Smith, Frederick James. "Alice for Short." *Photoplay* Oct. 1917: 77–79. Web. 12 Nov. 2016.

St. Johns, Adela Rogers. "Gloria!" *Photoplay* Sept. 1923: 28+. Web. 18 Nov. 2016.

—. "How They Do Grow Up!" *Photoplay* Oct. 1923: 38+. Web. 18 Nov. 2016.

Studlar, Gayln. "The Perils of Pleasure? Fan Magazine Discourse as Women's Commodified Culture in the 1920s." *Silent Film.* Ed. Richard Abel. New Brunswick: Rutgers UP, 1995. 263–97. Print.

Underhill, Harriette. "All Feminine Except the 'Billie.'" *Photoplay* Dec. 1917: 55–58. Web. 22 Nov. 2016.

Winship, Mary. "Raising Riches." *Photoplay* Dec. 1920: 32+. Web. 22 Nov. 2016.

York, Cal. "Plays and Players." *Photoplay* Apr. 1920: 86. Web. 17 Jan. 2017.

—. "Plays and Players." *Photoplay* Dec. 1921: 78. Web. 18 Jan. 2017.

Unlikely Documents, Unexpected Places: The Limits of Archive

By Mark Celinscak

My first book, *Distance from the Belsen Heap: Allied Forces and the Liberation of a Nazi Concentration Camp*, examines how Allied military personnel responded to the surrender and relief of the notorious Bergen-Belsen concentration camp in northwest Germany at the end of World War II in Europe (Celinscak). It is a work deeply indebted to the scholarship of Marlene Kadar, one of my doctoral studies advisors at York University in Toronto.

Kadar's work demonstrates that archives are always incomplete because we simply cannot preserve everything ("Things" 9). Individuals in unique positions of power determine what is irreplaceable and worthy of preserving. During my research, I was prompted constantly to reimagine what constitutes an archive. In short, my project required that I look beyond official repositories. I came to realize that an archive can be anything that keeps, maintains, and shelters.

A Past Intensity

The initial inspiration for my project was to explore how British military personnel responded to the liberation of Bergen-Belsen. This was a concentration camp well known to have been surrendered to the British Army at the end of the war. However, early in my research I came across items relating to Canadian military personnel who also encountered the camp. This generally came in the form of a name in a newspaper article, a reference in a soldier's letter home, or a passing mention in an interview. I had already consulted books on Bergen-Belsen, the Holocaust, and World War II, but never once came across any mention of Canadians at

This article was originally published with errors, which have now been corrected in both the print and online versions. Please see Correction (http://dx.doi.org/10.1080/08989575.2019.1588527)

the camp. According to these sources, the British alone were involved in the liberation of Bergen-Belsen.

As my research progressed, I continued to come across traces of Canadian involvement at this dreadful camp. Kadar once wrote, "It is better never to assume that a trace is too faint to be plumbed" ("Resisting" 117). I thus began my venture into the depths of the archive to explore the connection between Canada and the camp's liberation. I spent time working at Library and Archives Canada, the Archives of Ontario, the Ontario Jewish Archives, and the Canadian War Museum. These national and regional archives contained only a smattering of documents relating to Canada's role at Bergen-Belsen. There was not enough material readily available in these archives to explore adequately how Canadians responded to their encounter with this particular camp. If I found anything, it was simply more traces, such as, for example, a reference in a letter home by a soldier telling his family that a Canadian colleague encountered the horrors of Bergen-Belsen.

As I continued to gather documentary evidence, the name of one Canadian often led to another, which often led to a few more. Eventually, one name turned into ten, and then ten turned into a hundred. However, names alone cannot tell a nuanced story. First and foremost, I was after eyewitness accounts by Canadian military personnel. Consequently, these national and regional archives did not reveal the treasure trove of letters, diaries, and reports I was hoping to find. I merely had a long list of names of Canadians who had some sort of connection to Bergen-Belsen. What the precise connection was, I still did not understand.

At this point I knew that I wanted to expand the scope of my project and explore how both British and Canadian military personnel responded to Bergen-Belsen. It was clear to me that this would reveal an untold aspect of the story. While the official archives had offered hundreds of British responses, they revealed little about the Canadian involvement. Therefore, I faced a scholarly predicament. I was quite certain that Canadians were involved in the liberation and relief of the camp, but I had little substance to answer my many questions. Why were Canadians at Bergen-Belsen? What was their role at the camp? How did they respond? Kadar explains that "your desire to complete a task is almost always delayed, deferred and frustrated; this is because you never know how things will turn out in an archive, never mind afterwards" (Kadar, "Historiography").[1] I was fumbling around in the dark, unsure of how things would evolve.

Working with Kadar challenged how I looked at the past and the manner in which I collected my materials. Previously, I viewed an archive as a concrete, formal entity. It was a place with trained staff, visiting hours, rules and regulations—an official repository created by the state or an organization for the collection of data and the production of knowledge. After studying with Kadar for so many years, I altered my conceptualization of what constitutes an archive. Her work reveals a preoccupation with fragments and traces not found in official archives. If I was to write about how military personnel responded to the liberation of Bergen-Belsen, it would be problematic to have hundreds of British responses from which to draw and only a few by Canadians. I recognized that I would need to find a way to locate more Canadian accounts concerning the camp's liberation. Therefore, I had to go beyond traditional channels.

A Name in a Notebook

The following description is simply one example of how I reimagined what constitutes an archive. This process helped me build a larger database of sources for my project. I had no master plan for how to proceed. In fact, I was still unsure of whether I could even tell this story. Kadar advises, "One thing leads to another; keep your nose to the grindstone; and what goes around comes around" ("Historiography"). Years later, her words became prophetic.

On an overseas research trip, I worked at the Contemporary Medical Archives Centre at the Wellcome Institute in London, where I examined the notebook of Martin Lipscomb, a British doctor whose assignment was to help plan a special diet suitable for Bergen-Belsen's starving inmates ("Photographs"). On a page featuring notes about patient treatment, I came across a name: "S/Ldr. Proskie, RCAF." In a notebook by an important British doctor working at Bergen-Belsen appeared the name of a squadron leader in the Royal Canadian Air Force.

I did further research at the archive at the Wellcome Institute but never found anything beyond the surname. Kadar explains that even a "benign piece of paper … [can] be an informative auto/biographical fragment, a trace that put[s one] … on the right track" ("Resisting" 116). This handwritten scrawl in a British doctor's notebook helped reveal something about the Canadian involvement at Bergen-Belsen. It would take time before the particulars were revealed.

I later pulled a personnel file from Library and Archives Canada and learned that there was a John Proskie who served in the Royal Canadian Air Force. However, there was no mention of any involvement at Bergen-Belsen in his file. It was certainly possible that Proskie's mention in the doctor's notebook was immaterial or unrelated, but, at the very least, I continued to keep a lookout for his name.

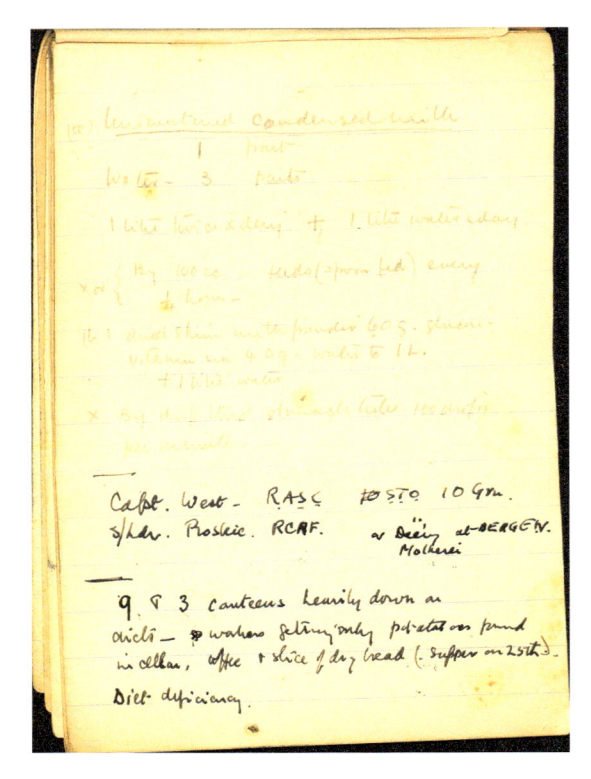

"S/Ldr. Proskie, RCAF" is mentioned in the notebook of Brigadier F.M. Lipscomb, Royal Army Medical Corps. RAMC/776. Contemporary Medical Archives Centre, Wellcome Institute, London, England.

Later, and using the Proskie surname in Google News Archive, I found a short article buried in the *Toronto Daily Star*. It was titled "23,000 Hungry at Belsen Fed by Canadian Expert." The article told the story of John Proskie of Edmonton, Alberta. A food and agricultural expert, Proskie was rushed to Bergen-Belsen to assist the starving inmates. The article revealed that Proskie was in sole charge of locating and gathering food for the sixty thousand survivors at Bergen-Belsen, which was liberated on 15 April 1945. By July 1945, when the article was published, Proskie was still gathering food for the twenty-three thousand survivors who remained in the camp.

I was utterly staggered by what I read. Previously, I thought Canadians were mostly onlookers at Bergen-Belsen. However, this was someone who was part of the liberating forces and who clearly played a significant role at the camp. Who was John Proskie? How did he find himself involved at Bergen-Belsen? How did he grapple with his enormous assignment? And

23,000 HUNGRY AT BELSEN FED BY CANADIAN EXPERT

With the R.C.A.F. In Germany, July 18—(CP)—Sqdn.-Ldr. John Proskie of Edmonton is the man who has 23,000 hungry mouths to feed.

Technically a Canadian education officer, this 39-year-old westerner has taken over the job of nursing back to health the survivors of the Nazi's notorious Belsen murder camp. Assisted by a British sergeant, Proskie at one time fed 61,-000 inmates of the camp, but now his meal-call is answered by only about one-third that number.

When Proskie was first rushed to his appointment on April 17, he found fighting raging on all sides of the camp and the starving internees looting food stocks. It looked like an almost impossible job to bring order out of that chaos.

But Proskie went to work. Farmers were visited, food reconnaissances made, and, in a surprisingly short time, meals were being supplied.

In one week alone Proskie, his sergeant assistant and commandeered labor gathered 40,000 pounds of fresh meat, 68,000 pounds of onions and leeks, 1,000 pounds of fresh strawberries and more than 13,000 pounds of rhubarb. R.A.F. and British Second Army men went on short rations, both for food and little luxuries such as cigarette and soap, to allow the camp to be supplied.

Soon the internees, starving until their liberation, were receiving a diet containing 26 different items, not counting fresh vegetables. The death rate dropped, from 500 daily at the end of April to between 20 and 40 in June.

A food and agricultural expert, Proshie, joined the R.C.A.F. in 1942 and was commissioned a year later to become a meteorological officer instructor. He went to France Oct. 1, 1944, with the job of supervising agricultural production and distribution in distressed areas.

Robert Renison

PRISONER FIVE YEARS LT. RENISON HOME

Flt.-Lieut. Robert Renison, 28, arrived in Toronto last night after being a prisoner of war for five years. Son of Bishop and Mrs. R. J. Renison of Iroquis Falls, this fighter-pilot of the R.A.F. was captured by the Germans before the fall of France.

"My base was at Lille, France, during those early days of 1940," he recalled. "On one of my sweeps during the battle for France, I was over Cambrai in my Hurricane when flak struck my kite. It promptly blew up and I bailed out. I was wounded and burned when the Germans picked me up and spent a month in a German military hospital."

NINE TORONTO AIRMEN WIN D.F.C. AWARD

The D.F.C. has been awarded to nine Toronto men, a r force headquarters announced today. They are Sqdn.-Ldr. C. F. L. Hare, Patterson Ave.; Sqdn.-Ldr. G. S. Patchel, Glenmanor Drive E; Sqdn.-Ldr. H. J. Reeves, Kapelie Ave; Flt.-Lieut. W. M. Buck, Cowan Ave.; Flt.-Lieut. J. N. Carson, Orchard View Blvd.; Flt.-Lieut. H. J. Colli.

A newspaper article detailing John Proskie's efforts at Bergen-Belsen. *Toronto Daily Star* (17 July 1945), 24.

why, in all the books written about Bergen-Belsen, was Proskie never mentioned? I desperately wanted answers to these questions.

Proskie was proof that Canadians assisted at the Bergen-Belsen concentration camp after liberation and performed crucial functions. Of course, I still had nothing in Proskie's voice. I was stifled, frustrated, blocked, yet I could not stop searching. Kadar reminds us that "The power of the fragment or trace is undeniable" ("Devouring" 225). There was clearly more to Proskie's story, and I was determined to find it.

I started a real-life search for John Proskie of Edmonton. Since the surname was somewhat distinctive, I looked up Proskies in Alberta phone books, but to no avail. I contacted Proskies online but came up empty. I wrote letters and heard nothing back. I searched for his obituary but could not locate one. In some respects, I felt as though I were writing a message in a bottle, throwing it out to sea and hoping someone would answer it. However, nothing ever materialized from these attempts at locating a real-life Proskie or a family member.

Months later, I came across the obituary of a woman named Rosalie Rector of Edmonton (Rector). The obituary noted: "Rosalie is a fine example of making a positive difference in the world by helping others. When Rose's brother, John Proskie, died, [she] put his money into scholarships and endowment funds for students at the University of Alberta and the University of Ottawa. Over the years, Rosalie received many letters of appreciation from grateful students." I immediately began pursuing this new lead.

I contacted the University of Ottawa, and staff members confirmed that while they still offered such an award, they had no further information about the man whose name was on it. I then contacted the awards office at the University of Alberta in Edmonton. I expected that Proskie's hometown would at least have some biographical information about him. I contacted several staff members in the hope of obtaining a response. As was the case in Ottawa, I was informed that the scholarship was established before many of the staff had been hired.

It appeared unlikely that I would learn anything further about the Proskie whose name was attached to this scholarship. Fortunately, I continued to exchange email with a staff member in the awards office at the University of Alberta who took a great interest in my inquiry. She agreed that it was a shame we did not know more about the identity of the man behind this generous scholarship. She kindly agreed to look into the matter further.[2]

Sometime later, she contacted me and said that she had located a dusty old file relating to the scholarship. Inside the folder was a treasure trove of material for which I had searched for so long. Jeanne Perreault and Kadar remind us that "unlikely documents [are often found] in unexpected places" (4). Among other items, it contained a typewritten biography, articles about his efforts that had been published in small local newspapers, official photographs, and documentation from his service in the Royal Canadian Air Force. In short, the file contained Proskie's uncataloged archival collection.

As luck would have it, this exciting discovery led to an interview with the Canadian Broadcasting Corporation's *Radio Active*, based in Edmonton (Celinscak). Because of the new material I had at my disposal,

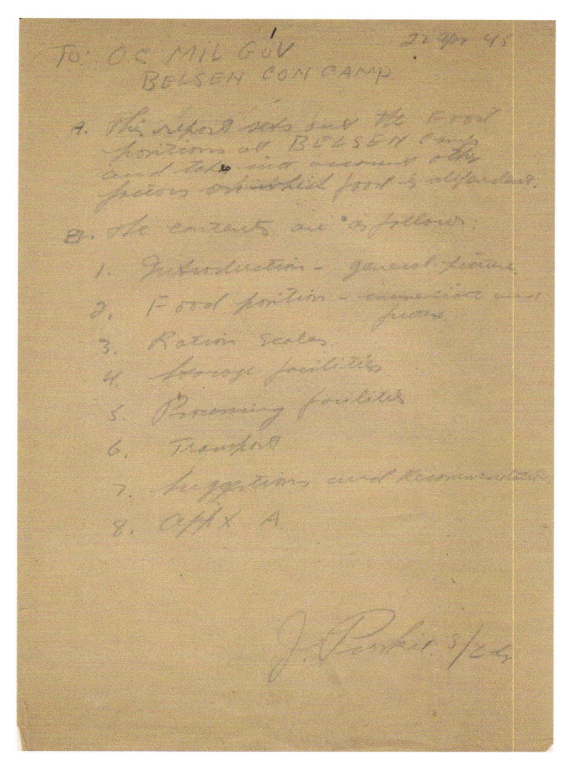

Handwritten report about Bergen-Belsen by Squadron Leader John Proskie dated 22 April 1945. 201811.16 BMOC/4/1, Royal Engineers Museum.

I was able to discuss the efforts of Squadron Leader Proskie during the war. Subsequently, the University of Alberta's Department of Resource Economics and Environmental Sociology, where Proskie earned one of his degrees, published a piece about the efforts of their notable alumnus in their newsletter, *Momentum*. The story of this remarkable Canadian was reaching a larger audience. Indeed, sharing Proskie's story with the public ultimately led to my greatest discovery.

A while later, I was contacted by the son-in-law of Warrant Officer Alfred Snow of the British Army's Royal Engineers who worked with Proskie during the war.[3] Proskie gave Snow several original wartime documents. After Snow passed away, the documents were left to his daughters. These documents were kept for more than seventy years. Of utmost interest to my research was a twenty-three-page, handwritten report about Bergen-Belsen by Squadron Leader John Proskie.[4] The report, signed by Proskie, told the story, his story, of the liberation of Bergen-Belsen. "The living use the dead as pillows at night," he notes hauntingly in the report, "and in the daytime a place that is convenient to sit and eat their rations. There apparently is little concern and no marked line is drawn between the living and the dead, for those who are alive today may be dead tomorrow" (2). It is a deeply moving narrative. In the report, Proskie reveals how he became involved with this infamous camp, his personal reaction to encountering the scenes firsthand, the state of the survivors, and the challenges facing him and other military personnel in tending to those in such desperate need.

It is an incredible account. It reveals the efforts of an extraordinary Canadian whom scholars had overlooked. The discovery of Proskie's report also became a sign that my research was on the right track. It encouraged me to push further. The lesson was that when we overlook or cannot access key documents, it can result in a misinterpretation of the past. In this instance, the British Army was completely overwhelmed and unprepared for the situation at Bergen-Belsen. They were in dire need of assistance, and Canadian military personnel offered their time, labor, and expertise. Canadian doctors, nurses, and other experts rushed to help.

Squadron Leader John Proskie, Royal Canadian Air Force. Courtesy of the Faculty of Graduate Studies and Research, Killam Centre for Advanced Studies, University of Alberta.

A Biographical Sketch of John Proskie

Born in 1906 in Edmonton, Alberta, John Proskie spent his life dedicated to agricultural science. In 1934, he graduated with a Bachelor of Science degree from the University of Alberta. He continued his studies at the university and, in 1937, he received a Master's degree from the Department of Political Economy. Upon graduation, Proskie worked with the Dominion of Canada's Department of Agriculture Research and Economics at the University of Alberta. Three years after the outbreak of World War II, Proskie enlisted in the Royal Canadian Air Force.

Rising to the rank of squadron leader, on 17 April 1945, Proskie was called on to assist at the recently surrendered Bergen-Belsen concentration camp. Because of his expertise as an agricultural economist, Proskie was responsible for planning the collection and employment of resources from the local area. The monumental task of organizing food for the inmates was left to Proskie and his lone assistant, a sergeant in the British Army. The two men surveyed the surrounding area, visiting local farms and food stocks to gather the necessary supplies (Proskie). In a given week, it was reported that Proskie delivered forty thousand pounds of fresh meat, sixty-eight thousand pounds of onions, one thousand pounds of strawberries, and thirteen thousand pounds of rhubarb to the camp. Conditions slowly improved at Bergen-Belsen. The efforts of Proskie and his assistant helped save countless lives. He remained at the camp for several months. At war's end, and because of the world's sugar shortage, he was assigned to survey the sugar-beet stocks in the British zone of Germany. His efforts ensured that enough seed was planted from the 1947 crop.

On receiving an honorable discharge from the air force in 1946, Proskie accepted a contract with the British Foreign Office. This led him to become involved in one of the first major international crises of the Cold War: the Berlin Blockade. Proskie was summoned to organize and administer the supply and distribution of food during the Berlin Airlift. His efforts helped restore the economic balance to the sectors of Berlin under Allied control.

After his foreign service, Proskie returned to Canada to work for the Department of Fisheries. He authored a number of books on the Atlantic fishing industry. He retired from the Department of Fisheries in 1970 after twenty-one years of service. He developed an interest in philately during retirement.

Proskie passed away in 1993 after a short battle with an illness. In 1994, his sister, Rosalie Rector, established the John Proskie Memorial Scholarship at both the University of Alberta and the University of Ottawa. The scholarship is offered to promote financial assistance and encouragement to graduate students studying agricultural economics.

Conclusion

The above account is merely one example of how I built a database for my project that explores the Canadian involvement in the camp's liberation. The manner in which I obtained Proskie's uncataloged archival documents was repeated countless times. I received numerous personal narratives from people over the last decade. These important documents were often left sitting—waiting—in basements, closets, cabinets, shelving units, desks, and boxes, under beds and in storage. These primary accounts were collected from lifelong friends of the dearly departed, comrades in arms, neighbors, children, grandchildren, great-grandchildren— and yes, even staff working in university award offices in Edmonton, Alberta. I was given access to rare, often never-before-examined documents relating to one of the twentieth century's most horrific crimes. It allowed me to reveal a long-ignored narrative in Canadian history.

In order to tell this particular story, I reimagined what constitutes an archive. Official state repositories are, of course, necessary and essential to reconstructing the past. However, we must also be mindful of who decides what is to be kept in an archive and what gets rejected. During my research, family members often told me of their struggle to get a parent's wartime correspondences accepted by authorized institutions. I have seen devastating artwork and photography of Bergen-Belsen that was rejected by national and regional institutions. Archives are privileged sites. Therefore, we must be aware of the dynamics and the tensions between the archived and the nonarchived.

There is history because there is absence. Kadar asks whether uncataloged archival collections can be "the skeleton for the story that exists out there but can never in its totality be told?" ("Things" 9). We should recognize that there will always be a gap between the past and our retelling of it, and that gap will never be entirely closed off. By expanding the parameters of what constitutes an archive, we can increasingly narrow that divide as we attempt to arrive at a more nuanced understanding of our shared history.

Notes

1. The author has received permission to quote from Kadar's unpublished work.
2. My thanks to Ms. Donna McKinnon for her help.
3. My thanks to Mr. John Wade for reaching out to me.
4. Proskie's report was later verified at the National Archives in London, England.

Works Cited

"23,000 Hungry at Belsen Fed by Canadian Expert." *Toronto Daily Star.* 18 July 1945: 24. Google News. Web. 23 May 2018.

Celinscak, Mark. *Distance from the Belsen Heap: Allied Forces and the Liberation of a Nazi Concentration Camp.* Toronto: U of Toronto P, 2015. Print.

—. Interview by Kim Trynacity. *Radio Active.* CBC, Edmonton. 26 Oct. 2011. Radio.

Kadar, Marlene. "The Devouring: Traces of Roma in the Holocaust: No Tattoo, Sterilized Body, Gypsy Girl." *Tracing the Autobiographical.* Ed. Kadar and Susanna Egan. Waterloo: Wilfrid Laurier UP, 2005. 223–46. Print.

—. "Historiography, Memory Studies and the Archive." Humanities Graduate Seminar, York U, 2010. Unpublished TS.

—. "Resisting Holocaust Memory: Recuperating a Compromised Life." *Working Memory: Women and Work in World War II.* Ed. Kadar and Jeanne Perreault. Waterloo: Wilfrid Laurier UP, 2015. 111–28. Print.

—. "Things Gone Astray: The Work of the Archive." *Working Memory: Women and Work in World War II.* Ed. Kadar and Jeanne Perreault. Waterloo: Wilfrid Laurier UP, 2015. 7–10. Print.

Perreault, Jeanne, and Marlene Kadar. "Tracing the Autobiographical: Unlikely Documents, Unexpected Places." *Tracing the Autobiographical.* Ed. Perreault, et al. Waterloo: Wilfried Laurier UP, 2009. 1–8. Print.

"Photographs and other memorabilia of Brigadier F.M. Lipscomb." RAMC/776. Contemporary Medical Archives Centre, Wellcome Institute, London, England.

Proskie, John. "Belsen Concentration Camp." WO 219/3944A. National Archives, London, England.

"Rosalie Rector." Obituary. *The Edmonton Journal.* Postmedia Network, 10 Feb. 2007. Web. 6 May 2018.

Frayed Edges: Selfies, Auschwitz, and a Blushing Emoticon

By Rachel E. Dubrofsky

Over a decade and a half ago, at my thesis defense, Dr. Marlene Kadar, one of my committee members, pushed me to dig deeper, encouraging me not to be deterred by the messiness: "Your work is interdisciplinary. It will always have frayed edges. That is part of the richness."

Marlene never let me get away with trying to take the easy route. Lovingly but sternly—the tilt of her head, the inflection in her voice, the brief twinkle in her eye—she let me know I *should consider* pursuing that PhD in communication in the cornfields of Illinois. I wanted to stay in Toronto. I knew better than to ignore Marlene's hints. Off I went to Illinois. More than fifteen years later, I am an associate professor in communication who does critical cultural-studies work. I look at popular media—in particular, reality television, television, film, and newer forms of media, with attention to surveillance. My scholarship tries, as Marlene might say, to "emancipate an overdetermined subject" (Kadar 12)—that is, to resist the surface, easy readings, to complicate them, raise more questions than can be answered. As Marlene's work shows beautifully, critical, innovative, groundbreaking scholarship is never neat and tidy. It is irreverent. It defies boundaries, genres, disciplines. The significance of the scholarship is in the tensions and paradoxes. The power of critical work is its resistance to giving a single answer, its refusal to foreclose the possibility of other stories. The very form of critical scholarship is part of the activist imperative: defy fixity, certainty, and insist we look at the many ways things come to be the way they are, rather than make affirmations about what should or should not be.

This article was originally published with errors, which have now been corrected in both the print and online versions. Please see Correction (http://dx.doi.org/10.1080/08989575.2019.1588530)

My work lays bare the conflicted stories of how women are presented in popular culture and opens up larger questions about the mundane, everyday ways in which misogyny and racism are made normal. To that end, I share with you some stories about Breanna Mitchell, a white seventeen-year-old girl, a US citizen, who, on 20 June 2014, took a smiling selfie in front of a building at the Auschwitz concentration camp. She posted the selfie on her public Twitter account with the line "Selfie in the Auschwitz Concentration Camp," accompanied by a blushing smiling emoticon. In telling this story, part of my hope is to impress Marlene with what I can now do.

Setting the Scene

This work is from a chapter for a book I am working on. In that chapter, I examine twenty-five mainstream press articles about what came to be known in the press as the "Auschwitz selfie"—mostly articles from the US, but also three from Australia, three from the UK, and one from Israel. All of the articles I found were written between 22 and 24 July 2014, even though the dates I used to search for articles were between 20 June 2014 (the day Mitchell posted the selfie) and 1 September 2014.

A month after Mitchell posted her selfie, it went viral and sparked outrage among some Twitter users and beyond, and became a trending topic. By 20 July 2014, Mitchell's selfie had been retweeted four thousand times and favorited 2200 times, with countless angry tweets directed at Mitchell (Perez). The media event that followed Mitchell's posting of the selfie, and the subsequent response on Twitter, was intense and explosive, but lasted only a few days.

At no point in the stories, or in the tweets and interviews by Mitchell used in the stories, is there any mention of Mitchell's ethnicity, race, nationality, culture, or religion. My assumption is that she is not Jewish. The absence of identifying information suggests Mitchell is a white, Christian US citizen, the default normative identity in the US.

I focus on the mediated event surrounding the Auschwitz selfie: how it was discussed in the popular press. I do not look at what Mitchell may or may not have actually done, her intentions, her tweets (except as mentioned in the articles), or the tweets of the people commenting on her actions (except as mentioned in the articles). The focus is on the stories told about Mitchell's actions, with attention to the presentation of emotion, selfies, gendered displays, authenticity, and performance. I ask: How might the selfie complicate displays of authentic-seeming emotion? How might authenticity and performing be problematically positioned in displays of emotion? What are the implications of emphasizing personal feelings in telling the story about the Auschwitz selfie?

In the articles, Mitchell is condemned and saved via affect. Sara Ahmed notes that affect and emotion "are not only treated as distinct but have, at least by some, come to be defined against each other" (208). Affect, according to Brian Massumi, is prior to feeling and emotion, preconscious, and cannot be fully put into language since it is outside of consciousness—what Sarah Banet-Weiser articulates as authenticity, which resides in the inner core of the self. Affect is what happens in the body when we feel something, before it becomes a feeling and before it is turned into a social expression via emotion. Ideas about authentic emotion, I argue, are what is imagined as the inner, nonperformative emotional self when nobody is watching. This construction of authentic emotion conflates what affect theorists sometimes divide into three separate things: affect, feeling, and emotion (Shouse). Authentic emotion, in the sites I examine, is framed as a transparent display of affect, of visceral instinct.

Paradoxically, while overwhelmingly the stories morally condemn Mitchell for narcissism (she is focused on herself rather than on the historical significance of Auschwitz) and her incongruent emotional display in this setting, it is her personal feelings about her father that ultimately redeem her: we are told he passed away a year earlier, that she had studied the Holocaust with him, and that they had planned to take a trip to Auschwitz together. When she got to Auschwitz, she felt close to him and was happy—hence the smiling selfie.

As Marlene will tell us, to write anyone's story is to fictionalize, which as a scholar can mean practicing critical theory (Kadar) that lays bare paradoxes, contingencies, and the inability of anyone to tell a definitive story. Today, I look at how the articles fictionalized a story about Mitchell. I fictionalize this story as part of my critical practice in my retelling.

Selfies

Selfies are a hot topic. A few years ago, in 2013, the *Oxford English Dictionary* declared "selfie" its Word of the Year. That same year, a photograph of US president Barack Obama, Danish Prime Minister Helle Thorning-Schmidt, and UK Prime Minister David Cameron taking a selfie at Nelson Mandela's memorial sparked "an international media frenzy nicknamed 'Selfiegate'" (Miltner and Baym 1701). Not surprisingly, selfies are becoming a focus of scholarship in communication, as illustrated by the special issue of the *International Journal of Communication* dedicated to the selfie. As Theresa Senft and Nancy Baym note in the introduction to this special issue, "Selfies are suddenly ubiquitous" (1588).

Selfies, by definition, are expressly performative. The selfie, as a photograph one takes of oneself, centers the process of posing—performing—for the camera for eventual public display, usually in social media. There is no possibility of a spontaneous photograph since the person taking the photograph is the same as the person featured in the photograph—though one never knows what could happen in the background (nature can intervene or someone might decide to photobomb by appearing in the frame, for instance) The staged nature of the selfie complicates the authenticity of the display of emotion by the person taking the selfie, since authentic displays are usually framed as unpremeditated expressions of affect. One article about Mitchell sums up the tension: "The selfie could provide a sacred pausing if it didn't involve so much posing" (Detweiler). In effect, the selfie cannot capture authentic, unmediated expression of feeling—what seems to be required in the space of Auschwitz.

Not only is performing a problem when it comes to expressions of authentic feeling; technology inhibits authentic—unmediated—expression. One article about the Auschwitz selfie laments that the selfie "involves a level of performance that pulls us out of the place itself" (Detweiler). Here, performing dissociates people from their physical contexts, making them unable to connect with and fully experience a moment. Our digital devices, it would seem, create a conundrum: how to be fully present in the moment we are trying to broadcast (Detweiler).

Selfies are often primarily about the timely display of the self in a context (Hess 1631), making selfies somewhat anachronistic to the type of photograph encouraged at Auschwitz, or expected as a representation of Auschwitz, which appears to be object-oriented, with the purposes of documenting evidence of the Holocaust. While, as one article puts it, "Auschwitz is not, by any means, a place that discourages pictures" (Molloy), there are expectations for what these will look like—and they do not look like selfies. Indeed, the website for the Auschwitz-Birkenau Memorial and Museum provides instructions for taking photographs: "Taking pictures on the grounds of the State Museum Auschwitz-Birkenau in Oświęcim for own purposes, without use of a flash and stands, is allowed for exceptions of hall with the hair of Victims (block nr 4) and the basements of Block 11. Material may be used only in undertakings and projects that do not impugn or violate the good name of the Victims of Auschwitz Concentration Camp. Photography and filming on the Museum grounds for commercial purposes require prior approval by the Museum."

This reflects what one article about the Auschwitz selfie notes: "Auschwitz seems flawlessly designed to lay out the simple truth of what happened" (Molloy)—pinpointing a desire that photographs of Auschwitz will tell a truth, capture an already existing truth. Photographs of Auschwitz should not be expressly performative or aesthetic; rather, they are meant to provide evidence of a singular, irrefutable truth. Mitchell's selfie does not fit these expectations.

Narcissism and Bad Selfies

Gender comes into play, of course, when it comes to selfies. Senft and Baym highlight the "damned-if-you-do and damned-if-you-don't rules of visual display [that] apply more to some social groups than others" in relation to selfies (1592). Not surprisingly, women, queers, and people of color "tend to be more socially policed" and surveilled (1592), their selfies coming under a particular kind of scrutiny. Derek Conrad Murray remarks that "most talk of selfies is focused (unfairly) on young women … [as] a critique of their apparent narcissism as a kind of regressive personality trait" (490). As Anne Burns notes, the articulation of white women and their activities with selfies sustains gendered power relations that perpetuate "negative feminine stereotypes that legitimize the discipline of women's behaviors and identities" (1716).

Senft and Baym detail how stories about selfies inevitably incorporate "discourses of pathology" (1589), and as Burns highlights, selfies are largely identified as feminine—used by women to express themselves—and thus are laden with assumptions that "the selfie indicates selfishness or narcissism" (1729). Articles about Mitchell, without exception, begin by condemning her for the selfie. Patronizing and paternalistic language is used to detail Mitchell's immoral and narcissistic actions, suggesting she should have known better. One story in *USA Today* is emblematic of the tone: "In truth, it's hard to think of anything less sensitive, less appropriate or less self-aware than a 'selfie in the Auschwitz Concentration Camp'— smiley—as if the suffering of millions of people was somehow subsumed by Breanna's own personal narrative. She was there, sure, but so were tens of thousands of others, and her willful minimization of that fact is, frankly, pretty gross" (Durando). The presentation of Mitchell as lacking empathy for lives lost at Auschwitz is especially problematic for women, who are expected to be relational and caretaking in their outlook on the world and in their interactions with others, since, as Burns reminds us, "selfishness is a particularly barbed insult when directed at women, as it references the subject's transgression of the norm of feminine self-sacrifice" (1729).

Burns details the press coverage of a selfie that the popular press labeled "the Worst Selfie Ever," featuring a woman in front of the Brooklyn Bridge. Showing the rare potential for a spontaneous nonperformative element in a selfie, in the background is a person about to jump off the bridge, committing suicide. The woman is crucified in the popular press for being self-centered (1730). Mitchell is presented similarly—oblivious to her surroundings because she is so self-centered. However, unlike the woman in the bridge selfie, so absorbed in her image that she failed to notice what was going on behind her, Mitchell is portrayed as aware of the significance of Auschwitz (she was quoted as saying she studied the

Holocaust). The term "willful minimization" in the *USA Today* story situates Mitchell as expressly discounting the historical significance of Auschwitz, agentically deciding to ignore the history of Auschwitz and the pain of millions, and instead opting to focus on her feelings of happiness.

This kind of language, characterizing Mitchell as willful, is used in many of the stories. One person writes, "The despicable nature of all of this is self-evident, right? Smiling teen with one earbud in. Blushing emoji, as if she realizes she should be ashamed—but isn't" (Dewey). Mitchell's actions are presented as intentional—she should be ashamed, she knows she should be, but she is not. The stories suggest that the history of Auschwitz and Mitchell's feelings are concomitant: she knew about Auschwitz, knew better, but was so self-centered that she *expressly* put her happiness *above* the suffering of millions.

Further damningly, many stories note that Mitchell revels in the media attention she receives by reporting that Mitchell tweeted "I'm famous y'all" after an article in *Business Insider* was published, framing her tweet with statements like this from the *New York Post*: "Once the attention began to pour in, Mitchell seemed to be relishing her newfound notoriety" (Perez). Now Mitchell is not only narcissistic; she is also opportunistic, using the pain of others to further her personal ambitions.

Authenticity, Emotional Transparency, and Redemption

The narrative movement that unfolds in all the articles shifts from clear condemnation of Mitchell's actions at the beginning of the article to humanizing personal details that give a context for understanding Mitchell's behavior. The stories use Mitchell's feelings about her father while taking the selfie as a sense-making framework, providing an affective structure for readers to understand her actions. Readers are invited to move from disbelief and horror to empathy. Banet-Weiser outlines how transparency is key in displays of authenticity, since it suggests that one is "ostensibly giving viewers a complete view of one's 'authentic' self" (60). An authentic self is therefore "transparent, without artifice, open to others. Authenticity is demonstrated by allowing the outside world access to one's inner self" (60). The press stories about Mitchell attempt to do this—make Mitchell transparent, particularly her feelings.

Lauren Berlant details how affect is used as a logic of legitimation, noting a sense that "people ought to be legitimated because they have feelings and because there is an intelligence in what they feel that *knows* something about the world that, if it were listened to, could make things better" (2). Stories about Mitchell follow this trajectory: revealing details about her personal life and feelings, making her transparent in Banet-Weiser's sense, implying that if we can understand her feelings, we can understand her actions. The suggestion is that if we can connect on an emotional level to her story, then she is verified as authentic, and we will understand her.

All of the articles make clear from the outset that Mitchell's selfie is offensive, with sentences like "Her picture, although having a personal significance, is *understandably* going to cause offence" (Driscoll). Many articles follow up with something like "[but] the selfie isn't exactly what it appears to be" or that it is not what it looks like "on its face" (Molloy), or a comment about how viral images can be misunderstood (Dewey), suggesting not only that there is more than meets the eye, but also that there is a correct reading that can be uncovered, inviting the reader to dig deeper, look below the surface.

While many of the articles are not explicit in their sympathies for Mitchell, they use standard journalism tactics by devoting more than half the piece to details about Mitchell's personal life, which highlight how Auschwitz was a personally meaningful place for Mitchell because she had planned to go with her father, who passed away. These details humanize Mitchell, revealing her to readers—making her emotions transparent in Banet-Weiser's sense and using feelings to translate her actions to us, feelings that rely on gender conventions about loving daughters.

As noted earlier, although the form of the selfie is problematic in expressing authenticity because of the inherently performative nature of the genre, many articles use a quote from an interview with Mitchell, which functions to frame her as authentic. Mitchell is quoted saying, "Honestly I don't think I would do anything differently just because I didn't mean any harm. I told everybody my story behind it and that's the only reason I don't regret taking it" (Koziol). This quote verifies Mitchell's feelings as authentic and does this despite *and because of* the backlash about the Auschwitz selfie. In retrospect, after all the backlash, Mitchell is presented as having no regrets and standing by her actions: she would do it all over again if given the choice. This framing authenticates Mitchell because her intentions are presented as good—she did not mean to dishonor Auschwitz. She took the selfie to express authentic and strong feelings about her father, which are captured in the selfie once appropriately contextualized as being about her father and not Auschwitz, despite the inherently performative nature of the selfie.

Concluding Thoughts

Feelings damn Mitchell but save her in the end. The tension about what is presented as disrespectful and abhorrent behavior at the outset of the

articles—Mitchell smiling at Auschwitz—is resolved by making this incident a pivotal piece in a personal story about how one girl deals with her
grief about her father's death. While the articles begin by criticizing
Mitchell for using Auschwitz as a background for her happiness, they
ultimately background Auschwitz to tell a sympathetic personal story
about Mitchell. Auschwitz is the red herring.

Paradoxes and contradictions, Marlene. In my head, you implore me
to follow the different threads—pull on one, see what happens … I
pulled a bunch. I return to your statement about the importance of
derailing the once-objective speaker or narrator (Kadar), or, in this case,
the many narrators seeking objective status: the authors of the articles
telling Mitchell's story, the incontrovertible story of the Holocaust,
myself narrating the story of the articles, Mitchell's story. Feminist work
is, as you insist, about recuperating women's texts—here, about recuperating Mitchell's selfie as text, refusing a neat story about her text, laying
bare how her story is written by others, and the implications. Marlene,
you taught me to tell a messy story, to leave open the possibility of
other stories that can be told, and never to mistake my story for the
only story.

Acknowledgments

I am tremendously grateful to Eva C. Karpinski and Ricia Chansky for their generative and thoughtful feedback on this piece.

Works cited

Ahmed, Sara. *The Cultural Politics of Emotion*. 2nd ed. Edinburgh: Edinburgh
    UP, 2014. Print.
Auschwitz-Birkenau Museum. *Państwowe Muzeum Auschwitz-Birkenau*, 2018.
    Web. 31 May 2018.
Banet-Weiser, Sarah. *AuthenticTM: The Politics of Ambivalence in a Brand
    Culture*. New York: New York UP, 2012. Print.
Berlant, Lauren. *The Female Complaint*. Durham: Duke UP, 2008. Print.
Burns, Ann. "Self(ie)-Discipline: Social Regulation as Enacted through the
    Discussion of Photographic Practice." *International Journal of Communication*
    9 (2015): 1716–33. Print.
Detweiler, Craig. "Smiling for 'Auschwitz Selfies,' and Crying into the Digital
    Wilderness." *CNN*. Cable News Network, 22 July 2014. Web. 6 May 2018.
Dewey, Caitlin. "The Other Side of the Infamous 'Auschwitz Selfie.'" *The
    Washington Post*. The Washington Post, 22 July 2014 Web. 6 May 2018.
Driscoll, Brogan. "Breanna Mitchell's Smiling Auschwitz Selfie May Be Bad Taste,
    but the Backlash Is Far Worse." *Huffpost*. Oath Inc, 20 Sept. 2014. Web. 6 May
    2018.

Durando, Jessica. "Auschwitz Selfie Girl Defends Actions." *USA TODAY*. USA Today, 23 July 2014. Web. 6 May 2018.

Hess, Aaron. "The Selfie Assemblage." *International Journal of Communication* 9 (2015): 1629–46. Print.

Kadar, Marlene. *Essays on Life Writing: From Genre to Critical Practice*. Toronto: U of Toronto P, 1992. Print.

Koziol, Michael. "'I Regret Nothing', Says Auschwitz Selfie Teen." *The Sydney Morning Herald*. Fairfax Media, 23 July 2014. Web. 6 May 2018.

Massumi, Brian. *Parables for the Virtual: Movement, Affect, Sensation*. Durham: Duke UP, 2002. Print.

Miltner, Kate M., and Nancy K. Baym. "The Selfie of the Year of the Selfie: Reflections on a Media Scandal." *International Journal of Communication* 9 (2015): 1701–15. Print.

Molloy, Tim. "'Auschwitz Selfie' Outrage: But You're Supposed to Take Pictures." *The Wrap*. The Wrap News Inc., 23 July 2014. Web. 6 May 2018.

Murray, Derek Conrad. "Notes to Self: The Visual Culture of Selfies in the Age of Social Media." *Consumption Markets & Culture* 18.6 (2015): 490–516. Print.

Perez, Chris. "Smiling Auschwitz Selfie Sparks Twitter Outrage." *New York Post*. NYP Holdings, 21 July 2014. Web. 6 May 2018.

Senft, Theresa M., and Nancy K. Baym. "What Does the Selfie Say? Investigating a Global Phenomenon." *International Journal of Communication* 9 (2015): 1588–606. Print.

Shouse, Eric. "Feeling, Emotion, Affect." *Media-Culture* 8.6 (2015): n. page. Web. 6 May 2018.

Kim Thúy's *Ru* and the Art of the Anecdote

By Helen M. Buss

> No matter what we do to autobiography, it continues to flourish in one form or another… . the varieties of representation of the autobiographical are multiplying, and…need to be examined as seriously as their predecessors.
>
> —Jeanne Perreault and Marlene Kadar, "Introduction: Unlikely Documents, Unexpected Places"

In introducing my subject, I have quoted from Jeanne Perreault and Marlene Kadar's introduction to *Tracing the Autobiographical* to claim the art of making anecdotes as an autobiographical form. Kadar and Perreault place the responsibility for the act of "tracing" on those of us who carry out the "practices of auto/biographical scholarship" (2). Kim Thúy's book, *Ru*, the winner of the Governor General's Literary Award for Fiction and the "Canada Reads" contest in 2012, is named a "novel" on its cover. However, Thúy herself says in an online interview that it is based on her own memories as a child as well as her family's experience as Vietnamese "boat people" ("Following"). She decided not to claim the text as an autobiography because her family's experience as refugees fleeing Vietnam after the south fell was much less devastating than so many other refugees whose conditions she describes in *Ru*. Her mixed feelings about the generic placement of the book invites the practice of tracing. In my own reading of *Ru*, and in my desire to trace it as a gendered as well as a generic form, I would like to examine it as "autography," in the manner Perreault identifies that term as a gendered form in her book *Writing Selves* to describe the way that women "writers make 'I' and 'we' signify both continuity with an ongoing life in a body and a community, and dissociation within that life" (4). I want to trace the generic choice of anecdote as one particularly appropriate to autography.

Ru is a series of anecdotes, or perhaps more appropriately for a text originally written in French, a series of vignettes. This generic tool, which grows out of the oral use of the anecdote in every human society, transfers easily to fiction and nonfiction forms and exhibits, in Jurgen Heine's words, "a special realism" and "a claimed historical dimension" (qtd. in "Anecdote" 15). The French term *vignette* translates as "a little vine," suited for a book named *Ru*, which means "a small stream" in French and "a lullaby" in Vietnamese, all three terms, little vine, small stream, and lullaby, implying short, modest forms, seemingly as unassuming as the anecdote, a word that dictionaries usually classify as "unpublished documents."

The word "vignette" also has a special use in theories of psychology to describe involuntary memories. The short anecdotal style of the book imitates the suddenness and quick movement of involuntary memory, which can stem from traumatic experiences. Traumatic memory is a common result of the refugee experience and can extend into the immigration and settlement that follows, even when that settlement experience is as successful as Thúy's has been in her real-life roles as seamstress, interpreter, lawyer, and restaurateur as well as wife and mother, and now writer. At present we generally associate traumatic memory with posttraumatic stress disorder (PTSD), but such memories may also be part of normal involuntary memory. As viewed by psychologists Anne Rasmussen and Dorthe Berntsen in their article "The Possible Functions of Involuntary Autobiographical Memories," involuntary memories, often called flashbacks, are not to be compared to voluntary memory, which is contextualized in various conscious ways. Such flashbacks, in Rasmussen and Berntsen's view, are not contextualized by consciousness, and they form the core of spontaneous thought. In tracing the "autography" of Thúy's anecdotes, the life writing of a survivor of war, of the refugee experience, of resettlement, and of the adult return to the place of birth, I would like to explore Perreault's term *autography*, along with definitions of anecdote and the uses of involuntary or traumatic memory, as guides to reading *Ru*. I propose that in addition to the negative implications of traumatic memory, such memory may form the core of what can become creativity and, for my purposes, can shape the act of life writing. Flashbacks can guide a writer to a generic choice of anecdotes, which are often seen as incomplete and not always logically joined, unlike the narrative styles of traditional autobiography. This choice, in my reading, emphasizes the aspect of "dissociation" identified in Perreault's concept of autography, differentiating anecdotal life writing from the very consciously shaped historical "bio" typical of auto*bio*graphy. In the brief flashbacks of memory of traumatic times, Thúy uses short anecdotes that inform the present moment of her own "auto" or self-in-progress while avoiding a dominant "bio" that more traditional generic approaches would emphasize.

Jane Gallop's complaint in her book *Anecdotal Writing*, that theory never considers anecdotal forms, seems to remain true today and leaves folk like me to search for our own theoretical ground. So, at this point I need to take a short anecdotal detour of my own to another, very different autobiographical text to make my point about anecdote as a generic and gendered practice. In the same month that I read *Ru* for the first time, I also read Romeo Dallaire's *Waiting for First Light*, his autobiographical account of decades-long suffering from the intense disability of PTSD as a result of witnessing the Rwandan genocide as a UN peacekeeper and being told by the United Nations to do nothing but observe the tragedy because any interference to save lives through the use of weapons did not come under the umbrella of "peace keeping." Dallaire's text was inspired by a gift from Iqbal Risa, who, as a UN executive involved in making the decisions against interference and living with the results of those choices, understood the traumatic pain Dallaire was suffering and sent him an illustrated edition of Coleridge's *Rime of the Ancient Mariner*, verses of which Dallaire uses to head the chapters of his autobiography.

Coleridge's poem, which I first read in the late 1950s, my undergraduate years, is one of the longest in the English language and is the story of a man constantly retelling his story of survivor guilt to anyone who will listen. I remember that at that first reading, I was completely bored by the sad sailor who must stop "one in three" of everyone he meets to retell his tale of guilt and woe. But from the wisdom of my present three score years later, and with some survivor guilt of my own, I suddenly recognized what the three texts, Coleridge's, Dallaire's, and Thúy's, have in common: traumatic memory. Being a reader fascinated with how differences in both genre and gender can change the reading act, I observed the now rather obvious fact that each of the three writers describes quite different results of traumatic memory through their generic differences.

It is no surprise that autobiographical texts generally imitate the dominant generic forms of their era: for example, the detail of Christian confession in the earliest texts, such as St. Augustine's; the biography written as personal memoir, such as Godwin's late-eighteenth-century remembrance of his wife, the mother of feminism, Mary Wollstonecraft; or the first-person novelistic texts of the last two centuries. Dallaire's text, with its careful attention to character and plot in portraying the events of his life in historical order and in creating an ending emphasizing that a central character (a subject with a well described "bio") can change for the better, is an imitation of the novel format. Ru imitates none of these previous formats, but in its poetic short anecdotes it does evoke some aspects of Coleridge's long poem. For me, long poems always have a kind of haunting quality produced by the repetition of the same message with small variations of plot and setting but with incremental repetition, like a recurring dream that one finally comes out of understanding a basic truth about living, as in Coleridge's conclusion: "he prayeth well who loveth well." The incremental repetition of the anecdote/vignette form Thúy uses conjures a lesson for me as well: she writes well who loves well. Coleridge's mariner and Thúy's self have their need for love in common while choosing quite different generic (and gendered) routes.

Hopefully my anecdote of reading three texts to arrive at what is central for me in *Ru* has done what Wikipedia says an anecdote should do, that is, "reveal a truth more general than the brief tale itself." I can now offer a closer reading of a portion of Thúy's text to show the typical devices of the anecdote, the manner in which it starts with only a brief awareness of the first-person teller, but then goes quickly to an emphasis on significant others as actors with limited emphasis on the self as central. In Thúy's text these three realities are informed by the traumatic memory manifesting itself through the anecdotal or flashback nature of the teller's story. The anecdotes are usually less than a page in length, often only a few lines with the rest of the page left blank. Those from pages one to thirteen show the larger world of past and present as intertwined, beginning with, "I came into the world during the Tet offensive," then moving quickly in thirteen lines through the horror of a country "ripped in two" and the grounding of the self in the significant other: "The purpose of my birth was to replace lives that had been lost … . My life's duty was to prolong that of my mother" (1). In these first pages, this pattern of self as other, the world of war, and the central maternal figure moves from the traumatic past through to Thúy's traumatic present as mother of an autistic child, a pattern in which we begin to see the value of traumatic memory as her guide to loving. Flashback-like anecdotes into the traumatic past serve as support in a traumatic present. Thúy ends this first overview of her life thirteen pages later, writing of how her mother had been "preparing us for the collapse," preparing her family for the refugee camps because she knew that soon they would no longer have even "a floor beneath our feet" (13).

It is left to the reader, as often it is in the briefness of anecdote or the economy of poetry, to connect past and present and the manner in which present trauma seeks past trauma as guide. In this way, on page seven of *Ru* the childhood past is interrupted by a sudden jump from the refugee condition to Thúy's own maternal present. It is necessary to read this anecdote in full:

> I didn't cry out and I didn't weep when I was told my son Henri was a prisoner in his own world, when it was confirmed that he is one of those children who don't hear us, don't speak to us, even though they're neither deaf nor mute. He is also one of those children we must love from a distance, neither touching, nor kissing nor smiling at them because every one of their senses would be assaulted by the odour of our skin, by the intensity of our voices, the texture of our hair, the throbbing of our hearts. Probably he'll never call me Maman lovingly, even if he can pronounce the word poire with

all the roundness and sensuality of the oi sound. He will never understand why I cried when he smiled for the first time. He won't know that, thanks to him, every spark of joy has become a blessing and that I will keep waging war against autism, even if I know already that it's invincible. (7)

The anecdote seems over, but then, in a one-line paragraph used like a pause before the punch line of an anecdote ("punch" meant here not as in its comic form as in many anecdotes, but in a more serious meaning as in a blow to the body, perhaps also to the psyche), she adds, "Already, I am defeated, stripped bare, beaten down" (7). Thus, trauma is recognized as an already known part of the self but also as a power to be used to recognize sparks of joy in the present.

In an online interview on YouTube with Lilou Mace, Thúy asserts, "I'm in survivor mode all the time." She adds that her writing style is learned through mothering an autistic child who has taught her lessons in "slowing down," "alertness," "detail," "seeing color in a special way," in order to become "a messenger of joy." This attitude gives trauma and its ongoing memory reoccurrence in our lives an entirely different dimension than our perception of traumatic memory as always a negative influence in ongoing life and invites exploration of the idea that traumatic memory may be our brains' ability to push us toward an exploration of how such memories can inform, change, and enhance our selfhood.

In the next seven pages of her text, Thúy moves us through aspects of the refugee and immigrant experiences in a series of flashbacks|anecdotes, whose first lines begin with small observations on the beauty of snowbanks and the magical nature of experiencing her first Canadian winter. She then moves back to her son Henri, comparing her own situation as refugee-|immigrant to her son's dilemma: "I was like my son ... unable to talk or to listen ... . I had no points of reference, no tools to allow me to dream, to project myself into the future, to be able to experience the present, in the present" (8). This joining of her own past inabilities to her son's problems leads not to failure but the beginning of a new way of being in the world, as remembered in the next anecdote, describing her first school experience: her first teacher in Canada begins Thúy's learning of new "tools" as she takes the children into a world of "colours, drawings, trivia" (9). When the teacher moves to speaking to the silent child in the new language, saying, "My name is Marie-France, what's yours?" Thúy tells us,

> I repeated each of her syllables without blinking, without needing to understand, because I was lulled by a cloud of coolness, of lightness, of sweet perfume. I hadn't understood a word she'd said, only the melody of her voice, but it is enough. More than enough. (9)

The traumatized child—after the reassurance of safety given by a loving teacher who offers "colours, drawings, trivia" that arouse the senses—

finds new ways, such as mimicry of the melody of the teacher's voice, the felt sense of coolness and lightness, and sweet perfume, to enter language. The implication here, for the reader, is that just as her teacher offered a variety of ways to enter language, Thúy can find new tools to help her child enter language.

Before this reader is asked to enter the memories of the dreadful refugee camps five pages later, early anecdotes prepare me for the challenges of the move from refugee to immigrant, which seem difficult and sometimes insulting, to read the much worse past of the refugee camp. This constant reverse movement of the anecdotes through the past and back to various present times carries on throughout the text as we learn to experience traumatic memory as both trauma and an inventive guide to new ways of being, just as the adult mother of an autistic child learns new ways to communicate with her child.

When Thúy does begin to describe the horrors of war, the breakup of a country, the refugee and immigrant experience, the lives of Vietnamese women past and present, the anecdote continues to be her choice of form. Thúy moves into the past to recover the lives of women in traditional Vietnamese society, such as her many aunts, who lived in the past as prisoners of wealth and tradition. She then moves beyond the past to the stories of former Viet Cong women soldiers and poor women, whom Thúy writes of after her return to Vietnam as an adult writing short, effective anecdotes of women who are always in survival mode as she is, from the female victims of war to the stories of prostitutes who perform sex acts for as little as a bowl of soup. These anecdotes build on top of one another to create a gendered genre of anecdotal autography. The increasingly female gendering of this anecdotal autography moves outside the intimate community of family to a wider world of female experience and traces a female self that is a not a "center," nor a "core" nor a "site" nor a "space," but in Perreault's naming an "energy" (17), in Thúy's case the maternal energy of the survivor, who uses traumas of the past to create the energy of love in the present informed by living as a survivor.

Kadar and Perreault end their argument for the value of tracing in "Unlikely Documents, Unexpected Places" with questions about the value of such scholarship to "help us evade or at least recognize the overwhelming colonizing forces of global economies and media … . Will the possibility of connection among readers, writer and theorist of life documents dissipate the ill effects of exile? Will the powers of analysis and the recreation of life narratives we enact here counteract forces that seem ranged against life itself?" (6). I suggest that tracing the "energy" of Thúy's anecdotes of a life affected by all of these concerns as well as the power of love is a good place to start.

Disclosure Statement

No potential conflict of interest was reported by the author.

Works Cited

"Anecdote." Wikimedia Foundation, Inc., n.d. Web. 20 May 2018.

Coleridge, Samuel Taylor. *The Rime of the Ancient Mariner*. 1834. *PoetryFoundation.org*. Poetry Foundation, n.d. Web. 7 Apr. 2018.

Dallaire, Romeo. *Waiting for First Light: My Ongoing Battle with PTSD*. Toronto: Random House Canada, 2016. Print.

Gallop, Jane. *Anecdotal Theory*. Durham: Duke UP, 2002. Print.

Perreault, Jeanne. *Writing Selves: Contemporary Feminist Autography*. Minneapolis: U of Minnesota P, 1995. Print.

Perreault, Jeanne, and Marlene Kadar. "Introduction: Unlikely Documents, Unexpected Places." *Tracing the Autobiographical*. Ed. Kadar et al. Toronto: Wilfrid Laurier UP, 2005. 1–7. Print.

Rasmussen, Anne S., and Dorthe Berntsen. "The Possible Functions of Involuntary Autobiographical Memories." *Applied Cognitive Psychology* 23 (2009): 1137–52. Applied Cognitive Psychology, n.d. Web. 15 Apr. 2017.

Thúy, Kim. "Following Where Life Leads You." Interview by Lilou Mace. *YouTube*. 25 May 2014. Web. 7 Apr. 2018.

—. *Ru*. Trans. Sheila Fischman. Toronto: Random House Canada, 2012. Print.

Drawing a Narrative Landscape with Women Refugees

By Ozlem Ezer

Finding My Path to Life Writing as a Genre Through Marlene Kadar's Works

In summer 2003, I was preparing for my comprehensive exams at York University as a PhD student in women's studies (now gender, sexuality, and women's studies).[1] In planning my talk for the 2017 IABA-Americas conference, I revisited my comprehensive exam essay after almost fourteen years and found a metaphor for contrasting Marlene Kadar's oeuvre to more traditional and mainstream texts: "The conversation taking place in Kadar's work on life writing reminds me of a friendly, informal gathering among peers versus a traditional family dinner where each member knows her place and dare not cross" (Comprehensive 3). *Essays on Life Writing* and the anthology *Reading Life Writing* proved to be extremely useful not just for my dissertation but also for my book in Turkish on women's travel writing. Kadar's work helped me to extend beyond the reach of autobiography in the traditional sense. As she indicates in the introduction to *Tracing the Autobiographical*, her and her three co-authors' approach to life writing underlines the potential and multiplying possibilities as well as reinventions regarding the ways to address the lives of individuals, in my case, selected Syrian women's life stories (1). I hope that my work on the diversity of Syrian women's representations will find a voice and space despite my relentless questioning of disciplinary and historical demarcations.

Representing Displaced Women of Syria

Since March 2011—after the brutal and complex war fueled by political and sectarian divisions had claimed many lives—images of chaotic

This article was originally published with errors, which have now been corrected in both the print and online versions. Please see Correction (http://dx.doi.org/10.1080/08989575.2019.1588530)

crowds, rubble, screaming people, and dead bodies either in Syria or on the shores of Turkey and Greece have dominated the global media. Mostly, refugee representations in the media are often of victimized, vulnerable, and subordinate Syrian women and children. They trigger feelings of pity, revulsion, and estrangement, among other emotional states, leaving hardly any room for the many untold stories of Syrians who do not fit these dominant narratives and who can blend into their host countries in Europe, Turkey, and Canada; these Syrian refugees can speak English and maintain a life outside of the refugee camps as invisible survivors.

To challenge the dominant stereotypes and to explore displacement as one aspect of a woman's life, rather than *the* defining aspect, I interviewed ten Syrian women refugees for approximately fifteen to eighteen hours each between February 2016 and January 2018. The process of recording and compiling these personal narratives illustrated confusions and ambiguities of human nature while revealing several gender-specific expectations of being a girl-child, teenager, married or single woman, or mother in Syria and as a Syrian refugee since 2011. The chosen host countries are the ones with humanitarian asylum policies, unlike the rest of the so-called democratic regimes.

The interviews began in Istanbul and continued in Germany, Sweden, Canada, and Greece, in that order. The participant in Sweden pulled out because of unforeseen personal reasons, but the rest persisted. Except for Halima, the women were able to express themselves in English at different levels of proficiency, and their profiles reflect the diversity of the group. Rose defines herself as a Kurdish Yazidi and an educator. She is fifty-one, was born in Damascus, grew up in Aleppo, and is married with three children. We met in Istanbul (2016), but she has been in Germany since fall 2017. Halima (forty-seven) is from Dara, is married with three children, and lives in Istanbul with her husband and in-laws. She is a practicing Sunni Muslim and wants to focus on Syrian children's education in Turkey.

Lamia's family moved to Damascus in 2008 from Deir Ez-Zor. Lamia (twenty-five) was studying environmental engineering in Aleppo when the war broke out. Her transfer application to Istanbul University in 2013 was successful, and her mother recently joined her there. Muzna (twenty-seven) is from Aleppo, and she was raised as a Muslim with her two brothers. She is a human rights activist with a degree in French linguistics. In 2016, Muzna received a grant from the Nobel Women's Initiative in Canada. She began her MA in peace studies at Sherbrooke University in fall 2017.

Emile (twenty-eight) and her four older brothers were raised by a Muslim single mother in Homs. She traveled alone through Dubai, Jordan, Lebanon, and Yemen before arriving in Canada in fall 2014 thanks to a scholarship.[2] She graduated with honors in political science in January 2018. Sama (twenty-eight) is from Damascus, is a practicing Muslim, and has a degree in translation.[3] After living in Lebanon and Turkey, she crossed the Aegean on a boat with her parents and a younger sister in 2015 and reunited with her brothers in Germany. Zizinia (thirty-eight) is a single mother with two daughters and has a degree in economics from the University of Aleppo. She works in Gaziantep (Turkey), leading an NGO called Space of Hope.

Sara (twenty-six) is from Latakia, the eldest of four siblings, a self-proclaimed atheist and bisexual, born into a conservative Alawite family. She has a degree in pharmacy. She left Syria in December 2015, first for Istanbul, then Athens, where she sought asylum. She found a job at an international NGO after six months of homelessness. Born in Aleppo in 1984, Bidaa grew up in a close-knit family with compassionate Sunni parents. She practiced law for several years and has been an asylee in Athens since March 2016. She gives Arabic lessons to the children of Arab expatriates and is learning Greek.

All women experienced separation from their immediate families because of the war at some point; yet technology allows them to stay connected through a virtual network. One example is WhatsApp: two of the women I interviewed talk to their mothers two or three times a day through this app. They share everyday things, such as asking what to cook for dinner. The strength of individuals' virtual presence and assistance to each other by the use of their phones and certain apps needs to be acknowledged in their stories. In other words, the narrative landscape that I have been painting is inclusive of virtual communication and contributes to the boundary discussions regarding the forums used in interactions between the participant and the researcher.[4] Digital and mobile technologies have become inextricable from our relationships, and this life-writing project is no exception. In fact, mobile technologies have proven to be lifelines in multiple ways for all documented and undocumented people in transition.[5]

The Importance of Bonding and Blurring in Life Writing: The Writer and the Co-participants

My project's title is "Lifelines: Syrianwomanhoods in Transition," and the word "lifeline" as a metaphor has a bidirectional function. The selected

Syrian women are not the only ones who are excluded from authentic knowledge resources. With so-called post-truth politics, "alternative facts," and fake news sites that have been disproportionately circulated and consumed, readers also need narrators' lifelines, as in the case of projects like this one, where the voices of refugees are not cut for an ideology or media company and are made accessible to the reader only after each narrator signs off her consent upon reading their stories. In other words, these stories serve as lifelines for the consumers of knowledge so that they are not drowned in a polluted ocean of unreliable data or hearsay, and enabling them to make efforts to improve their understanding of Syrian life and culture and the women of Syria.

The narratives in this project are not limited to the tragedies of recent Syrian history, although they do acknowledge the facts and incidents that have been a preferred focus of global news and humanitarian aid organizations' agendas since March 2011. Instead, they offer diverse firsthand life accounts, including the women's family backgrounds, childhood memories, favorite foods or music, their early years of formal and informal education, the most significant people in their lives, and marriage and children (if applicable). Each narrative is structured so that the war and the displacement are presented as one aspect of a fuller life. In summary, my project explores the lives of Syrian women who have immigrated after surviving a major conflict and now redefine themselves as postcrisis humans.[6]

Having the concept of "womanhood" in the title instead of "women" and choosing the term "co-participant" over "narrator" or "subject" are intentional feminist interventions. In fact, "womanhoods" in the plural was suggested by the Syrian ex-participant in Stockholm during our meeting in December 2016, to which I eagerly agreed. I mention it here as one source of evidence of bonding with the participant and blurring the boundaries between the two of us in regard to authorial and authoritative realms of life-writing projects. I also played with the idea of referring to the co-participants as "oral historians," as Susan Geiger did in her article "What's So Feminist About Women's Oral History?" (180). Then my role and designation can dance around the terms "ethnographer," "recorder," and "researcher." Although only four of the ten co-participants refer to themselves as feminist activists, and some have patriarchal views regarding the role of family and women in a society, the collection stands out as a feminist project in its prioritization of women's life stories over those of men. The following email is a part of the diversified narrative landscape and is included here as evidence of the transparency that we, the Syrian co-participant and I, have developed since our first meeting in

Istanbul in June 2016. Muzna Dureid shared her attorney's Facebook post after she was accepted to Canada as a refugee in January 2017:

> Among the privileges of being a refugee lawyer is helping people change their lives by obtaining protection in Canada. Yet rarely in my 27-year career have I been so moved. The 25-year-old Syrian woman recognized today by the immigration and refugee board brings honor, joy and inspiration to my heart. Is it the authenticity, the peacefulness, the passion for defending human rights? It is all of those things and more. Canada has gained a leader, who has already made a career of working for refugee protection, feminist causes and human rights. She is fluent in English and French. She exudes emotional and intellectual intelligence. She is a gem. She is on a path to being a great leader. My client is thankful to Canada but it is Canadians that should be grateful that this amazing young soul has chosen out land. Mitchell J. Goldberg.

Marlene Kadar's contribution to incorporating online correspondences into auto|biographical projects have been very inspirational for me throughout. In fact, it was because of her work as much as the faculty whom I met during my postdoctoral studies at GexCel Linkoping University in Sweden that I survived academia after my dissertation. Creativity and jargon-free language can breathe life into certain mostly marginalized academic spaces, to which I have eagerly contributed (for example, "Exotic"; "Re-Constructing"). One needs to reach out, though, and ask for assistance, preferably with some written material at hand.

Some Terminology and the Content of *Lifelines*

I have used the term "oral history" to describe my work in order to satisfy the disciplinary demands of academia, grant applications, and publishing houses. However, depending on the context and the audience, my preference is to refer to it as either "polyphonic writings," borrowing words that are used to describe Svetlana Alexievich's prose ("Svetlana"), or life writing, since the term used is likely to affect a grant committee member differently from public lecture attendees. Both descriptions indicate opportunities for experiments with the interviewer's self-inscription and representations along with the narrators. In short, polyphonic writings and oral histories leave doors open for multiple narrators and occasional personal commentaries from the interviewer, and they display transparency in the author|interviewer—participant interaction. *Lifelines* explores "ordinary" middle-class Syrian women's lives, emphasizing communication and sharing rather than cataloguing evidence-based research. Through careful documentation, the co-participants reflect on certain demands, events, sentiments, and social aspects of being a woman in Syria but also being a displaced individual.

The other unusual aspect of this life-writing project lies in its suggestion to view displacement as a potential for transformation, particularly for women who were expected if not forced into certain gender roles in Syria and now are based in another country. Through access to language courses and quality education, the abused or repressed people in the country of origin can thrive in the hosting country through some unplanned and unpredicted ways. However, this process needs to be taken cautiously because of the loss of the women's networks and communities back home, which can be disempowering. There is plenty of evidence in the narratives to demonstrate the complexity of the gender-role shifts in the process of resettlement (e.g. attempts by male authority figures to increase control during the transition and resettlement processes). For example, one of the co-participants who had her own car and a full-time job was in no rush to get married in Aleppo. She told me that once in Germany, her father became very controlling and began to monitor the time that she spent outside the house by calling and texting her. She tried to reason with him and told him to trust her. Her father thought Germany was not as safe as prewar Aleppo, especially after dark (also expressed by another participant in regards to Athens), and the unfamiliarity with the culture and language aggravated his new fears for his daughter. As a consequence, the pressure for single daughters to get married, preferably to another Syrian refugee, increased when they were relocated in Europe or Canada.

My research can be approached in two ways. One is locating the life stories in a broader literature on forced displacement, including but not limited to economic and natural-disaster-induced displacements. Second, these life stories can be embedded into the resettlement narratives of refugees from different geographical areas, time periods, classes, educations, and gender sensibilities.

Conclusion: Life Writing as a Political Practice

I have tried to do justice to the co-participant women, to their concerns and experiences, but the resulting text is bound to be partial. Besides, the narratives have been filtered through many layers since the time of our recordings and have survived several negotiations. I used online forums for the purpose of clarifying many statements or completing several unfinished sentences from the participants, and I structured the narratives in a semichronological style. These follow-ups sometimes gave birth to new stories or corrections to what was initially recorded. In accordance with standard ethics protocols of emancipatory research, each participant was informed from the beginning that they had the opportunity to intervene at any stage of the narrative inquiry process. They had immediate access to the transcripts and were free to edit or take out certain passages with which they did not feel comfortable.

The time and labor invested in examining a person's life generate the potential to dispel the "spreading epidemic of misinformation," popularly known as "alternative facts." In an era when "misinformation pushes aside knowledge," being an academic and researcher requires the utmost sensitivity against stereotyping (Will). Life writing serves as a fitting multidimensional tool and political practice because of its dynamic and productive nature. These life-story narratives are apt to expose the confusions, contradictions, and ambiguities that are part of our everyday experience and ourselves, and they are compatible with the textual freedom that life writing offers to its practitioners. In this sense, regardless of the terminology or categorization, recording and publishing women's life stories is a valuable project, and it illustrates the need for a flexible and holistic perspective toward our understanding of refugees worldwide.

Notes

1. The word *landscape* offers an incredibly rich array and history of meanings whose resonances are too abundant to expand on here. The following is my selection of definitions, but the word is not limited to: adumbration, outline, a faint or shadowy representation, compendium, plan, view, and background.
2. The university name has not been revealed in order to protect participant anonymity.
3. The university name has not been revealed in order to protect participant anonymity.
4. There has been a proliferation of articles and special issues of academic journals regarding digital ethnographies in the past decade (e.g. *Forum: Qualitative Social Research* 8.3 (2007) and *Visual Ethnography—Tools, Archives, and Research Methods* 5.2 (2016)).
5. For refugees, smartphones act as GPS in boats, and once landed on shore, dialing 112 (the European equivalent to 911) to ask for immediate rescue teams saved many lives.
6. Ricia Anne Chansky suggested the term "postcrisis humans."

Disclosure Statement

No potential conflict of interest was reported by the author.

Works Cited

Ezer, Ozlem. "'Exotic Sweden': A Nordic Quest in the Winter of 2010." *Telling and Re-Telling: The Mosaics of Traveling Narratives and Narrators, a Spec. Issue of Utah Foreign Language Review* 19 (2011): 33–54. Twentieth Anniversary Edition. Print.

—. "Re-Constructing Konya through Woolly Wanderings." *Liminalities: A Journal of Performance Studies* 13.2 (2017): 1–19. Liminalities.net, n.d. Web. 17 May 2018.

Geiger, Susan. "What's So Feminist About Women's Oral History?" *Journal of Women's History* 2.1 (1990): 169–82. Print.

Goldberg, Mitchell J. Facebook post. 10 Jan. 2017.

Kadar, Marlene. "Coming to Terms: Life Writing—From Genre to Critical Practice." *Essays on Life Writing: From Genre to Critical Practice.* Toronto: U of Toronto P, 1992. 3–16. Print.

Kadar, Marlene, ed. *Essays on Life Writing: From Genre to Critical Practice.* Toronto: U of Toronto P, 1992. Print.

—. *Reading Life Writing.* Toronto: Oxford UP, 1993. Print.

Kadar, Marlene, et al., eds. *Tracing the Autobiographical.* Waterloo: Wilfrid Laurier UP, 2005. Print.

"Svetlana Alexievich—Facts." *Nobelprize.org.* Nobel Media AB, 2014. Web. 8 Apr. 2018.

Will, George. "The 'Alternative Facts' Epidemic Goes Way beyond Politics." *The Washington Post.* 5 Apr. 2017. Web. 8 Apr. 2018.

Essays

Translanguaging and Autobiogeography as Decolonial Strategies for Writing Life Narratives within Displacement

By Manoela dos Anjos Afonso Rodrigues

ABSTRACT

In this article, the author presents research that explores individual and collective autobiographical acts aiming at the creation of places of enunciation for decolonial selves through practices in the visual arts. This practice-based research benefits from interdisciplinary crossings between feminist geography, life writing, and decoloniality, through which the author designed the network of concepts that gave form to the epistemological approach to practice and research used. The first stage of the practice is a self-reflective response to personal experiences within geographical displacement and dislocation in language. The second part comprises collective writing processes conducted with twelve Brazilian women who live in London. Writing is a cross-element in this practice-based research, and visual arts offer a space for exploring decolonial acts. Thus, the author sought in decoloniality a path to offer a contribution to knowledge by proposing decolonial strategies for writing life narratives within displacement through translanguaging and autobiogeography.

Turning

A few months before starting my doctoral research project at the Chelsea College of Arts, I came across a remarkable traffic sign in London (Figure 1). Its text warned "Diversion Ends," but someone had accented the word "Diversion," scratched out the word "Ends," and answered in Spanish, "La Diversión Ha Empezado!!!" ("The Fun Has Begun!!!").

This traffic sign shows how powerful an acute accent can become: it converted English into Spanish, opened the public space for a different dialogue, and gave place to another language, tone, meaning, author, and readers. This accent turned a space for warning into a place for *diversión*, *diversidad*, *diversidade*, diversity. All these words are related to the Latin verb *vertere*, which means "to turn" and can be translated into Brazilian Portuguese as *desviar*, "to divert," or *mudar de posição*, "to change

---

This article was originally published with errors, which have now been corrected in both the print and online versions. Please see Correction (http://dx.doi.org/10.1080/08989575.2019.1588530)

Figure 1. *"La Diversión Ha Empezado!!!" 2011. Photograph.*

position." When I first read this message, I immediately felt I was being addressed and I was brought out of the place of muteness I entered when I became a newcomer in London with difficulties in communicating in the English language. I noticed that "turning" could become a powerful strategy for creating places where other presences, voices, meanings, and stories can coexist. At that moment, I understood that belonging, in the context of immigration, can be directly related to being addressed and invited to a conversation that is conducted in a "pluriversal" environment where languages and cultures are not only related to each other, but also entangled among themselves (Mignolo, "Pluriversality").

My project found its starting point in the middle of personal changes in geography, language, self, and identity. It branches into myriad fragmented stories written in-between languages through my practice in the visual arts and is inspired by life-writing genres such as diary, memoir, and correspondence. While I invented forms to express myself in English and write my own stories about displacement in this language, I also unfolded artistic methods for knowing other Brazilian women's stories. In this process, art practice helped me to reach higher levels of consciousness about my subject positions as a woman who came from central-western Brazil to study in London. Such awareness led me to reflect in more depth on power relations between language and place, and their impact on my self-perception and agency.

The objective of my investigation is to understand how practices in the visual arts can engender individual and collective decolonial acts for exploring experiences of displacement, raising an "immigrant consciousness" (Mignolo, "Geopolitics" 132–33), and opening places of "enunciation" for decolonial selves (Gaztambide-Fernández 198–200). For the purposes of this project, I employ Walter Mignolo's approach to decoloniality, since it highlights "attitudes, projects, goals, and efforts to delink from the promises of modernity and the un-human conditions created by coloniality" ("Further" 27), stimulating critical analysis of "the construction, transformation, and sustenance of racism and patriarchy that created the conditions to build and control a structure of knowledge" (*Darker* xv).

Therefore, my research topic emerged from my own experience as a newcomer in London who entered a place of muteness after being challenged by a new language in a new place. Although I became mute, I refused to be silenced by the coloniality of being, sensing, and knowing that was operating in my subjectivity, and decided to face the shame of not knowing the language through creating strategies for "turning" the place of muteness into a place of enunciation. Thus, with|in silence but not silenced, I experimented with decolonial acts through my practice in the visual arts to articulate life stories and reinvent my voice by critically positioning myself in the middle of my own muteness. This experience led me to coin the idea of "autobiogeography as decolonial methodology" ("Autobiogeografia"), which stimulates the creation of situated autobiographical acts through art practice to confront the coloniality of power and raise an immigrant consciousness. This experience changed my practice as an artist: now, rather than creating artworks, I first want "to create in order to decolonize sensibilities" (Gaztambide-Fernández 201) and open paths toward my decolonial self.

Writing

Inspired by the traffic sign (Figure 1), I developed a writing process that consists of assembling photographs of words collected in the city into

Figure 2. *"Memoir (London, 2010–2013)." Red book. Artist's book, 18 × 18 cm, single edition.*

Figure 3. *"Memoir (London, 2010–2013)." Red book. Artist's book, 18 × 18 cm, single edition.*

artist's books. In this article, I present the first pair of books created by using "turning" as a mechanism for changing the meaning of words and writing personal narratives. It is called "Memoir (London, 2010–2013)" and comprises two books: a red book (Figures 2 and 3) and a black book (which will be shown later in this text).

The photographs used to write the red book were taken during my first walks on the streets of London. Differing from the other books produced afterwards, in "Memoir (London, 2010–2013)" I was not conscious that I was collecting words in the city. I only realized this fact when I decided to apply for a doctoral degree and needed to look back carefully at my visual work to design my art-based research project. I was surprised by my own collection of words because it perfectly addressed my experiences as an immigrant living in London. By looking at and reading my photographs, I realized that my feelings of unease were directly connected to the messages I was receiving from the city, which constantly reminded me that I did not belong there (Figure 2). Then, I framed my research project on the relationship between language and place, and decided to start by investigating which stories were hidden in the words that I had collected. When I realized that the hidden stories were about the colonial traces in my own being, I answered to|through the city, with|in silence: "Remember Me | We Are Here to Create Purpose for Life" (Figure 3).

Writing by combining images to unveil the coloniality of being, sensing, and knowing became a key element for my art practice in this project. In this process, photography came to work as a kind of "type machine," through which I "wrote" words by clicking—that is, by photographing them on the streets (Figure 4).

As I started to position myself as a writer, I sought to find a life-writing genre that could be in dialogue with what I was doing with the images of words in my artist's books. Language memoir (Kaplan) seemed to be the perfect genre to guide conceptually this writing-making process, since it focuses on the experiences about learning a language. In addition, as G. Thomas Couser reminds us, memoir is a relational and democratic life-writing genre rooted in the ways people represent their lives, make identity claims, and locate themselves through personal stories connected to everyday life. Rather than registering preexisting selfhood, memoir nurtures processes that bring new selves into being and "has been a threshold genre in which some previously silent populations have been given voice for the first time" (Couser 12).

Writing about crossings from one language to another, and thus from one culture to another, highlights the problem Mignolo pointed out by regarding the complicities between language and the notions of empire and nation. Mignolo argues, "While the imaginary of the modern world system focused on frontiers, structures, and the nation-state as a space within frontiers with a national language, languaging and bilanguaging, as a condition of border thinking from the decolonial difference, open up to a postnational imaginary" (*Local* 253). From the colonial perspective, translation is rooted in the principles of epistemic colonial power and might work as a tool to stress colonial difference, which tends to racialize people and make them "seen as inferior by the dominant discourse" (*Darker* 214). This is a kind of translation that leads to conversion instead

Figure 4. *"Writing," 2014. Photograph by Alexandre Strapasson.*

of conversation, reinforcing "the colonial difference between Western European languages (languages of the sciences, knowledge, and the locus of enunciation) and the rest of the languages on the planet (languages of culture and religion and the locus of the enunciated)" (Mignolo and Schiwy 10).

In my case, the hierarchy between languages can be felt in two ways: from the Brazilian Portuguese to the Portuguese language, and from the Brazilian Portuguese and its accent to the British English language. The former is related to my own family history, since I was born to a Portuguese father and a Brazilian mother, who does not know very much about her own Indigenous heritage. The latter refers to my experience of learning British English in the UK, where different levels of prejudice are connected to the different types of accent that people in this country have. In the first case, I experienced linguistic prejudice when I first

Figure 5. *"Get Rid of Your Accent," 2015. Poster affixed on the canteen wall of the Students' Union at the University of the Arts London.*

traveled to Portugal to get to know my family on my father's side. There, I was told that what we speak in Brazil is not Portuguese at all: it is "Brazilian." Curiously, in London I heard the same story: in the US, people speak "American," not English. In the second case, while I lived in London, I discovered that learning "standard English" would not be enough because, in British society, there is discrimination against people because of their accent (Figure 5). It became clear that there is a hierarchy between not only western and non-western languages, but also between western languages and the languages that are a legacy of colonization, such as the Brazilian Portuguese and the American English languages.

In the Zapatista movement, for example, another kind of relationship between languages emerges: the "double translation" (Mignolo and Schiwy 17–20), which differs from the one-way translation process implied by the modern colonial world system based on metropolitan interests. Thus, the Zapatistas' theory of translation is conceived as a re-educational process called "translanguaging," which is "a way of speaking, talking, and thinking in between languages" (27). Therefore, as another option, translanguaging offers places for border thinking where new perspectives to conceptualize translation and transculturation can be built through the "double consciousness of subalterns in confrontation with hegemony"

Figure 6. *"Memoir (London, 2010–2013)." Red book. Artist's book, 18 × 18 cm, single edition.*

(22). In this way, translanguaging "turns" hegemonic languages into tools for communication, connection, struggle, justice, and transformation.

In my practice, I used "turning" as a decolonial act for creating translanguaging possibilities through writing with images of words collected in the city. This process helped me to reposition my voice and self in order to transform a place of muteness into a place of enunciation. Through "turning," I activated voice with|in silence and became aware of the traces of coloniality operating in my own being|sensing|thinking. As Mignolo argues, in the decolonial option, one must "engage in epistemic disobedience" if one intends "to take on civil disobedience," because only in this way is it possible to go beyond reforms and provoke transformations (*Darker* 139). This kind of disobedience demands a decolonial courage to confront coloniality and deal with the colonial wound (Figure 6). In order to heal the colonial wound, one needs to create processes of delinking for "regaining your pride, your dignity, assuming your entire humanity in front of an unhuman being that makes you believe you were abnormal, lesser, that you lack something. How do you heal that? Through knowing, understanding, decolonial artistic creativity and decolonial philosophical aesthesis, and above all by building the communal" (Gaztambide-Fernández 207).

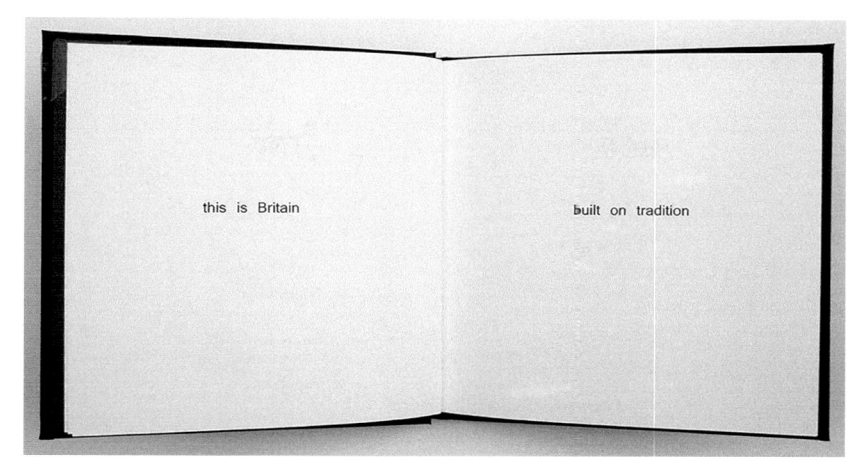

Figure 7. *"Memoir (London, 2010–2013)." Black book. Artist's book, 18 × 18 cm, single edition.*

Voicing

Assembling images of words into the red artist's book allowed me to craft an accented, visual, and textual voice. Through this process, I started to map my dynamic subject positions within displacement. However, when I first held the printed copy of this book in my hands, I felt dissatisfied after a while. My written, personal voice was not visible enough because it was immersed in all the imagery of those photographs. This is why I decided to erase the images and produce a new book, the black one, which included only the words (Figure 7).

The new book had a profound impact on me because I "saw my voice" through the act of crafting my own words. By subtracting its visual surroundings, this accented voice built through diversion got "louder." I also realized that I had divided the book into six chapters: arrival, surveillance, taking action, university, life goals, and meeting loved ones. This became an unprecedented writing-making process that involved three phases: selecting words through photography, composing narratives through assemblage, and subtracting images to make the textual voice appear (Figure 8).

If the notions of image and reality are complimentary and the camera may be seen as "the ideal arm of consciousness," as Susan Sontag suggests (2), then photography can work not only to capture images or mirror realities, but also to build and disclose meanings, as Victor Burgin points out (1–14). In my writing-making process, when the image is gone, "voice" appears. It seems that images were distracting me while I sought understanding about why I photographed those words and not others.

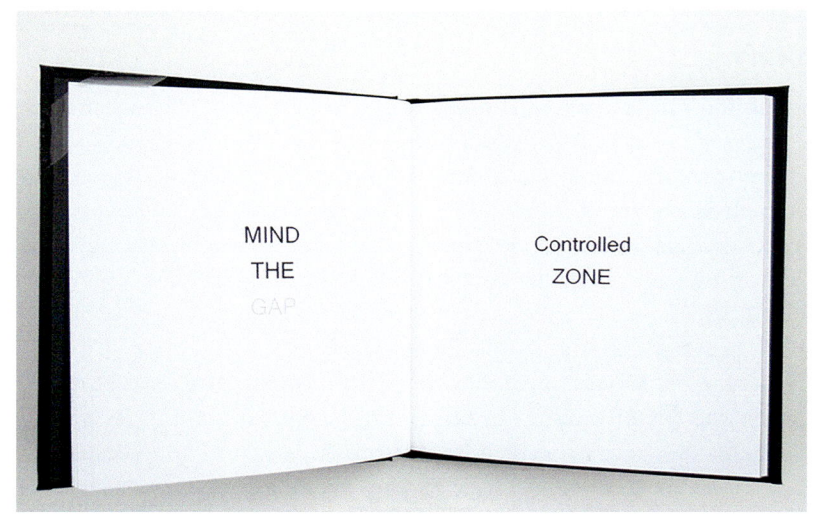

Figure 8. *"Memoir (London, 2010–2013)." Red and black books. Artist's books, 18 × 18 cm, single editions.*

The narratives in both the red and black books are born from strategies of appearance and disappearance, location and dislocation. The appearance process, in the red book, is related to the formation of a personal, experiential, material, and embodied vocabulary. The disappearance process, in the black book, ultimately involves getting rid of the visual in favor of the textual.

In this project, the situated autobiographical writing became the modus operandi of my autobiogeographical practice in the visual arts. I created decolonial approaches to writing to express experiences of displacement that were unfolding in-between languages. Photography worked as a tool for building a vocabulary comprising words collected in the city, and played a crucial role as a disclosure (rather than only a picturing) device. In this writing-making process, the complex relationship established between appearance and disappearance, "turning" and "accent," the assemblage and erasure of images and words, generated life narratives written through border thinking at the same time as I inhabited the borderland. Gloria Anzaldúa argues that "Living in a state of psychic unrest, in a Borderland, is what makes poets write and artists create. It is like a cactus needle embedded in the flesh" (95). People know that they are living on the border when they feel ashamed, invisible, and illegitimate. From this place, the borderland, one can engage in border thinking and start to delink from the coloniality of being, sensing, and knowing. This is how Anzaldúa deals with her cactus needles as a writer who departs from her own experience: "I get deep down into the place where it's rooted in my skin and pluck away at it, playing it like a musical instrument—the fingers pressing, making the pain worse before it can get better. Then out it comes. No more discomfort, no more ambivalence. Until another needle pierces the skin. That's what writing is for me, an endless cycle of making it worse, making it better, but always making meaning out of the experience, whatever it may be" (95).

Bridging

The collective practice developed in my research is informed by critical pedagogy, especially Ivan Illich's notion of conviviality (16–55), Paulo Freire's approach to dialogue (*Pedagogia* 107–19), and Pablo Helguera's transpedagogy (77–81), which are the pillars of my collective art projects. These three concepts inform the way I work to build bridges between the individual and collective spheres of my practice as an artist, a teacher, and a researcher. In my research with Brazilian women, I used three methodological strategies to approximate both spheres and investigate life stories of language and place beyond my personal experience: semi-structured interviews, diaries, and collective practices developed in a convivial place.

The semi-structured interviews offered an initial overview of language and place, beginning with the interviewees' arrival in London, exploring their perception of language in the current moment of their lives, and looking at future perspectives in relation to (im)possible returns to Brazil. Considering Linda Sandino's notion of oral history in the arts as a source of elements and operations that might create collaborative engagements within social and relational practices, I took interviews not only as a qualitative method for collecting data, but also as a dialogical practice that can build bridges between the individual and the collective dimensions of my work. Therefore, supported by a questionnaire comprising fifteen questions, I carried out individual, audio-recorded, semi-structured interviews with twelve Brazilian women who live in London.

In order to diversify the group and build a horizontal environment from the first contact with each participant, I employed a decentralizing strategy to form the group of interviewees. First, I invited four Brazilian women whom I had met on different occasions in London to take part in the research. Then, I asked them whether they would like to invite another two women each to participate and work together with them in the future steps of the research. All of them answered positively to this idea, and as soon as they suggested other women, I contacted them and scheduled the other eight interviews. This strategy helped build trust among us and diversify the group in terms of time of residence in London, class, ethnicity, and professional backgrounds. These aspects added relevant intersections to the whole collection of stories of language and place gathered at this stage of the research.

The interviews led us to moments of conversation in which I was not just asking questions unilaterally. As they reflected on their own experiences with language, some of them asked me how I was dealing with the new language not only in my daily life in the city, but also at the university, since I was doing doctoral research. I shared some of my experiences, uncertainties, and thoughts with them, and we started to build a dialogical environment within this interview process. This experience led me to an understanding of oral history not only as a research method, but also as a source of materials (narratives) and a relational resource that can connect the individual and collective spheres of my practice (Rodrigues "Histórias" 1–12).

Four of the meetings took place in public areas of London, and the other eight interviews took place in the interviewees' homes, depending on where they felt more comfortable sharing their feelings and stories. Each interview lasted about an hour and a half, resulting in approximately fifteen hours of audio-recordings in total, which I started to transcribe after I conducted the last interview. I published selected parts of each interview in an artist's book called "Língua&Lugar: Relatos, 2015–2016" (Figure 9). The book focuses on the participants' experiences with the British English and Brazilian Portuguese languages within displacement, and comprises twelve chapters, one per person.

Each chapter of the book offers a different collection of stories about the English language in relation to distinct ages, class backgrounds, ethnicities, levels of proficiency in English, regions of origin in Brazil, and

Figure 9. *"Língua&Lugar: Relatos, 2015–2016." Transcription of interviews. Artist's book, 20.3 × 12.6 cm, single edition.*

periods of residence in London. Many interesting stories emerged, such as, for example, about the impacts of the English language on childbirth experiences, prejudices connected to a lack of proficiency in the English language and its relation to the Brazilian accent, language and loneliness, the relationship between high levels of proficiency and better job opportunities, the specificities of language within intercultural marriage and the education of bilingual children, and comparisons between Brazilian and British culture.

For instance, one of the participants observed that the level of proficiency in the English language could function as a leveler within the Brazilian community in London because it approximates people from different class backgrounds who, in Brazil, would never share the same space. She recounted that people who do not know the new language will lose their previous class status: "We are just another one here. In Brazil, people who we would never meet, here we meet, because the language equalizes. You lose your status. One from the middle class, the other from the working class, we will live together, all levels" (my translation).

Another participant shared stories about her difficulties in speaking with doctors during her pregnancy, childbirth, and postpartum periods. Difficulties in speaking during childbirth resulted in postpartum depression: "My childbirth was an emergency. They doped me because I wanted to talk. I started to speak in Portuguese and English, all mixed up, and I

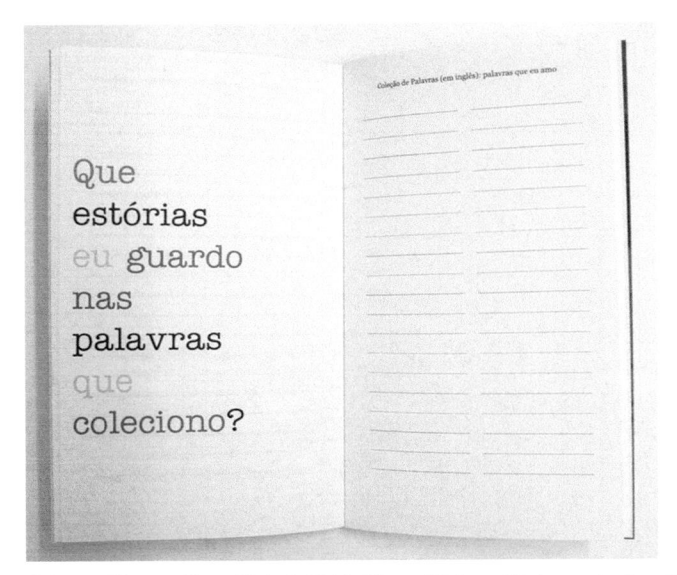

Figure 10. *"Língua&Lugar: Um diário,"* 2014. Diary, 20.3 × 12.6 cm, single edition.

felt desperate. I think because of all this, of not speaking the language, of needing things, I ended up having postpartum depression, because it was difficult to want to speak and not be able to express myself" (my translation).

The book, as a collection of stories, became a place where other people can access, know, and relate to particular stories in specific ways. I noticed that making these stories accessible through the artist's-book format (rather than an academic article or report) aroused the interest of many people from different spheres, from university researchers to other Brazilian women living abroad who have no relation to the arts or the academy. I welcomed this positive response because one of my concerns as an artist, teacher, and researcher is to circulate research results broadly and beyond academia.

At the end of each interview, I offered each participant a blank diary that I had previously prepared and printed out (Figure 10). The diary worked as a strategy to keep the interviewees thinking of stories about the English language in their lives in London until our next meeting, which took place a few months later in a residential flat. The diary contains pages to be filled out and is divided into two parts. The first part gives direction to the writing process: "These are stories about English language in my life in London." In the second part, there is a question: "Which stories do I keep in the words I collect?" This question is followed by seven pages containing columns to be filled with words, in English and Portuguese, according to specific feelings and uses: words in

English that I love, that oppress me, and that I use the most, words of my life story, and words I need the most. In Portuguese, there are spaces for writing "words I miss the most" and "words I keep using daily."

I assured the participants that the contents of the diary would be private, and all of them were relieved to hear this. I told them that they were free to decide what information and stories they should disclose during our future encounters. This strategy worked well, and during the transition from the interview to the convivial place, some of the participants kept sending messages by e-mail and social networks in order to share the pleasure of filling out the diary. Two of the participants mentioned that they thought they had nothing to tell about "language," but when they started to write, many stories came up. Two other participants showed an interest in continuing to write about their life experiences independently of the research, since they found their own stories interesting. They demonstrate that the diary helped them to dig out forgotten stories and made their feelings related to learning a new language clearer. Moreover, only two participants were previously involved with writing practice: one kept a diary about her past experience with breast cancer and the other wrote poems. Two other participants who did not practice writing even bought notebooks to continue their writing.

At this stage of the research, the diary worked as a presence kept at a distance, which respected the intimacy of each participant, built trust, and strengthened their critical reflection not only about the theme, but also about themselves. The positive response to this proposal produced a durational aspect connecting the researcher and participants. Therefore, while the interviews established a starting point for a conversation and worked as a bridge between individual and collective spheres of the art practice, the diary (which I also filled out) strengthened relationships, built trust between the researcher and participants, and culminated in the convivial place where we met later to continue this conversation in person and write life narratives through practices in the visual arts.

The flat became our temporary convivial place for writing-making together. Working in a residential place rather than an institutional space was a conscious decision. I wanted to provide an unmonitored place where we could speak in our own language without any further concern and where the participants could bring along their children and pets if necessary. Therefore, my intention was to provide a space that could offer respite from oppressive environments and relationships mediated by competition, productivity, speed, or spectacle. I also hoped that, together, we could transform such space into a "homeplace" (hooks 41–49), an act that can be empowering in the context of immigration, since housing issues can become a very serious problem in the lives of immigrant women.

I argue that art, as a convivial tool (Illich 16–55), can also stimulate the creation of convivial places where people can build relationships, explore liberatory practices, enunciate counternarratives, and create modes of freedom. With this in mind, we spent our time in the flat sharing and making stories about language and place. We experienced writing-making processes, from drawing and mapping to cooking and music, but for the purpose of this article, I will present only one: "writing life with words that aren't mine."

In this exercise, I offered the participants the exact same words I used to write my first pair of artist's books (Figure 8). I printed the words out, put them in envelopes, and addressed them to each participant. Obviously, my intention was not to fill the participants' minds with pre-conceived words. Rather, I wanted to propose a challenge about overcoming the place of muteness created by the encounter with unknown words. I was curious to know what kind of strategies each participant would use to claim those words in order to articulate their narratives. While they took the words out of the envelopes and tried to figure out where I had extracted them from (I did not give any clues), other stories came up, since they looked at some words and remembered places and specific events pertinent to their own experiences. After this initial discussion, they started to concentrate on this activity, exploring, combining, and cutting words in order to rebuild them to create narratives that could express their life stories (Figure 11).

Those who were more familiar with the English language transformed the words immediately by cutting and composing other words with pieces of syllables (Figure 12). On the other hand, those who knew the language less well tried to write their stories without changing any of the words (Figure 13). Those who knew the language well started to adapt the words according to what they needed to express for the stories they already had in mind, whereas others tended to adapt themselves to that limited vocabulary, communicating their thoughts in a more fragmented and hesitant way. I provided a dictionary for the group, just in case some of the participants might feel more comfortable with that, but practically no one wanted to look at it.

As soon as everyone had produced their writing pieces, we displayed them on the living-room and kitchen cabinets, thereby making our home-place a reading place, and gradually the house came to embody our narratives of language and place (Figure 14). Those who knew the language demonstrated a proactive attitude in relation to promoting changes in the words and making them more meaningful. It was possible to observe how powerful the act of transforming words is in order to learn how to say one's own word (Freire, *Pedagogia* 107–19). Knowing the language made

Figure 11. *Writing-making process, 2015.*

Figure 12. *Writing-making process, 2015.*

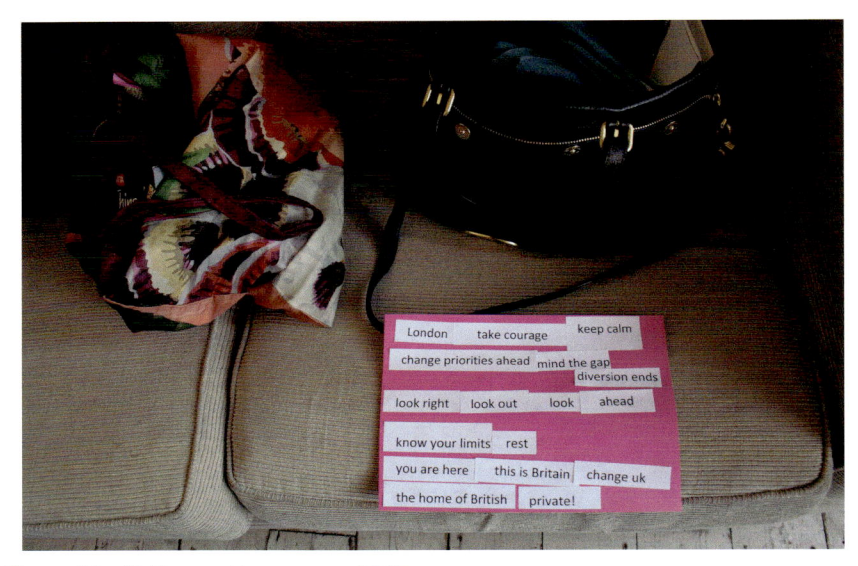

Figure 13. *Writing-making process, 2015.*

Figure 14. *Homeplace as writing and reading place, 2015.*

them able to take decisions according to specific purposes because "the human word is more than mere vocabulary—it is word-and-action" (Freire *Cultural* 20).

The activities developed in the convivial place generated a series of photographs about the meetings and our writing processes. These images were used to write a collective language memoir (Figures 15 and 16).

Figure 15. *Collective language memoir, 2015/2016. 28 × 21.5 cm, single edition.*

Figure 16. Collective language memoir, 2015/2016. 28 × 21.5 cm, single edition.

Some of the participants mentioned that spending those moments together in the flat, sharing experiences, eating and laughing together, reflecting and making things, were pleasurable and comforting experiences, and they wished that other people experiencing displacement could take part in those kinds of activities. Writing collaboratively about sensitive topics opened a space for dialogue and helped the groups build solidarity, overcome the shame of not knowing, and regain confidence through the discovery of self and others.

Leaving

This project is grounded in the visual arts and benefits from interdisciplinary crossings between feminist geography, life writing, and decoloniality, through which I designed the network of concepts that gave form to the epistemological approach to practice and research I used. The first stage of my practice was a self-reflective response to my life experiences within geographical displacement and dislocation in language. The second part, a collective writing process conducted with women, originated from the first stage, where I developed methods for investigating life stories of language and place as told by a group of Brazilian women living in London. Writing became a cross-element in this practice-based research, and visual arts offered a space for exploring decolonial acts and turning the place of muteness into a place of enunciation. To this end, I sought in decoloniality a path to understand the potentiality of my "not knowing" and offer a contribution to knowledge by proposing decolonial strategies for writing life narratives within displacement through translanguaging and autobiogeography. The autobiographical aspect of this whole process is informed by a politics of location grounded in feminist geography and decoloniality, which serves as a basis to articulate life stories, individually and collectively, into|as artworks as a way to be epistemologically disobedient in-between languages and thus to move toward our decolonial selves.

Acknowledgments

The author thanks Ricia Chansky from the University of Puerto Rico Mayagüez, Eva Karpinski from York University, Emily Hipchen from the University of West Georgia, David Cross and James Swinson from the University of the Arts London, Linda Sandino from the University of Sussex, Hayley Newman from University College London, Maria Tamboukou from the University of East London, and the research participants, Alba Cabral, Allane Viana, Alessandra Leighton, Alessandra Molina, Carolina Angrisani, Cristiane Pederiva, Jamile Kollar, Joselita Padilha, Marisa Aranda, Marta Fernandes, Rosa Gonçalves, and

Talita Bolzan. The author acknowledges the support of the CAPES Foundation, Ministry of Education of Brazil, and Federal University of Goiás, Brazil.

Disclosure Statement

No potential conflict of interest was reported by the author.

ORCID

Manoela dos Anjos Afonso Rodrigues (iD) http://orcid.org/0000-0003-4994-4291

Works Cited

Anzaldúa, Gloria. *Borderlands, La Frontera: The New Mestiza*. San Francisco: Aunt Lute, 2012. Print.

Burgin, Victor. *Thinking Photography*. London: Macmillan, 1982. Print.

Couser, G. Thomas. *Memoir: An Introduction*. Oxford: Oxford UP, 2012. Print.

Freire, Paulo. *Cultural Action for Freedom*. Boston: Harvard Educ. Rev., 2000. Print.

—. *Pedagogia do oprimido*. Rio de Janeiro: Paz e Terra, 2011. Print.

Gaztambide-Fernández, R. "Decolonial Options and Artistic/AestheSic Entanglements: An Interview with Walter Mignolo." *Decolonization* 3.1 (2014): 196–212. Web. 31 Mar. 2018.

Helguera, Pablo. *Education for Socially Engaged Art: A Materials and Techniques Handbook*. New York: Pinto, 2011. Print.

Hooks, Bell. *Yearning: Race, Gender, and Cultural Politics*. Boston: South End, 1990. Print.

Illich, Ivan. *Tools for Conviviality*. New York: Harper, 1973. Print.

Kaplan, Alice. "On Language Memoir." *Displacements: Cultural Identities in Question*. Ed. Angelika Bammer. Indianapolis: Indiana UP, 1994. 59–70. Print.

Mignolo, Walter. *The Darker Side of Western Modernity*. Durham: Duke UP, 2011. Print.

—. "Further Thoughts on (De)Coloniality." *Postcoloniality-Decoloniality-Black Critique: Joints and Fissures*. Ed. Sabine Broeck and Carsten Junker. New York: Campus, 2014. 21–51. Print.

—. "Geopolitics of Sensing and Knowing: On (De)Coloniality, Border Thinking, and Epistemic Disobedience." *Confero* 1.1 (2013): 129–50. Web. 31 Mar. 2018.

—. *Local Histories/Global Designs: Coloniality, Subaltern Knowledges, and Border Thinking*. Princeton: Princeton UP, 2000. Print.

—. "On Pluriversality." *Waltermignolo.com*, 20 Oct. 2013. Web. 31 Mar. 2018.

Mignolo, Walter, and Freya Schiwy. "Transculturation and the Colonial Difference: Double Translation." *Información y Comunicación* 4 (2007): 8–30. Web. 31 Mar. 2018.

Rodrigues, Manoela dos Anjos Afonso. "Autobiogeografia como metodologia decolonial." *ANPAP* 26 (2017): 3148–63. Web. 31 Mar. 2018.

—. "Histórias sobre a língua inglesa na vida de doze mulheres brasileiras em Londres." *XIV Encontro Nacional de História Oral*. Campinas. 2–4 May 2018. Web. 1 June 2018.

Sandino, Linda. "Oral History in and about Art, Craft, and Design." *Oral History in the Visual Arts*. Ed. Sandino and Matthew Partington. London: Bloomsbury, 2013. 1–13. Print.

Sontag, Susan. *On Photography*. London: Penguin, 1979. Print.

Sick Women, Sad Girls, and Selfie Theory: Autotheory as Contemporary Feminist Practice

By Lauren Fournier

ABSTRACT

In autotheory as contemporary feminist practice, artists, writers, philosophers, activists, curators, and critics use the autobiographical, first person, and related practices of self-imaging (Jones, Self/Image 134) to process, perform, enact, iterate, subvert, instantiate, and wrestle with the hegemonic discourses of "theory" and philosophy. The term "autotheory" circulates specifically in relation to third wave and fourth wave feminist texts, such as American writer Maggie Nelson's The Argonauts and American filmmaker and art writer Chris Kraus's I Love Dick even as the act of theorizing from the first person is well-established within the genealogies of feminism; as a post-1960s practice it takes on a particularly conceptual and performative valence. This article serves as a historicization of what we are referring to in the present as "autotheory," with autotheoretical antecedents having been referred to as "critical memoir," "theoretical fiction" (Hawkins 263), "life-thinking" (Samatar), and "fiction theory" (Brossard). I turn my attention to "Sick Woman Theory" and "Sad Girl Theory" as twenty-first century examples of autotheoretical feminist practices that span out across social media. I consider how these post-internet practices of making space for sickness and sadness in autotheoretical ways can be understood in relation to the imperatives of intersectionality and the complications of neoliberalism in the present.

> The ease with which the label "narcissistic" is deployed to condemn a particular cultural practice relates to its conventional link to a specifically feminine degradation of the self.
> —Amelia Jones, *Body Art: Performing the Subject*

> Theory can do more the closer it gets to the skin.
> —Sara Ahmed, *Living a Feminist Life*

"Autotheory"[1] has emerged as a term to describe the practices of engaging with theory, life, and art from the perspective of one's lived experiences; an emergent term, it is very much in the zeitgeist of contemporary feminist and queer feminist cultural production today. While the term "autotheory" circulates specifically in relation to third-wave and fourth-wave feminist texts, such as American writer Maggie Nelson's *The*

This article was originally published with errors, which have now been corrected in both the print and online versions. Please see Correction (http://dx.doi.org/10.1080/08989575.2019.1588530)

Argonauts and American filmmaker and art writer Chris Kraus's *I Love Dick*, theorizing from the first person is well established within the genealogies of feminist practice; after the 1960s—the parameters of my focus here—it takes on a particularly conceptual and performative valence. In my research on autotheory across media, I contextualize it as emerging from conceptual art, performance, and body art practices, including what Amelia Jones refers to as "self-imaging" (*Self/Image* 134), such as performing for the camera or, to use today's terminology, taking selfies. In this view, autotheory becomes a way of rereading earlier feminist texts, such as Brazilian writer Clarice Lispector's musically influenced *Água Viva* or African American conceptual artist Adrian Piper's ritual of photographing herself while reading Immanuel Kant in *Food for the Spirit*. Given its discursive entanglement with, and self-proclaimed divergence from, genres like memoir, autobiography, and life narrative, autotheory bears consideration within the scholarly spaces of autobiography studies. This article introduces autotheory as a performative post-1960s practice with a well-established feminist genealogy, contextualizing what we are referring to in the present as autotheory, with autotheoretical texts that have previously been designated as "critical memoir," "theoretical fiction" (Hawkins 263), "life-thinking" (Samatar), and "fiction theory" (Godard 6). I turn my attention specifically to the subsets of "Sick Woman Theory" and "Sad Girl Theory" as twenty-first century examples of autotheoretical feminist performative practices that span out across web-based social media platforms. I ask, what constitutes criticality and theory at the present moment of autotheoretical practice? Taking up works by fourth-wave feminist artists and writers Johanna Hedva, Kevin Brophy, Audrey Wollen, Carolyn Lazard, @gothshakira, and Sarah Maple, I consider how postinternet practices of making space for sickness and sadness in autotheoretical ways can be understood in relation to the imperatives of intersectionality and the complications of neoliberalism in the twenty-first-century feminist present.

Incorporating different theoretical turns, including poststructuralism, the affective turn, the queer turn, and the performative turn, autotheory presents the question of whether it constitutes a theoretical turn itself. Writing in 1991, Nancy K. Miller considered the possibility that "personal criticism"—a mode of feminist scholarship that bridges the personal and the political—had already become an academic trend (3). At the time of my writing, autotheory is gaining traction, especially among young feminist artists and writers who exist between academia and the art world. The history of feminist theory and practice has encouraged an exploration of the personal and the embodied alongside the critical and the theoretical. With autotheory, the "master discourse" (Irigaray 149) of theory as "power through knowledge" (Jameson 192) is processed and iterated toward feminist and queer ends. Given the contemporary climate in which terms like posttheory, antitheory, and "the death of theory" circulate with a certain ease, I consider the ways in which autotheory offers a different way of doing theory: a renewed aesthetic practice that spans intermedial art, art writing and criticism, conceptualism, performativity, comedy, new media, sound, postinternet spaces, manifestoes, and other experimental writing and art practices, all resonant with the twenty-first-century context of pervasive social media.

Rather than focusing specifically on literary genres like memoir, autobiography, and life writing, I choose to foreground autotheory's relationships to contemporary art, cross-disciplinary, and transmedial practices. Explicit engagement with visual culture, sound, conceptualism, performance, body art, and art writing and criticism is a trait not only of recent autotheoretical work but of earlier autotheoretical texts as well: take for example the work of Lispector, who between the 1940s and 1970s was writing innovative (and arguably autotheoretical) work that evaded description (Moser xiii) and, later, artist Roni Horn's autotheoretical exhibition *Rings of Lispector (Agua Viva)* in London in 2004. In the 1960s, coexistent modes of cultural production—video art, performance art, body art, conceptual art, installation, happenings, sound art—intersected with the politics of gender, race, sexuality, and representation, leading to a feminist art movement in the 1970s.

One of the terms used to describe autotheory, "critical memoir," embodies this conjoining of life-writing practices and perhaps a more "distanced" criticality. Guided by Eve Kosofsky Sedgwick's elucidation of Judith Butler, as well as the work of other queer feminist affect theorists such as Lauren Berlant, Sara Ahmed, and Sianne Ngai, Anna Poletti theorizes life narrative as performative—as enacting or constructing the life through the act of "life writing"—rather than expressive—as describing "a life" that exists prior to the performative act of writing about it. Experimental writers in the late-twentieth century mobilize this postmodern approach to the self or "I" in their work, having inherited the post-structural lineage of performativity from Butler. A relatively recent term, "autotheory" is rife with a history of intellectual problems and paradoxes that have been taken up in different ways in philosophy, theory, art, literature, and feminism. Indeed, the history of feminism is, in a sense, a history of autotheory—one that actively seeks to bridge theory and practice and that upholds tenets like "the personal is political." From Hélène Cixous's writing the body and the self in *écriture féminine* and Luce Irigaray's philosophical critiques of phallocentrism to Adrienne Rich and Donna Haraway engaging a politics of positionality, to writing by radical women of color in *This Bridge Called My Back* and Audre Lorde and other Black feminists theorizing a politics of difference, feminists have critiqued male-authored theory for not acknowledging its own subjectivity or its gendered and racialized aspects.

Work in the genre of autotheory takes one's embodied experiences as a primary text or raw material through which to theorize, process, and reiterate theory to feminist effects. Autotheory provides a means of consolidating, integrating, and more rigorously conceiving of seemingly disparate modes of contemporary feminist cultural production—particularly those modes of production that do not easily fit into preexisting categories of genre or feminism, in a manner not unlike earlier feminist practices that experimented with the creation of new modes of writing and theorizing, such as Nicole Brossard's *fiction théorique,* as found in works like *The Aerial Letter* and *Picture Theory*. With the publication of Nelson's *The Argonauts* in 2015, "autotheory" surfaced as a term that might better describe her form of life writing populated by citations from the history of philosophy, theory, and art inscribed in the margins of the page. In twenty-first-century autotheoretical practices, the writers and artists take up the discourses of theory as artistic material to perform, iterate, reenact, and transform. Of course, the problems that neoliberalism and capitalism present to the capacities for subversion—specifically the risk of conflating criticality with the cultural cachet engendered from associating oneself with the learned edge of theory—remains worthy of analysis.

On 1 October 2015, British Indian writer Bhanu Kapil tweeted, "This is the year I heard the words 'autotheory' and now, from Sofia Samatar, 'life-thinking'—for the first time." Here, Kapil is retweeting Somali American writer Sofia Samatar, who describes the blogs of Kapil and Gukira as "a kind of life-thinking." Autotheory, Samatar explains, is "a word for writing that integrates autobiography and social criticism." Arguably, most of philosophy and theory, as well as literature and contemporary art, are modes of "life-thinking"; and yet terms like "autotheory" and "life-thinking" seem to be breaking new ground within contemporary literary, artistic, and theoretical networks, foregrounding criticality alongside the personal in ways that are being received as new. In the same year, Dutch cultural theorist, curator, video artist, and documentarian Mieke Bal wrote a chapter entitled "Documenting What? Autotheory and Migratory Aesthetics." She defines autotheory as both a "practice" and an "ongoing, spiraling form of analysis-theory dialectic" that she turned to after being "confronted with the shortcomings of written documentation especially for the understanding of contemporary culture, which is by definition still 'in becoming'" (124). For Bal, the practice of making documentary films and then approaching them "as *theoretical objects*" (133) in their own right is necessary to be able to adequately understand and theorize what she has been calling "migratory aesthetics."

Before the 2015 wave that saw autotheory surge forth in contemporary art and literary discourse, it appeared as a term coined in Stacey Young's *Changing the Wor(l)d: Discourse, Politics, and the Feminist Movement*, a work of feminist social-movements theory grounded in social science methodology. Young reads feminist "autotheoretical" texts as "counter-discourses" and as the "embodiment of a discursive type of political action, which decenters the hegemonic subject of feminism" (61), that is, the white, heterosexual, cisgender woman with class privilege. Focusing on the field of American feminist publishing between 1970 and 1990, Young cites Minnie Bruce Pratt's *Rebellion: Essays 1980–1991*, Rosario Morales and Aurora Morales's *Getting Home Alive* (1986), and the 1981 anthology *This Bridge Called My Back: Writings by Radical Women of Color*, edited by Cherríe Moraga and Gloria E. Anzaldúa, as three originary examples of autotheoretical texts. Young maintains that it is from women of color and lesbian women's theorizing from the perspective of their own lived experiences that the women's movement learned to address intersectionality as a feminist imperative.

Aside from Young's usage—which more closely resembles Miller's "personal criticism" than it does the more performative,[2] conceptual, cross-medial works that I read as autotheoretical—the only other definitions of the term have appeared in personal blogs. In a post from April 2017, artist Valeria Radchenko's cites Young and Preciado in her definition of "autotheory" as "a method of using the body's experience to develop knowledge." In April 2016, a writer named KC, who self-describes as "a white, able-bodied, queer/trans/non-binary person, as a survivor, as a person navigating mental health issues, and as a person with a deep commitment to critical analysis and political revolution" ("About"), wrote a blog post entitled "the academy, autotheory, and the argonauts," which opens with an anecdote from their experience in a seminar class on queer affect theory. The post becomes KC's account of "quit(ting) the academy" or opting out of academia; yet they concede that, despite their exit from academic institutions, "there was a particular genre of work that i craved … . testo junkie, ann cvetkovich's depression, s. lochlann jain's malignant, audre lorde's zami …" ("academy"). Put another way, these autotheoretical texts mark KC's point of affinity with the discourse called "theory," a discourse embedded in academic institutions that might be seen as inaccessible—at best daunting, at worst hostile—to particular bodies, such as those who are mentally ill or who are survivors of sexual violence. In the 2010s, the impulse to write autotheoretically as a way of making theory and philosophy more accessible to wider publics manifests in collections of nonfiction essays such as Erin Wunker's *Notes from a Feminist Killjoy*, Roxane Gay's *Bad Feminist*, or Sara Ahmed's *Living a Feminist Life*. The same decade also sees works that once would have been described as manifestoes now being framed as "autotheory," from third wave, postpunk, French feminist Virginie Despentes's *King Kong Theory* to fourth-wave, social-media feminists Hedva's Sick Woman Theory and Wollen's Sad Girl Theory. It is these latter examples that I turn my attention to now.

Sick Woman Theory

The late-nineteenth to the early-twentieth centuries include many literary and philosophical precursors to autotheory as a feminist practice of writing from one's own lived experience. In 1892, Charlotte Perkins Gilman wrote "The Yellow Wallpaper," a short story inspired by the writer's personal experience of so-called madness; Gilman disclosed the autobiographical nature of the story in her 1913 "Why I Wrote 'The Yellow Wallpaper.'" Another thinly veiled autobiography of a woman's experience of madness under patriarchy is Sylvia Plath's *The Bell Jar*. The Confessional movement of the 1950s, with its poetry of the personal, saw poets like Plath and Anne Sexton exploring in verse their taboo experiences of mental illness, suicidal ideation, and personal relationships. Similarly, the ongoing presence of diaristic and epistolary practices—feminized as they are—has been evidenced from the dawn of the novel in the eighteenth century to the recent publication of the collected diaries of German American artist Eva Hesse, whose pioneering practice in the 1960s American art world integrated concerns of abstract expressionism, feminism, sexuality, and the themes of Confessionalism, including trauma, illness, familial, and mental health issues.

Queer feminist affect theory creates a context in which contemporary feminist writers and artists can unpack their own experiences of illness and mourning through an autotheoretical practice grounded in these earlier contributions. A large body of autotheoretical texts that engage with the politics, aesthetics, and ethics of illness, injury, and grief could be described—to take Hedva's term—as Sick Woman Theory, influenced by Sedgwick's autotheoretical writing. In addition to Hedva, it includes works by artists, writers, poets, and scholars like Amy Berkowitz, Lazard, Dodie Bellamy, Leslie Jamison, Gillian Rose, Eula Biss, Susan Brison, Saidiya Hartman, Kate Zambreno, Leah Lakshmi Piepzna-Samarasinha, Meghan O'Rourke, S. Lochlann Jain, Mari Ruti, Kapil, and Claudia Rankine, as well as earlier works by Lorde, Susan Sontag, Elaine Scarry, and Lisa Steele. They all use autotheory to make visible and then theorize experiences of illness, disease, pain, trauma, and grief—either personal or experienced by others—and to connect these experiences to political, social, and structural issues of concern to feminists, including the delegitimization of women's pain and the interrelatedness of sexual trauma with mysterious, feminized illnesses like fibromyalgia.

Feminist theory, critical disability and crip studies, mad studies, and critical race theory converge in Hedva's Sick Woman Theory, which resembles a manifesto in its line of reasoning and tone and is disseminated online in an effort toward greater accessibility of information—yet she does not call her work a manifesto. Her title was inspired in part by two other autotheoretical works, Wollen's "Sad Girl Theory" and Zambreno's *Heroines*. Hedva draws on autobiographical contributions to the thinking and advocacy around invisible disabilities, autoimmune diseases, and the feminist politics of illness, wellness, and ability, including Christine Miserandino's "The Spoon Theory." In a similar manner, Despentes's *King Kong Theory* performs the function of a manifesto, providing succinct and sophisticated arguments around the politics of prostitution, pornography, and rape. Yet she does not frame her text as a manifesto or a collection of autobiographical essays but, like Hedva, as theory.

Hedva uses her ongoing experience of living with chronic illness to write a new, intersectional feminist theory that upholds the lives, agency, and limits of those (young feminists) who are experiencing illness and disability. She grounds her theory in contemporaneous political contexts, specifically the Black Lives Matter movement in Los Angeles in 2014, and her inability to participate in the protests. Citing the work of Butler and Lorde as well as Hannah Arendt, Ann Cvetkovich, and Starhawk, and placing their theories alongside her gendered, racialized, and class-based experiences as someone with an autoimmune disease, Hedva engenders a space that resonates both with the second-wave "personal is political" mantra and a more intersectionally capacious, explicitly queered twenty-first-century feminism; she explains her use of the term "woman" in Gayatri Spivak's sense of strategic essentialism, emphasizing the long-standing feminist imperative of making one's particular subject position known while at the same time queering the "woman" label through trans, nonbinary, and genderqueer subjectivities (Hedva).

Sick Woman Theory can be aligned with Lazard's "In Sickness and Study" and Alize Zorlutuna's "Labour for the Horizon," both web-based art projects that advance the ideas that Hedva articulates in her autotheoretical manifesto; all three combine active interdisciplinary art and critical writing practices. In Lazard's project, a series of digital photographs posted to Instagram, she metaphorically arms herself with her favorite books of contemporary theory and literature—often feminist or queer texts that engage with biopolitics, medicalization of bodies, and related issues—each time she is in the hospital receiving blood transfusions for an autoimmune disorder. The series repeats over the course of two years, with Lazard's arm—bandaged and connected to an IV drip—holding books like Cvetkovich's *An Archive of Feelings*, Lorde's *Sister Outsider*, and Alison Kafer's *Feminist, Queer, Crip*. This act of "posing" with books as part of an autotheoretical gesture on Instagram and related platforms like Tumblr and Twitter is a trend among postinternet feminist artists, to varying effects. Wollen (@tragicqueen), who is credited with coining the term "Sad Girl Theory," engages in a similar, iterated performance as Lazard does, taking selfies with books during her regular visits to the hospital. These practices mobilize one's lived experiences of illness, trauma, and disability to generate theory and practice that is both resonant with and relevant to present-day intersectional feminist politics and aesthetics, including a practice of "failing" to be as active as one would like to be—as a feminist activist, as a scholar, and so on.

There are other texts that more closely resemble essays and long-form prose poems that cluster around the practice of Sick Woman Theory and its concomitant feminist approaches to illness, injury, disability, and grief. For example, American prose poet Berkowitz in *Tender Points* writes through her experiences of past trauma—specifically childhood sexual abuse—and present chronic illness—living with fibromyalgia—in a manner that is autotheoretical. Her experiences become a kind of subjective-empirical material through which to process these issues alongside the works of contemporary theory, literature, and medical texts, citing bell hooks, Sontag, Rankine, Berlant, Kapil, Despentes, Anne Carson, Diane di Prima, Scarry, David Wojnarowicz, Sigmund Freud, doctors and specialists writing on fibromyalgia like Leslie Crofford, and Miserandino's "Spoon Theory." Berkowitz is particularly interested in exploring the ways in which trauma becomes "lodged" (122) in the brain and in the body over the long term.

Tender Points bears resemblance to other autotheoretical feminist texts that are more straightforward than they are conceptual. Still, Berkowitz's accessible feminist arguments on trauma are not without a conceptually complicated ambivalence. Even as she theorizes and enacts the need to disclose lived accounts of rape to reveal it as a systemic problem, she also concedes her frustration that this topic should consume "brilliant women" who, had they not been raped, could be engaging instead in conversations about art, including their own (112). She titles a speculative painting *Brilliant Women Talking about Rape Again (Instead of Talking about Their Art or Any Other Topic* (112) in a darkly comic riff on the Bechdel test.[3] Berkowitz's work is part of the larger drive in feminist spaces to publicly disclose rape, sexual assault, and harassment; she takes this further by embedding it within a larger autotheoretical practice that critically ties the trauma of rape and sexual assault to her specific experience of chronic illness as a woman interacting with a Western medical establishment that fails to understand her and her pain.

As a postinternet practice, Sick Woman Theory takes earlier feminist positionings such as the hysteric and performatively reinhabits them in a way that is self-reflexive, embodied, and grounded in discourses of theory. Shannon Bell describes the "post-hysteric" as a site of discursive agency in the context of Lacanian theory ("Fragment" 1). Bell's own theoretical practice is grounded in her work as a performance artist who includes self-imaging in her academic publications like *Fast Feminism*. Certain media, like performance for video, are particularly well suited to the autotheoretical mode because of its enmeshment in aesthetic issues related to self-imaging and the history of conceptual art. In "Video: The Aesthetics of Narcissism," feminist art historian Rosalind Krauss argues that the medium of video is not a particular material or technology but is in fact the psychic mechanism of narcissism. In "The Rhetoric of the Pose: Hannah Wilke and the Radical Narcissism of Feminist Body Art," Jones defends artist Hannah Wilke's work against the critiques of narcissistic self-indulgence she has received from both the patriarchal art world and other feminist artists. According to Jones, both audiences tend to read Wilke's body—conventionally attractive and figuratively wounded—as complicit with patriarchy rather than subversive in a feminist way. She provides a convincing reading of Wilke's work as subverting the patriarchal biases of the mid-twentieth-century American art world. Jones ultimately argues that feminist body art and performance art of the 1960s onward create a condition of possibility for the female artist to be "both body and mind, subverting the Cartesian separation of cogito and corpus that sustains the masculinist myth of male transcendence" (*Body* 157). Third and fourth-wave feminists who draw on self-imaging practices to theorize contemporary issues in an autotheoretical way are indebted to this longer history of poststructuralist feminist experimentation.

The turn toward the self, and the use of one's positioning to generate politically efficacious work, is a theme in the history of feminism more broadly, and Jones's scholarship makes a convincing case for a radical feminist politics of "narcissism" in feminist body art practices. In the twenty-first century, social media platforms enable a widespread, daily narcissism, with a large population having access to writing their own Facebook statuses and tweets, posting images to their Instagram pages, and responding to posts on their newsfeeds. In the postinternet, neoliberal, capitalist context of new media technologies and social media, how do we understand the politics and aesthetics of autotheory? Does a white-passing woman with class privilege taking a selfie with a book of feminist theory and posting it to Instagram constitute an autotheoretical feminist practice? What if she is in a hospital bed (Wollen)? I am cognizant of potential problems with such modes of postinternet practices, including Sarah Sharma's coining of the term "selfie-care" to critique the individualistic compulsion to publicly display one's own self-care rituals at the expense of cultivating "the conditions of possibility for people to be cared for in common" ("Selfie-Care" 14). As a practice that integrates self-imaging and public acts of self-display with the criticality of theoretical discourse and a more politicized or "woke" self-reflexivity, autotheory has the potential to resist the ossification of selfie-care and instead stand as a contemporary practice of theorizing that is accessible beyond the borders of academic institutions.

Neoliberal Feminism and Intersectional Feminist Memes

Reflecting on Canadian feminist performance art of the 1970s through the 1980s, Johanna Householder notes the expediency of the medium and women's turn to performance art because they had immediate access to the required materials—namely, their bodies (13). It is conceivable that selfies are a similarly "expedient, almost involuntary" (Householder 13) practice for young women artists in the twenty-first century, given their access to iPhones and various social media platforms to produce, present, and disseminate their images. The selfie debate is not unlike the debate that feminist performance artists have faced over the past century: how to comprehend the willing self-objectification women engage in through these media, especially in a context in which women are always already commodified, and whether such "narcissistic" work can also be conceptually rigorous. There is a spectrum of feminist autotheory within this cluster: in some cases, the theory becomes an accessory or a fetish object in service of the selfie—making the selfie appear to be more intellectual, possessing a cultural capital that certain reading practices connote. This is the case in much of Wollen's tragicqueen work, where selfies by a white-passing woman with perceived class privilege are repeated in a context that uncritically, and vaguely ironically, accepts neoliberal capitalism's grip on culture.

One problem I perceive in Wollen's work is her upholding the idea that one's identity is based on the things one consumes, including theory and feminism. Even if these objects are feminist or theoretical-philosophical, it is still advancing a Consumerism 101 view—that a person is constituted by what they consume. For example, Wollen's "The 'Sad Girl' Starter Pack" collage includes fashion accessories like a dog-collar choker and a plaid skirt and commodities like a car (Prius) and Moon Juice, along with feminist theory texts: Valerie Solanas's *SCUM* and the Invisible Committee's *The Coming Insurrection*—the latter intervened by Wollen, with Sailor Moon supplanting the original cover art. The motif of juxtaposing Sailor Moon with texts of (mostly feminist) theory is seen throughout Wollen's Instagram feed:[4] while intelligible as a postmodern gesture, it does not feel particularly complex or interesting. The work, like much of the general tone of Sad Girl Theory, is suffused with irony and implicit (ambivalent, complicit) capitalist critique: the whiteness and class privilege (disposable income) that Moon Juice functions as a metonymy of, alongside the Invisible Committee's French theory tract which "predicts the imminent collapse of capitalist culture" (Moynihan). Reading her work as performative, it is possible that Wollen is instantiating the theory that she is taking up—the Invisible Committee's view of capitalism as reaching a limit point where it will collapse—while at the same time acknowledging her own ambivalent desires and complicity in late capitalism. She includes the caption "is seeing yr own starter pack the Internet version of the mirror stage???" (Wollen, "Starter Pack"), which reads as a playfully memetic riff on Lacanian psychoanalytic theory.

Another problem with Wollen—particularly consequential with regards to charting a history of autotheory as feminist practice—is the way in which she takes credit for coining the term "Sad Girl Theory" as "a gesture of research that is structured around the idea that the internalized suffering women experience should be categorized as an act of resistance" (Wollen, "Sad") without giving due acknowledgment or credit to those who advanced a similar theory or thesis before her, as Chris Kraus did, for example, more than a decade earlier. Wollen says, "Sorrow, weeping, starvation, and eventually suicide have been dismissed as symptoms of mental illness or even pure narcissism for girls" (Wollen, "Sad") which is simply a reiteration of Kraus's thesis articulated with more nuance and sophistication in *Aliens and Anorexia*, where she takes the example of Simone Weil, "the anorexic philosopher" (Kraus, *Aliens* 28) to discuss anorexia as a stance of resistance and affirmative activism that women take in rejection of (patriarchal) culture. Even if unacknowledged, Wollen's work is in conversation with Kraus's through her repeated reference to *The Coming Insurrection* and to ideas of Sad Girl Theory advanced by Kraus and then appropriated into, and transmuted through, the signifiers of late capitalism and its commodity fetishism. For example, Wollen's post on "Patron Saint of Depression and Anxiety St. Dymphna Gel Mouse Pad" combines feminist autotheory of Kraus and Zambreno with the commodity fetishism and ironic nostalgia of the typically obsolete object of the mousepad.

American non-binary conceptual artist Brophy, also working from a fourth-wave feminist tradition, preemptively responds to my hesitance around the status of Wollen's Sad Girl Theory as legitimately critical or theoretical. *Perfect Eyeliner Tutorial* is an autotheoretical performance for video in which Brophy subversively iterates the visual rhetoric and discourse of Sad Girl Theory. Embedded on YouTube, and not differentiated as "art" by any contextual cues, it features Brophy applying red eyeliner to her eyes with a large knife while the text-to-speech technology of PDF Reader reads out an essay that she wrote on Sad Girl Theory during her MFA studies. Brophy's work is metatheoretical and autotheoretical, since the artist performs a theorization of the Sad Girl phenomenon in the context of contemporary art while simultaneously generating a new work of Sad Girl culture using her own body and screened in a contemporary art gallery. In this performance on video—a medium Sad Girls often use—a non-binary artist performs a gesture that juxtaposes hegemonic rituals of beautification with the implication of self-harming. The streaking of red eyeliner with the knife across the eyelid momentarily tricks the viewer's eye into believing that the eyeliner is blood and that this woman is enacting a ritual of cutting onscreen. In my opinion, the power of this video lies not so much in its contribution to Sad Girl culture as in its adept autotheoretical articulation of the ambivalences central to this culture and to the problem of the reception of work by young women and non-binary artists. Brophy autotheoretically theorizes the online feminist art movement of Sad Girl Theory—a movement that foregrounds performances of the self online—using the form of a performance for video to do so, thus bringing the metatheoretical tendencies of autotheory as feminist practice full circle.

Both Jones and Brophy address the ongoing problem of disregarding women artists' work as narcissistic or uncritical if they use their own bodies—especially if their bodies are considered conventionally attractive, as is the case both for Wollen and @gothshakira. Brophy is hopeful for the work's potential, arguing that Sad Girls "use their body, their privilege, to speak about a larger issue. What is striking about Sad Girls is their awareness—social awareness and self-awareness—when discussing their work" (Brophy). This does not eliminate the issue of whiteness nor the potential collusions or conflations with capitalist systems that occur when this work uses avenues like Instagram and is not framed as *art*. I take issue with Brophy's implication that the artists' "awareness" might somehow exempt them from privilege; with the institutional relationships that they form, namely, the cooptation of this work by capitalist mechanisms;

with the work's likeness to uncritical equivalents in the world of fashion and design. There is a feminist politics to the affect of Sad Girl Theory: the claiming of women's right not to smile, to be a kind of cute feminist killjoy, to use Ngai's and Ahmed's terms, and the decisive saying no to capitalism's hailing of the happy and productive neoliberal subject. But the question remains as to the efficacy of this kind of work and the role that theory plays in its production and reception. Indeed, given the history of feminist performances of the self in art, one wonders what it is that Sad Girl Theory brings to feminism other than what appears to be a savvy move at self-branding in light of the influence that framing one's work as *theory* has for young women with class mobility who have been exposed to theory in art school.

Another question concerns the making of theory or philosophy into a fetish object in the service of a selfie that contributes to one's cultural capital. There are examples of young feminist artists working with selfies in autotheoretical ways, like Montreal-based Instagram artist @gothshakira, whose practice involves the production of what she calls "intersectional feminist memes" on Instagram ("Keynote"). As a self-identified "latinx" woman who positions herself as a "meme administrator"—with "GRAN SACERDOTISA DE LOS MEMES" as the headline on her Instagram—she produces lengthy autotheoretical memes involving the juxtaposition of appropriated or found imagery of Latina women—Jennifer Lopez, Shakira, Selena Gomez—with selfies (either as single images or as GIFs) or, more often, photos of herself posing that have been taken by others. As autotheory, @gothshakira's work is simultaneously confessional[5] and theoretical—that is, informed by ideas from feminist theory and literature, including hooks, Angela Davis, and Lorde. It is also politicized as explicit and articulate feminist and Latinx representation on the internet today, often functioning in direct confrontation with antifeminist internet trolls who target meme administrators like @gothshakira for articulating feminist positionings in the form of memes. Other artists, like British Muslim artist Maple, have received death threats from being visible and vocal as a feminist online, and Maple has used that experience to create politically responsive work.

Maple's *Freedom of Speech*, a performance on video featuring the artist as herself, opens with a shot of Maple facing the camera directly. Her gaze meets ours as she begins what seems to be a lecture or vlog to introduce the themes she will be taking up: she uses key words like "representation," "feminism," and "Disney princesses." As she continues to speak about feminism, a hand emerges from off camera and slaps Maple straight across the face. The first slap is barely registered, and as she goes on speaking the viewer questions what they just saw. The hand appears again and slaps her across the face, even harder this time. The performance continues, and it becomes clear that this is an endurance work: one in which the artist must compose herself in the face of literal violence. While the violence is wielded in an attempt to shut her up, she goes on speaking until, after nearly five minutes, she breaks and begins to cry. As Maple discusses this work at *The Practicing Feminist*, a roundtable event at the Tate Britain in 2016, she notes that 2012–2013 was an exciting time for feminism on the internet, yet there was also a terrible backlash that saw women speaking out or identifying as feminist online receiving rape threats and death threats. *Freedom of Speech* encapsulates what feminism often feels like for my generation, which began to come of age as fourth-wave feminists on the internet around 2012. The work anticipates the backlash and then literalizes its violence onscreen, implicating her body and facing the viewer in the postslap moments of vulnerability; it confronts the contradiction at the heart of "freedom of speech" discourse, such as in Trump's America, where anti-feminist trolls create a hostile environment for feminist expression, using language that verges on hate speech and inciting violence in the name of free speech. While it is a conceptual work, its message is quite clear to feminist audiences—that one is faced with literal violence when identifying as a feminist online, and that it takes endurance to continue as a feminist in the face of this violence. The accessibility that comes with such transparency is a big part of Maple's feminist work: "How can I take this idea and get it to as many people as possible?" she asks, noting that this question drives her practice. Her call for an accessible feminist theory resonates with earlier theorists, like hooks, and more recent work on Instagram, like @gothshakira.

@gothshakira attributes some of the vehemence of the antifeminist backlash she receives online to her work being both explicitly feminist and explicitly intellectual (Keynote). The text element of @gothshakira's memes or image macros is longer and more intellectual or theoretically informed than internet memes generally are, a matter that @gothshakira argues fuels the vitriol of antifeminist trolls.[6] She parodies this in a meme that reads, "When the confessional femme meme is longer than a sentence"; the image paired with the text is Aziz Ansari reading Sylvia Plath's *The Bell Jar* ("confessional"). @gothshakira considers the politics of syntax, discourse, and terminology from other perspectives than the cheeky, fourth-wave feminist one: some of her strongest memes, in my view, bring together theoretical insight and an intersectional feminist politics of accessibility to problematize academic buzzwords and the discourse of progressive leftist, feminist culture. In Xpace's group exhibition, "What Would the Community Think?" curated by Emily Gove, a

@gothshakira meme is printed in large scale vinyl and displayed on the wall. Paired with an image of Jennifer Lopez, the black text on the white gallery wall reads,

> when you realize that aggressively and abrasively shaming everyone who does not share the same fourth wave feminist views as u and/or has not been liberally educated and/or has not spent copious amounts of time on tumblr or in other social justice-oriented places whether tangible or intangible is classist, counterproductive, and is employing the same subversive strategies of the very systems of oppression that ur trying to circumvent and that, although the emotional and social labor reserves required from u may be great, the answer lies in compassionate understanding and patient/educational dialogue in the interest of coexistence/the forward progression of humanity as a whole. (Xpace)

This meme demonstrates @gothshakira's characteristic rhetorical form, beginning with the meme conceit "when you realize …" and concluding with an abbreviated intersectional feminist analysis of the accessibility and class issues around the discourse used by liberally educated fourth-wave feminists. In this way, it is simultaneously humorous, self-reflexive, and self-aware. Using the form of the meme,[7] @gothshakira argues, the personal experiences fueling the content of the memes (such as the second-wave mantra of "the personal is political," as taken up by the fourth-wave postinternet feminists) become, by virtue of the form, collective, social, and depersonalized. The focus of @gothshakira's work is not so much on her self as on using her self, as a Latinx woman, as a phenomenological and performative positioning from which to generate theory resonant with political, social, aesthetic, and cultural concerns. And yet, for all its transgressive posturing, @gothshakira's Instagram is also very much invested in a project of self-branding, juxtaposing her more politically resonant meme posts with selfies of her as a light-skinned, even white-passing and conventionally very attractive woman in different enviable outfits, hairstyles, and social situations around Montreal and New York.

While this kind of self-branding is more obviously visible on social media, as on @gothshakira's Instagram, it is also at work in older media like the novel. Readers should be attuned to the ways in which the self is performed and mythologized in works by Kraus or Nelson, just as they might be attuned to the ways the self is produced through social media platforms today. Indeed, there are interesting similarities between the work of @gothshakira and Wollen and the work of Kraus. Kraus's *I Love Dick* is a performative instantiation of Irigaray's mimetic mechanism, wherein Kraus moves from the positioning of "philosopher's wife" to "feminist autotheorist," all the while rhetorically indulging the phallocentric imperatives of academic and art patriarchy, symbolized by the figure of "Dick," in a brashly parodic way. In like manner, @gothshakira's self-described intersectional feminist memes—ripe as they are with social, cultural, political, and discursive analyses resonant to a contemporary feminist and queer readership—coexist with titillating selfies of @gothshakira; in this way, the artist shapes herself in relation to the context of Instagram as a social media, and the lines between criticality, accessibility, and complicity (with capitalism, with neoliberalism, with what Sharma calls "selfie-care") are dynamically blurred. I end my discussion of these fourth-wave practices on this ambivalent note, as I perceive an ambivalence at the heart of these autotheoretical projects themselves.

Working within a neoliberal, capitalist context, artists like Wollen readily take up feminism and theory as consumer objects with cultural cachet, couching their feminist actions in a certain kind of "coolness"; at worst, theory becomes a kind of fetish object that enhances the cultural cachet of a selfie. More generously, I might understand the inclusion of theory as an object in a selfie to be the artist's demonstration of their awareness of the centrality of theory as a discourse to contemporary art and academic practices, and their ensuing use of it within their work as a kind of sculptural object and signifier of a certain mode of patriarchal power. Given autotheory's resurgence in the context that incentivizes "followers" and "likes," as seen on the social media platforms that pervade contemporary social, political, and discursive life, one must be cognizant of the risks we run when theory becomes first and foremost a fetish and an image, rather than text being read and digested, or when practices of self-imaging become a substitute for critical thinking and informed discussions and debate.

Coda

In autotheory as a conceptual and performative feminist practice, artists, writers, and critics use the first person, or related practices of self-imaging (Jones, *Self/Image* 134), to process, perform, enact, iterate, and wrestle with the hegemonic discourses of "theory" and philosophy, extending the feminist practice of theorizing from one's subject positioning as a way of engendering insights into questions related to aesthetics, politics, ethics, and social and cultural theory. In autotheory, one's embodied experiences become the material through which one theorizes and, in a similar way, theory becomes the discourse through which one's lived experience is refracted. In the context of neoliberalism, with its imperatives of individualism, competitiveness, and productivity, Sick Woman Theory and Sad Girl Theory mobilize autotheory as a counterpractice for twenty-first century feminist life—as another way of understanding feminist agency, or what it means to be an activist, an artist, or a theorist. By couching the specialized discourse of theory in the language and media of twenty-first century popular culture, including selfies, self-branding, exposure, fashionability and trendiness, hashtags and followers and likes, and by using the form of the meme, artists like Audrey Wollen, Kevin Brophy, and @gothshakira translate feminist theory for new audiences. As a new form of feminist theory, the intelligent meme disseminates theory in a manner resonant with contemporary conceptions of what it means to be critical. As a transmedial, transdisciplinary, and transnational practice, autotheory has the capacity to trouble dominant epistemologies and approaches to philosophizing and theorizing, exposing the problematics of maintaining conceptual separations between self and theory—a project which feminism has long been engaged in.

Notes

1. While there are variations on the spelling of the term, my preferred version is "autotheory"; with the exception of those places where I am quoting a particular source, I use this spelling of the term throughout.
2. Miller's description of "personal criticism" and "narrative criticism" in *Getting Personal* integrates the sentiment of Young's term "autotheory" with the influence of the performative turn.
3. Conceived of by queer feminist graphic novelist Alison Bechdel, who has also created work in an autotheoretical mode, the Bechdel test reads the feminist viability of a given film against three criteria: whether there are 1) two woman characters who 2) talk to each other 3) about something other than a man. The test was first introduced in a 1985 comic strip in Bechdel's ongoing series *Dykes to Watch Out For*.
4. In her @tragicqueen Instagram feed, which since the time I wrote this article has been taken down, Wollen also juxtaposes images and characters from *Sailor Moon* with such texts as Judith Butler's *Gender Trouble*, Simone de Beauvoir's *The Second Sex*, and Shulamith Firestone's *The Dialectic of Sex*.
5. In her keynote address at the "no neutral art, no neutral art histories" symposium in Montreal (January 2017), @gothshakira describes her work as "confessional femme memes."
6. @gothshakira speaks of her experience being trolled and threatened by "self-identified beta males" who emerge from places like 4chan and target feminist meme administrators. She explains how these men "feel very alienated, very threatened, by the existence of left-leaning feminists"; some of the trolling she has received attack her memes both for being too personal and for being too intellectual ("Keynote").
7. In order to be a "meme" rather than an "image macro," the meme must be distributed virally through social media (@gothshakira, "Keynote").

Disclosure statement

No potential conflict of interest was reported by the author.

Funding

This work was supported by the Social Sciences and Humanities Research Council of Canada [767-2013-0110].

Work Citied

Ahmed, Sara. *Living a Feminist Life*. Durham: Duke UP, 2017. Print.

Bal, Mieke. "Documenting What? Autotheory and Migratory Aesthetics." *A Companion to Contemporary Documentary Film*. Ed. Alexandra Juhasz and Alisa Lebow. Hoboken, NJ: Wiley-Blackwell, 2015. 124–44. Print.

Beckles, Madelyne. *Theory of the Young Girl*. 2017. Video.

Bell, Shannon. "Fragment of a Case of Posthysteria: D'or Owns the Jewel." *ESC* 40.1 (2014): 1–22. Print.

—. *Fast Feminism: Speed Philosophy, Pornography, and Politics*. Autonomedia, 2010. Print.

Berkowitz, Amy. *Tender Points*. Oakland, CA: Timeless, Infinite Light, 2015. Print.

Brophy, Kevin. *Perfect Eyeliner: How to Put Eyeliner on with a Knife*. YouTube, 2015. Web. 10 June 2017.

Brossard, Nicole. *The Aerial Letter*. Trans. Marlene Wildeman. Toronto: Women's Press, 1987. Print.

—. *Picture Theory*. 1982. Trans. Barbara Godard. Montréal: Guernica Editions, 2006. Print.

Cvetkovich, Ann. *An Archive of Feelings*, Duke UP, 2003.

Despentes, Virginie. *King Kong Theory*. Trans. Stephanie Benson. New York: Feminist, 2010. Print.

Gay, Roxane. *Bad Feminist*. New York: Harper, 2014.

Gilman, Charlotte Perkins. "Why I Wrote 'The Yellow Wallpaper'," *The Forerunner*, 1913. CUNY, 8 June 1999. Web. 3 June 2018.

@gothshakira. Keynote. "whom tf invited a meem admin to a mf art history conference lmfoaaao." *no neutral art, no neutral art historians*. Concordia Art History Graduate Student Association Conference. Montréal: Concordia University. 27 Jan. 2017. YouTube. 4 July 2018.

—. "When the Confessional Femme Meme Is Longer than a Sentence." Meme. Instagram. 20 Oct. 2016. Web. 16 Feb. 2017.

—. Meme. "@gothshakira." *What Would the Community Think*? Toronto: Xpace Cultural Centre. Curated by Emily Gove. 9 Sept. to 15 Oct. 2016.

Godard, Barbara, et al. "Theorizing Fiction Theory." *Tessera* 3 (January 1986): 6–12.

Haraway, Donna. "Situated Knowledges: The Science Question in Feminism and the Privilege of Partial Perspective." *The Feminist Standpoint Theory Reader: Intellectual and Political Controversies*. Ed. Sandra G. Harding. London: Routledge, 2004. 81–102. Print.

Hawkins, Joan. "Afterword: Theoretical Fictions." *I Love Dick*. By Chris Kraus. Cambridge: Semiotext(e), 1997. 263–76. Print.

Hedva, Johanna. "Sick Woman Theory." *Mask Magazine*. Mask Media, n.d. Web. 5 May 2018.

Hesse, Eva. *Diaries*. Ed. Barry Rosen and Tamara Bloomberg. London: Hauser and Wirth, 2016. Print.

Householder, Johanna. "Apologia." *Caught in the Act: An Anthology of Performance Art by Canadian Women*. Ed. Johanna Householder and Tanya Mars. Toronto: YYZ, 2004. Print.

Irigaray, Luce. *This Sex Which Is Not One*. 1977. Trans. Catherine Porter and Carolyn Burke. New York: Cornell UP, 1985. Print.

Jameson, Fredric. "Periodizing the 60s." *Social Text* 9–10 (1984): 178–209. Print.

Jones, Amelia. *Body Art/Performing the Subject*. Minneapolis: U of Minnesota P, 1998. Print.

—. *Self/Image: Technology, Representation, and the Contemporary Subject*. New York: Routledge, 2006. Print.

Kafer, Alison. *Feminist, Queer, Crip*. Bloomington: Indiana UP, 2013. Print.

Kapil, Bhanu. "This Is the Year I Heard the Words 'Autotheory' and Now, from Sofia Samatar, 'Life Thinking'—for the First Time." *Twitter*, 1 Oct. 2015, 9:09 am. Tweet.

KC. "Academy, Autotheory, and the Argonauts." *aminotfemme* 22 Apr. 2016. Web. 10 June 2017.

Kraus, Chris. *Aliens and Anorexia*. Cambridge: Semiotext(e), 2000. Print.

—. *I Love Dick*. Cambridge: Semiotext(e), 1997. Print.

Krauss, Rosalind. "Video: The Aesthetics of Narcissism." *October* 1 (1976): 50–64. Print.

Lazard, Carolyn. "In Sickness and Study." *The Blackwood* 1 (2017): 23. Print.

Lispector, Clarice. *Água Viva*. 1973. Trans. Stefan Tobler. Ed. Benjamin Moser. New York: New Directions, 2012. Print.

Lorde, Audre. *Zami: A New Spelling of My Name*. Toronto, ON: The Crossing, 1982. Print.

Maple, Sarah. *Freedom of Speech*. 2013. Video.

—. *The Practicing Feminist*. Clore Auditorium, Tate Britain, London. 21 May 2016. Artist talk.

Miller, Nancy K. *Getting Personal: Feminist Occasions and Other Autobiographical Acts*. London: Routledge, 1991. Print.

Miserandino, Christine. "The Spoon Theory." *But You Don't Look Sick? The Stories Behind the Smiles*, 2003. Web. 3 Apr. 2017.

Moser, Benjamin. Introduction. "Breathing Together." *Água Viva*. Clarice Lispector. Ed. Benjamin Moser. Trans. Stefan Tobler. New York: New Directions, 2012. Print.

Moynihan, Colin. "Liberating Lipsticks and Lattes." *The New York Times*, 15 June 2009. Web. 1 July 2018.

Nelson, Maggie. *The Argonauts*. Minneapolis: Graywolf, 2015. Print.

Ngai, Sianne. *Our Aesthetic Categories: Zany, Cute, Interesting*. Cambridge: Harvard UP, 2012. Print.

Piper, Adrian. "Food for the Spirit, July 1971." *High Performance* 4.1 (1981): 34–35. Print.

Poletti, Anna. "Periperformative Life Narrative: Queer Collages." *GLQ* 22.3 (2016): 359–79. Print.

Radchenko, Valeria. "Autotheory." *Valeria Radchenko*, 22 Apr. 2017. Web. 5 May 2018.

Samatar, Sofia. "What @Keguro_ Does Here: gukira.wordpress.com Is a Kind of LifeThinking. Reminds Me of What @Thisbhanu Does Here: jackkerouacispunjabi.blogspot.com." *Twitter*, 1 Oct. 2015, 8:58 am. Tweet.

Sedgwick, Eve Kosofsky. "Melanie Klein and the Difference Affect Makes." *South Atlantic Quarterly* 106.3 (2007): 625–42. Print.

Sharma, Sarah. "Selfie-Care and the Uncommons." *Take, Care*. Ed. Greig de Peuter and Christine Shaw. University of Toronto Mississauga, Mississauga: Blackwood Gallery, 2017. 14. Print.

Solanas, Valerie. *SCUM Manifesto*. 1967. Introduction by Avital Ronell, Verso, 2004. Print.

The Invisible Committee. *The Coming Insurrection*. Cambridge: Semiotext(e), 2009. Print.

Wollen, Audrey (@tragicqueen). "The 'Sad Girl' Starter Pack." *Instagram*, 21 Feb. 2016.

—. "Patron Saint of Depression and Anxiety St. Dymphna Gel Mouse Pad." *Instagram*, 8 Nov. 2015.

—. "Tell Me about Sad Girl Theory." *Instagram*, 22 June 2014. Web. 1 Apr. 2017.

Wunker, Erin. *Notes from a Feminist Killjoy: Essays on Everyday Life*. Toronto: BookThug, 2016. Print.

Young, Stacey. *Changing the Wor(l)d: Discourse, Politics, and the Feminist Movement*. London: Routledge, 1997. Print.

Zambreno, Kate. *Heroines*. Cambridge: Semiotext(e), 2012. Print.

Zorlutuna, Alize. *Labour for the Horizon. MICE Magazine* 2 (2016). Vimeo. 5 May 2018. 3 June 2018. Video.

Remembering Forgetting: Graphic Lives at the End of the Line

By Kathleen Venema

ABSTRACT

This essay analyzes four graphic memoirs of a daughter's caregiving through a mother's final years, examining how each text chronicles the mother's health-care needs; the daughter's emergence as caregiver; the negative emotions of caregiving; and the processes of forgetting by which ugly emotions are refined and re-storied as elegiac compassion.

Introduction

Almost exactly at its midpoint, Roz Chast's award-winning graphic memoir, *Can't We Talk about Something More Pleasant?*, includes ten pages of photographs, all of ancient, shoddy, decrepit items discovered in the author's parents' apartment and promptly discarded (109–18). "It was pretty much dusty old junk," the narrator asserts in a text-filled comics panel preceding the photographs, and adds, in the next panel, "But it was our junk, and the thought of never seeing any of it again was troubling. So I took some photos" (108). The words in the second panel sit above a drawing of a camera, which is almost centered in the frame by the two drawn hands that hold it, inviting readers to imagine that they are the ones focusing in on the vase and flowers visible in the camera's viewfinder. In the insistently tension-filled space of comics (Hatfield xiii), however, readers remember that they both are and are not the focalizers. Chast's singularly visible hands act here as a synecdoche for her body, personality, and style, an instance of what Jan Baetens and Hugo Frey call "graphiation" (137), reminding readers that it is the artist's uniquely personal presence in the memoir that creates their subject position (Kadar ix).

The panel is the only instance of such explicit focalizing (Kukkonen 58) in the whole of Chast's memoir and is noteworthy for its layers of meaning. Through this carefully designed and positioned panel, Chast underscores the

This article was originally published with errors, which have now been corrected in both the print and online versions. Please see Correction (http://dx.doi.org/10.1080/08989575.2019.1588530)

ironic effort of taking photographs to *remember* her family's "junk," just as she is about to deliberately *forget* the junk, specifically by setting the photographed items—and hundreds and hundreds of others—metaphorically adrift (121). Over fifteen pages, that is, Chast simultaneously memorializes the overwhelmingly accumulated detritus (108–18), the few items she chooses to keep (119–20), and the wholesale discarding process to which she subjects her elderly parents' remaining life possessions (121). By doing so, Chast instantiates Gunnthorunn Gudmundsdottir's claim that one of the tasks of the autobiographical "work of memory is to rescue from the past what might otherwise be forgotten," at the same time as she confronts and embodies Gudmundsdottir's several corollaries: that the autobiographer must "come to terms with the fact that much … has [already been forgotten]" (*Representations* 7) and that, in order to remember, much must, in fact, *be* forgotten (7n).

Gudmundsdottir's proposal that autobiography be termed "the genre of memory" ("Future's" 367)—especially in the context of her extended argument that memory always entails both remembering *and* forgetting (*Representations* 1)[1]—is peculiarly relevant to the four graphic memoirs considered in this essay, each one a daughter's account of caregiving through a mother's or parents' final years. Like Chast's *Can't We Talk about Something More Pleasant?*, Joyce Farmer's *Special Exits: A Graphic Memoir*, Sarah Leavitt's *Tangles: A Story about Alzheimer's, My Mother and Me*, and Dana Walrath's *Aliceheimer's: Alzheimer's through the Looking Glass* document the years through which adult-artist daughters navigate the physical and cognitive losses of their mothers' aging selves,[2] and the demands those losses make on available forms of care. All four texts instantiate Amelia DeFalco's claims about graphic caregiving memoirs: they disrupt the "generic tendency for self-aggrandizing individualism," visually assert "embodiment and concomitant vulnerability," and counter the marginalization of anomalous bodies "by publicizing and humanizing bodies in need" ("Graphic" 225). By doing so, they also unsettle conventional equations of valid identity with intact cognitive-narrative memory,[3] ableist assumptions about aging and old age that do not go unchallenged (see, for instance, Gullette; Kontos and Martin; Lock; Mortimer-Sandilands).

Contemporary discourses on aging are still uncoupleable, though, from concerns about failing memory (Goldman; Gullette 4; Katz; Swinnen and Schweda 11), and certainly each of these four memoirs identifies memory loss as a central or complicating element in the mother's decline. I am particularly interested, however, in how they each also balance a dynamic I call *remembering-forgetting* with a selective process of *remembering to forget*. I argue that the artist-daughters in question deploy comics' resources uniquely to assert the mother's significance as a simultaneously physical, cognitive, emotional, and social being; chronicle the aging mother's increasingly "complex embodiment" (Siebers 25–26); track the processes by which the daughter emerges as caregiver; acknowledge the frequently negative emotions that caregiving prompts; and document the critical (and often very generous) *forgetting* by which ugly emotions are refined and re-storied as elegiac compassion.

G. Thomas Couser describes an unexpected preponderance of daughters' memoirs of their fathers' dementia, despite the slightly higher incidence of Alzheimer's in women (*Memoir* 154–56), but it is clearly female narrators who are drawing stories about their aging mothers.[4] Crucially, given the ways in which aging continues to be a dangerously undertheorized site of cultural difference (DeFalco, *Uncanny* xii–xvi; Gullette), these graphic daughters are insisting that we see and think about how aging women are, in Hillary L. Chute's terms, "looking and looked-at subjects in particular times and spaces and histories" (*Graphic* 2). DeFalco calls texts like Farmer's and Leavitt's "somatographies" ("Graphic" 224), Couser's term for memoirs that recount the experience of knowing intimately someone with an "odd or anomalous" body (*Signifying* 2). The texts share kinship, too, with the grief memoirs on which Amy-Katerini Prodromou focuses. Textured performances of protracted mourning, the four texts evidence grief's complicated, ambiguous, gendered, nonlinear, multiaffective nature (Prodromou 18–20) and demonstrate throughout what Priscila Uppal calls elegy's "capacity to remember" and "capacity to create memories" (32), and they do so, in part, by selective, generous, and deeply compassionate forgetting.

Can't We Talk about Special Exits?

Significantly, the four artist-writers I consider are all white, middle-aged professionals, and they all inhabit, broadly, the middle class (though there are marked and meaningful discrepancies between the suboptimal medical attention Famer's working-class parents receive and the ease with which Walrath accesses sophisticated levels of care). Three of the writers are American; Leavitt is Canadian. The women's texts similarly have much in common and readily evidence the unique styles each one brings to witnessing lives at the end of metaphorical and graphically literal lines. Farmer's almost suffocatingly regular, "democratic" structure (Chute, "Comics" 298), for instance, "realistically" renders the constrained space of, and limited resources available during, the cascading series of health crises that characterize her parents' final years (DeFalco, "Graphic" 230; "Special"). In contrast with *Special Exits*' recognizably comics form, Leavitt's *Tangles* documents her adored mother's experience of early-onset Alzheimer's and effects poignant insights into dementia's uncanny distortions by juxtaposing genre-defying series of gutterless panels with eerily extended open spaces (Venema 51). Walrath's *Aliceheimer's* uses a very different visual style to explore a daughter's shifting relationship with her mother after an Alzheimer's diagnosis. By pairing photographs of the author's collages—made using a repurposed copy of *Alice in Wonderland*—with narrative vignettes, *Aliceheimer's* repeatedly represents dementia care as a potential form of relational healing (Bercaw). If Walrath works explicitly to resolve decades of friction between herself and her mother, Chast approaches the fraught relationship to her parents more obliquely, often through hilarious frenzy, as she—like Farmer—provides care through the compounding series of health crises that ultimately lead to her parents' deaths.

Walrath and Chast are certainly among the "messy bunch" of graphic life writers, whom Candida Rifkind describes as creating, using, and blurring a variety of media (188); of the four texts considered here, Chast's comprises the greatest variety of styles and media. A longtime, award-winning *New Yorker* cartoonist, Chast erratically intersperses both single photographs and series of photographs into her characteristically angsty comics, and so regularly changes page layouts that it might be accurate to call hers a poetics of chaos (Baetens and Frey 123). She frequently resorts to text-heavy narrative *telling*, but she includes ample *showing* too, as in Figure 1, when the narrator discovers that her mother's standards of cleanliness have slipped precipitously (15).

"What I noticed first," the narrator announces, of her first visit to her parents' apartment in eleven years, "was the level of **G-R-I-M-E**"—the grime visually recreated in enlarged and repugnant detail. A textual definition of "grime" and a tier of small panels representing some of the many objects covered in grime appear underneath the pictorial "**G-R-I-M-E**," while most of the bottom half of the page is taken up by a large, borderless cartoon recalling the mother's adamant declarations from earlier years: "You have to **DUST**!" The narrator's sotto voce observation runs in a banner along the very bottom of the page: "It was clear that she had stopped worrying about that" (15). Readers know instinctively what scholars bring to conscious knowledge—that the size and boldness of letters in comics "correspond to the volume at which they are spoken and the emphasis which is laid onto them" (Kukkonen 9). Read as pictures, both the narrator's discovery of "**G-R-I-M-E**" and her mother's capitalized, bolded, and multiply underlined words are, in Charles Hatfield's terms, "freighted with meaning" (36–37). Specifically, that is, they convey the meaningful discrepancies that now exist—literally, between the mother's past and current housekeeping capacities, and

Figure 1. *Roz Chast's* Can't We Talk about Something More Pleasant? *(page 15).* © *2014. Used with the permission of Bloomsbury USA.*

symbolically, between the still-tyrannical mother and her lifetime of service to prefeminist codes of cleanliness.

Life-writing texts about Alzheimer's disease and other dementias uniquely thematize remembering and forgetting, but though neither *Special Exits* nor *Can't We Talk* exclusively narrates protracted forgetting, both tell stories in which memory loss exacerbates, and is exacerbated by, the accumulating illnesses, impairments, and indignities of aging. Importantly, too, both feature key narrative moments in which a dynamic of remembering-forgetting sets in motion a cascade of intensifying health crises. In an early chapter of *Can't We Talk*, for instance, the daughter's announcement that she is going to the Galapagos prompts the mother's recollection of a trip to the islands many years earlier and of having received a certificate signed by "King Neptune!" (45).

Prompted by the conversation to remember the certificate, and determined to find the certificate that she has now remembered (48), the mother—whom the narrative establishes from the outset as dangerously domineering—cannot be deterred from using a step stool to search the aptly named "Crazy Closet" (the source of most of the junk the daughter later sets adrift) (53). Not surprisingly, the already-unsteady ninety-three-year-old falls, which precipitates an attack of acute diverticulitis (55n), which requires hospitalization (60), which exacerbates the father's dementia (64n), which results in a series of increasingly dangerous mishaps (90, 94, 97, 101). The crucial narrative point is that remembering-forgetting precipitates the sequence of events that now fully implicates the daughter in her parents' care. "Of all the stressful days I'd had with them since my mother's fall off the ladder," the narrator writes when her mother comes home from the hospital, "this one had been the worst… . At least then there were people around… . Professionals in the land of the ailing. Now I felt like it was just me, my mom, and my dad. And none of us had a clue" (101, emphasis in original).

If Chast's memoir works by way of hilarious and sometimes ugly excess, Farmer's comics explore remembering-forgetting and its effects on relationships of care more subtly. About a quarter of the way into *Special Exits*, for instance, the stepmother's untreated glaucoma triggers a wracking headache that signals the onset of permanent blindness—an event that occurs over two pages of text. Figure 2 illustrates the way Farmer's painstakingly detailed, incremental style (Gallagher) enables microsecond shifts in perspective to communicate the mother's sudden agony (44). As readers proceed across the panels and down the tiers, they experience themselves moving so rapidly toward, away from, and around the mother as to mimic the disorienting distress that migraine sufferers readily recognize (Kukkonen 9). Anxiety eases slightly and time slows moderately on the next page, where, as Figure 3 illustrates, five of the eight panels provide crucial perspectives—each one from a slightly or significantly different angle—of the coffee table cluttered with the mother's medications (45).

Both the sixth and seventh panels of the previous page (Figure 2) also include the coffee table piled with medications, but it is in the fourth panel on the second page (Figure 3) that readers see—for the first time in

44

Figure 2. *Joyce Farmer's* Special Exits *(page 44).* © 2010. *Used with the permission of Fantagraphics Books.*

this sequence—the eye drops that might have made all the difference. "Where are your eye drops? Have you been taking them?" the father asks in that panel, to which the mother responds, "I take all my pills, you

45

Figure 3. *Joyce Farmer's* Special Exits *(page 45).* © *2010. Used with the permission of Fantagraphics Books.*

know that." Belying the mother's certainty, however, the final three panels show the father selecting the grubby bottle of eye drops, discovering they have expired, and realizing the horrifying consequences of the neglect.

"Glaucoma ... ," the text of the final panel reads, as the weeping father consults a medical manual:

regular use of eye drops prevents blindness ... otherwise ...

....

....

... damage is permanent .... (45)

Like Chast's pictorial "**G-R-I-M-E**," readers are cued to read the sticky dust attached to the eye-dropper bottle in the fourth panel as evidence that—in the midst of the various medications that the mother is remembering to take—she has been forgetting this critical part of her complicated health protocol. What is especially poignant about this pivotal moment of remembering-forgetting is the way *Special Exits* quietly references the eye drops early in the narrative, where we first see the bottle clearly in the foreground, at least a year and a half before blindness sets in (15). Indeed, engaging in a process very similar to the remembering-reconstructing dynamic that a medical diagnosis often prompts ("What were the signs?" we ask; "How did we not notice?" we lament; "Could this have been prevented?" we anguish), a careful rereading of *Special Exits* finds nine separate visual references, before the blindness episode, to the medications lined up on the coffee table, with no fewer than six showing the eye drops, each time fully accessible, each time still grime-free (15, 16, 17, 26, and twice on 27). As Gudmundsdottir does throughout her study, Farmer literally "map[s] the location of the forgotten" (*Representations* 15) here, using the extraordinary resources of graphic narrative to show us forgetting as it is happening. Of course, readers do not know, the first time through, that what they are seeing is forgetting, which means they cannot remember the eye drops until a second reading, when, with an almost visceral agony, it is already far too late to help.

Can't We Talk and *Special Exits* both structure remembering-forgetting as a narrative fulcrum, a catalyst for increasing dependence on care. From these respective narrative moments on—the mother's fall in *Can't We Talk* and the stepmother's blindness in *Special Exits*—both texts include increasingly frequent representations of the negative feelings that often attend, or accrue to, experiences of caregiving. These appear primarily visually in *Special Exits*, frequently and immediately following the blindness episode, starting on page 47 and then throughout. In *Can't We Talk*, negative feelings following the mother's fall are illustrated with frank, frenetic consistency and regularly put into words as Chast experiences repeated communicative impasses (56, 64, 70), exhausting personality clashes (57, 91), impossible time demands (58–59), logistical challenges (60), oppressive bureaucracies (62–63), the compounding effects of multiple ailments (73–75), administrative labyrinths (84–86), a caregiver's acute loneliness (101–03), and, repeatedly, the staggering costs of care. "My parents didn't have a clue," she recalls, about the facility to which she moves her parents when it becomes clear they can no longer manage in their apartment; "They never asked, and I never told them. … Everything took time and cost money. It was enraging and depressing" (128).

Indeed, Chast's text readily instantiates DeFalco's claims that graphic representations of care expose "the illusion of the disembodied, independent subject, while simultaneously problematizing optimistic visions of care relations," including by visualizing such negative experiences as "disharmony, neglect, [and] even cruelty" ("Graphic" 225). Though I think it does so inadvertently, Chast's account of caring for parents constrained by personal, familial, and historical traumas (5–7) also exposes what Margaret Morganroth Gullette calls the biopolitical sources of costly, age-related declining. Challenging what she calls the "despicable falsehood" of "supposedly 'naturally' accumulating" physiological weakness, Gullette underscores the ways in which "power foists biological declines on many. From the prenatal period on," she explains, "the body's fate is grounded on what money buys: access to nourishing food, healthy surroundings, higher education, medical attention, avoidance of dangerous work" (xvii).

If Gullette's list identifies deep-rooted deficits that Chast struggles to compensate for in her parents' final years, it sketches an ironic inverse of Farmer's parents' lives. Even more so than *Can't We Talk*, *Special Exits* regularly represents the ways in which responsibility for parents suffering the long-term effects of poverty, poor diet, minimal education, dangerous work, and economically inaccessible medical attention stretches caregivers to breaking points. While the politics of care is not these texts' explicit concern, each one invites further analysis of what it says and shows and—equally importantly—what it leaves unsaid and invisible. As I suggest above, Chast hints at the biopolitical sources of age-related decline, and Farmer, though she does not comment directly, visually details myriad flaws in the American healthcare system (DeFalco, "Graphic" 232). For her part, Leavitt frequently represents caregiving frustrations but fails to acknowledge the support of the Canadian medical system, while Walrath effectively mystifies the economics that underpin the exceptional care she is able to provide for her mother.

Remediating Alice in *Aliceheimer's*

After "a lifetime of mutually abrasive interaction" (Bercaw), Walrath moves her mother Alice hundreds of miles north of New York City to live with Walrath's family in the Vermont woods. This despite the fact that "Vermont winters are long and cold. She hated snow. I was the daughter who got on her nerves. The feeling was mutual" (1). "On the surface," Walrath adds, "I couldn't bear to see my mother in the lock-down 'memory care' unit," but she adds, "Although all of this was true, my real motivations were deep down and hidden. We had unfinished business. I wanted to create a bond with my mother, to redo the past, and to fill the hole inside of me. In the middle of dementia, somehow, my mother wanted to do the same" (1). Of the perhaps counterintuitive decision to move her mother away from accustomed surroundings, Walrath explains, "That [my mother] knew us might ground her. The unfamiliar fields and woods might curb her wandering and her attempts to walk home. Our farmhouse was peaceful. Nature could soothe her" (1). Walrath here echoes Catriona Mortimer-Sandilands' insights into "the inevitable involvement of place in the physical, cognitive, emotional, and social acts of remembering and forgetting" (283); ultimately, each of *Aliceheimer's* collage-vignette pairs roots dementia's remembering-forgetting dynamic in the intimate spaces that Walrath and her mother share.

"She's still here," an early collage caption insists, for instance, underneath a drawing of Alice's slippered feet blasting into space. "She's just losing her memory, the part that kept her grounded" (20). From its very first pages, *Aliceheimer's* articulates crucial insights into caring for a person with dementia, frequently illustrating aspects of Naomi Feil's "validation therapy" and instantiating principles of "relational" models of dementia care, which "stress that persons are more than their brains, that personal identity does not rest only on mental continuity, and that the story of dementia exceeds that of tragic loss and decline" (Swinnen and Schweda 11). "The dominant narrative is a horror story," Walrath acknowledges, but insists, "For Alice and me, the story was different. Alzheimer's was a time of healing and magic… . Reframing dementia as a different way of being, as a window into another reality, lets people living in that state be our teachers—useful, true humans who contribute to our collective good, instead of scary zombies" (4). Effectuating Mortimer-Sandilands' proposal that Alzheimer's caregivers jettison cognitive frameworks and offer familiar touch and motion, bodily rhythms, and rich perceptual relations instead (275), Walrath repeatedly *makes from* Alice's forgettings and misrememberings celebration-worthy new realities.

Every one of the text's thirty-one full-page spreads evidences Walrath's commitment to entering her mother's shifting sense of reality, variously relishing Alice's fun with linguistic losses (9, 19, 21, 23), Alice's insights into previously unspoken truths and experiences (11, 17, 43, 55), and Alice's immigrant history and the ways in which Alice's and Dana's histories are intertwined (17, 25, 39–43, 55, 57–59, 61, 65, 67). Three of the thirty-one spreads specifically engage Alice's many late-afternoon hallucinations (a phenomenon known as "sundowning" in the Alzheimer's literature): the pirates who kidnap and both frighten and entertain Alice (28–29), the witches who threaten (34–35), the death by drowning that Alice barely avoids (34–35), and the World War II soldiers creeping terrifyingly close (34–35, 36–37). Throughout, Walrath's lightly humorous, deeply intuitive, always sensitive treatment is fully evident, as it is in the four full-page spreads devoted to Alice's most frequent hallucination, of her late husband Dave up in the trees (26–27, 44–45, 46–47, 48–49). The collage opposite the vignette "The Lobster Quadrille" (47), shown in Figure 4, offers one version of this scene, with Alice drawn oversize and close up, her huge, dark eyes linked with Dave in a tree, shown in a medium long shot (Kukkonen 46) that underscores the distance—and the unequal distance—between them (Walrath 46).

"If characters look at something, chances are it's important," Karin Kukkonen notes about comics (13). Walrath's repeating images of Alice gazing at Dave certainly reiterate both his importance in Alice's life (13, 27, 45, 50, 52) and the important work Alice was engaged in, despite her dementia, of recuperating shortcomings in her relationship with her husband (27, 43). As many of Walrath's collages do (16, 18, 24, 26, 28, 30, 32, 34, 36, 44, 48–49, 50, 52, 54–55, 56, 68), this one includes a vertical line running through the center of the image. Likely a shadow of the margins in the sketchbook where the drawings originally appeared, the lines function as conceptual punctuation marks, separating Alice from both her

Figure 4. *Dana Walrath's* Aliceheimer's *(page 46).* © *2016. Used with the author's permission.*

hallucinations and the nondemented world. Michael Chaney, who writes about the mirrors, masks, and *mises en abyme* that characterize many pre-eminent comics, proposes that "These optic doublings compel reader-viewers to think twice about the drawings and their suspicious claims to representational authority" (15). "Apart from precipitating catharsis and cathexis," Chaney adds, "the comics' mirror also does reflective work outside of diegetic stories ... forcing reader-viewers to revise their assumptions about any text's capacity to reflect reality" (16). Walrath's mirrors (her "looking-glasses"), especially in the collages of Dave and Alice, signal a deliberate disconnection with rational reality and an engagement instead with the profoundly meaningful—and, crucially, emotionally contiguous—world that Alice now navigates.

"Alice practiced dying on a regular basis," the vignette opposite the collage begins, in confirmation of this interpretation. "Rehearsal usually happened around sunset. I would sit with her, my dead father and her parents hovering in the air around us. Alice took tiny steps toward them, then back to me ... . She was truly in between, liminal, ... transcending two worlds." "[A] person with Alzheimer's experiences a social death long before his or her heart stops beating," the narrator continues. "Somehow, for the rest of us, they are not as fully human as they once were when they no longer recognize their own families, can no longer speak. The rules for interacting with them and caring for them shift. In the middle of Alzheimer's, Alice somehow knew this death was already happening, so we needed to rehearse" (47).

In the context of life narratives that fully accommodate death as the intractable endpoint of aging processes, Gudmundsdottir's reminder that "death does not necessarily denote an absence of memory" but is, on the contrary, also traditionally "a point of remembrance" (4)[5] supports my claim that these four graphic texts are also, each in their own way, forms of elegiac witness, works of mourning that, in Christian Riegel's terms, "attempt to make present that which is irrefutably lost" (xix). Walrath's material is profoundly elegiac from its earliest moments, and definitively on the double-page spread shown in Figure 5, prefaced by the words "disappearing Alice ... " and tagged with the concluding lament " ... none is hard to draw" (14–15).

Multiplying the inexact mirroring of the pages that follow, this double spread simultaneously repeats and juxtaposes images from immediately previous pages. The left-hand page, that is, repeats an Alice collage from four pages earlier—one with words where Alice's head should be—but shifts the collage so far toward the right margin that it slides into the book's gutter, where it forms an inexact mirror to a plangent two-column collage (initially seen three pages earlier). The first of the columns is captioned "Days W/Alice" and consists of 28,126 marks of varying sizes,

Figure 5. *Dana Walrath's* Aliceheimer's *(pages 14–15).* © *2016. Used with the author's permission.*

shapes, textures, and colors, each one of which represents a day of Alice's life. On first glance, the second column, captioned "Days W/O Alice," looks empty. Careful examination, however, reveals the faint, textured outline of an image of Alice—a double image, in which a larger Alice appears to hold a smaller version of herself in her arms, the smaller version complete with her signature halo.

None is hard to draw, and Walrath's work reminds us over and over again that while Alice may be navigating a compromised memory, her life—and her life with her daughter—is emphatically not "none." Effectively instantiating Chute's claim that "graphic narrative asserts the value of presence, however complex and contingent" (*Graphic* 2), Walrath includes—even as she anticipates the "Days W/O Alice" that will be her future—a delicate afterimage of her mother's deep-eyed poignancy and entrancing otherworldliness. By doing so, she reiterates the text's powerful, counterintuitive truth: that there is much to be made, literally, aesthetically, metaphorically, psychically, emotionally, and relationally, out of what convention understands as the diminishments, the reducing-to-nothingness, of dementia's "progress."

Tangled Elegy

Unexpectedly, then, it is *Aliceheimer's*—the story of a daughter renegotiating a previously excruciating relationship with her mother—that wraps its benignly aging subject in the fantastical garb of a repurposed copy of *Alice in Wonderland* and renders her repeatedly as an eloquent-eyed, apple-cheeked, sunbeam-haloed, time-defying, superpowered icon of dementia's potential. *Tangles*, by contrast—a devoted daughter's heartbreaking account of losing her beloved mother to early-onset Alzheimer's—consistently traffics in vivid visual records of the ways that Alzheimer's disease ravages its sufferers' physical beings. As I argue elsewhere, Alzheimer's disease may be a disease of the brain, but *Tangles* reminds us repeatedly that "it wreaks its disintegrating effects on bodies too" (61). Indeed, when, as DeFalco puts it, "Leavitt refuses to shy away from the demoralizing, even repugnant aspects of caregiving" ("Graphic" 234), she underscores the way that it is bodies—ill bodies, damaged bodies, hurting bodies, anguished bodies, nonnormative, anomalous, lost, disoriented, baffled, and bewildered bodies—that one finds at the fraught intersection of aging, disability, grief, elegy, comics, and care.

According to Margrit Shildrick, "What is really unsettling about non-normative embodiment is ... the intuition that despite the privileging of mind in western discourse, our embodied selfhood is a matter of complex interweaving. Whenever the body is at risk, it is the stability of the self that is threatened" (75). Certainly, *Tangles'* plethora of monsters and otherwise grotesque human figures underscores the threat that Alzheimer's poses to both the mother's and the daughter's selves (Venema 54n). "As my mother changed," Leavitt writes in her introduction, "I changed too, forced to reconsider my own identity as a daughter and as an adult and to recreate my relationship with my mother" (7). "As Mom got sicker and their meals got smaller," the final two panels of *Tangles'* fifty-first page elaborate, "I turned into some sort of ... extreme Jewish mother, obsessed with making them eat" (51; Figure 6). Represented first in a head-on view, "ubiquitous ringlets standing on end,

Figure 6. *Sarah Leavitt's* Tangles *(page 51).* © *2010. Reprinted with the permission of Freehand Books, Canada, and the US publisher, Skyhorse Publishing, Inc.*

a furious expression, and threateningly outstretched arms," the daughter as caregiver "acquires a thoroughly grotesque appearance," witchlike in the final frame, wielding dangerous, oversized utensils, tongue extended, "an evocation of a rampaging monster" (Venema 57).

I read Leavitt's refusal to shy away from the monstrous truths of living and dying with Alzheimer's disease as a form of navigating what Prodromou defines as loss: the "depriv[ation] of a vital element necessary to the understanding and performance of a self." According to Prodromou, the loss of a beloved other requires "the whole concept of self [to] be reworked and revisited [as] we attempt to define ourselves within the … psychically altered space that results from this new absence" (6). Leavitt loses a vital understanding of her self as Alzheimer's both deprives her of the central, defining maternal force in her life and forces her to navigate the constantly altering space that her mother's unpredictable and increasing absence creates (7, 19, 22, 44, among many others). Her subsequent devoted, exasperated, heartrending, flailing, enraged attempts at reworking and redefining are evident throughout *Tangles*, especially when the text's often claustrophobically gutterless panels open out into swathes of disorienting space (8–9 and ff.). And they are uniquely at work in the text's final pages, when, after the mother's death, the narrative unfolds into what I have called its "fully elegiac conclusion" (Venema, 67).

Like the intractably double-sided process of remembering-forgetting that Gudmundsdottir explores, elegy's dynamics ostensibly enable forgetting while working to consolidate remembrances of those who are gone (MacDonald; Sacks; Uppal). Of the four texts I have considered here, *Tangles*' concluding lamentation most powerfully demonstrates comics' unique ability to make absence present (Chute, *Graphic* 2) as it plangently, reverently, and irreverently intersperses the mundane and the truncated-sacred into its slow, gutterless, grief-stricken, evacuated-of-humans stillness.

The first eight frames of *Tangles*' fifth-to-last page (Figure 7) are remarkable both because they are entirely devoid of human characters and because—at a point immediately following the mother's death—they mark the only moment where the text is structured by two separate narratives, two separate voices, and two separate time frames and durations. Consistently up to this point, *Tangles* proceeds as the account of a singular narrative focalizer, one who controls the whole of the telling, the recollecting, the organizing, the selecting, and the reproducing. Readers never doubt that it is Leavitt who recalls her mother at earlier points in her life (12, 14, 18, 38–39, and ff.), merges dual or multiple time frames within a single panel (15, 19, 24, 27, and ff.), or slows the narrative by inserting signature swathes of open space (8–9, 42–43, 45, 47, and ff.).

Figure 7. *Sarah Leavitt's* Tangles *(page 123).* © *2010. Reprinted with the permission of Freehand Books, Canada, and the US publisher, Skyhorse Publishing, Inc.*

The first eight panels on page 123 of *Tangles* thus offer an unprecedented instance of what Hatfield calls the tension between sequence and surface (48–52). There, a series of simple sentences—in printing that readers have learned to associate with the narrator—scrolls along or near the top of the panels, recounting the family's sequential activities: "We all went back to Dad's house"; "We drank a lot of wine"; "I read aloud Psalm 23"; "Then I made two huge batches of … cookies"; "There were no chips so I smashed up squares of Baker's chocolate"; "We ate all the cookies" (123). Following another chronology entirely—indeed, appearing to exist in an entirely different temporal frame—phrases from the twenty-third psalm appear in an unfamiliar, large, and bolded font along the bottoms of the panels. Despite the fact that only disjointed excerpts are visible, readers readily produce for themselves the whole of this most familiar of psalms, thereby engaging in "closure," the conceptual process that Scott McCloud describes and claims as comics' defining feature (63–67). "[T]he art of crafting words and pictures together into a narrative punctuated by pause or absence … mimics the procedure of memory," Chute reminds us, especially the procedure of traumatic memory (*Graphic* 4). Readers enter *Tangles*' mimicking of traumatic memory by imagining the whole of the liturgical fragments as cyclical, a ritual, sonorous evocation of loss that offers its own strange, insistent comfort and reassurance. Entirely counterintuitively, and yet apparently intentionally, *Tangles*' juxtaposition here of mundane activity and the telegraphed sacred also injects some of the text's funniest and subtlest humor.

Just before the narrator's announcement in the second panel, for instance, that "We drank a lot of wine," readers encounter the boldly solid psalmic assurance "**shall not want**" at the bottom of the first panel. Similarly subtle (or unsubtle), the fourth panel's announcement, "Then I made two huge batches of chocolate chip cookies," sits above an image of almost actual-size baking chocolate piled in the middle of the slyly comedic injunction "**fear no evil**," and just before the next panel's liturgical "**comfort me**." Entirely bare of images, the small seventh panel juxtaposes the narrator's confessional "Then I was so drunk I had to lie down under the kitchen table for a while" with the psalm's assurance of "**mercy**." Mercy appears to extend into the elongated eighth panel, moreover, which shows a detailed, head-on image of table legs, one of the text's myriad black cats, and the psalm's enduring promise of comfort "**all the days of my life**" (123).

According to Baetens and Frey, when a familiar narrative voice disappears from a comic's pages or panels, the disappearance is deliberate, intended to stress the given panels' emotional intensity (148). Here, of course, the narrator's voice is not absent but uniquely counterpointed, and so we understand that the panels' emotional intensity is created by what Hatfield calls "a 'soundtrack' for the images," the visual|verbal tension that "results from the juxtaposition of symbols that function diegetically and symbols that function non-diegetically … the mingling of symbols that 'show' and symbols that 'tell'" (40–41). Page 123 is not quite an instance of McCloud's "polyptych" (115), but like polyptychs, its panels blur "comics' equation of time with space," generating tensions between serial and synchronic readings, and requiring readers both to choose a reading and defer from choosing a reading (Hatfield 53).

As Hatfield predicts when he notes that "polyptychs tend to be used when time or space become the thematic concerns of the narrative itself" (53), time is the profound thematic concern of this most elegiac of

Leavitt's final pages. Not inadvertently, the spatially extended psalmic words "**all the days of my life**" are positioned directly above the page's final panel, in which a tiny Sarah is barely discernible, writing-drawing in bed. Repeating for the last time one of the narrative's most frequent images—of Sarah in and on beds, writing and drawing—the panel is unique for its rare inclusion of an image from Sarah's notebook. For one of the only times in the text, readers are invited here to view Sarah's drawings directly. And what they view are sketches of the mother's final stages, opposite a notebook page filled with the devastating handwritten realization that "there will be no more drawing, and I really thought there would be. Mom died today" (123). Beside and slightly below the notebook, a black cat walks off the page. Below the cat, the psalmic words "**for ever**" reiterate the finality of Sarah's new reality.

By including a representation of her last ever drawings of her mother, Leavitt conveys the heartbreaking finality of her mother's death and inadvertently parallels another—more surprisingly—elegiac conclusion, and that is Chast's. Surprisingly, that is, given its often hilarious, always angst-filled account of a deeply conflicted relationship, *Can't We Talk* ends on an unexpected visual note that—like Leavitt's—entirely shifts a reader's sense of narrative duration. Having made the merciful decision to tell, not show, some of her mother's final physical indignities, Chast closes with twelve plaintive portraits, one per page,[6] in a style utterly distinct from anything readers have seen in the preceding two-hundred-plus pages (Figure 8). Dignified sketches that quietly recollect Chast's formal art training, the slow series of portraits doubles as a requiem for the difficult, demanding, imposing, domineering mother who waited until the week

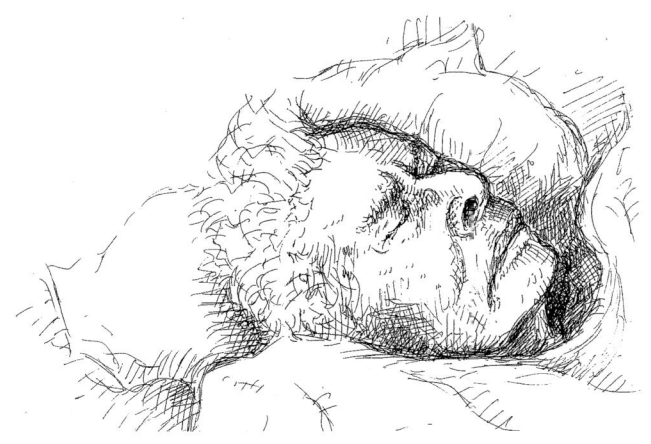

Figure 8. *Roz Chast's* Can't We Talk About Something More Pleasant? *(page 208).* © *2014. Used with the permission of Bloomsbury USA.*

before she died but did remember, finally, to tell her daughter that she loved her (208).

According to Frank Cioffi, Art Spiegelman's *Maus* books prompt a dissonance that "make[s] readers reflect on their own emotional mechanism—on the way that they can internalize, naturalize, and be seduced by a vision of the world. They awaken readers to how images can be used to create a world both believable and fantastic, linked to actual historicity but at the same time part of another realm or dimension altogether" (120). Not dissimilarly, I would argue, readers have so effectively been drawn in (pun intended) to a world that figures Chast's mother exclusively as a crazy-making drain on financial and emotional resources that we forget, until the final, elegiac portraits remind us, that she is also a real, human, detailed, complex, dignified body—dying. Readers readily answer Leavitt's invitation to remember and mourn the whimsical, appealingly accomplished, profoundly devoted mother around whom Leavitt's world revolved. Chast's concluding sketches require a more radical emotional shift, and could—if we were so inclined—prompt us to consider the ease with which we acquiesce to ready-made and deeply political generalizations about age, aging, memory loss, and dying.

Conclusion

In work that explicitly links materialist feminism with technoscientific world-making practices, Cecilia Åsberg examines Alzheimer's disease as an instance of the ways in which biomedical research focuses on molecular disorders, despite the fact that, in its most common form, Alzheimer's is not a clear-cut genetic disorder at microscopic levels of brain chemistry and "even more complicated and socially entangled if we scale up the perspective," specifically to its sociopolitical embedding at the intersections of age, gender, class, and racialization. "Add to that," Åsberg proposes, "Alzheimer's fearful and stigmatizing pop culture portraits of patients as vegetables, animals, crazies, zombies, and *dehumanized* creatures at the outer rim of personhood, and we glimpse how this disorder diffracts patterns of natureculture, embodied power relations, human-animal and human-inhumane continuums."

"What another person looks like to *you* is *your* responsibility," Gullette insists in her epigraph to *Ending Ageism, or How Not to Shoot Old People*[7]—a "gnomic" assertion, she acknowledges later, that may be "impossible to put into practice." Nevertheless, she insists, "being led to look properly at the Other can be a life-changing experience" (51). In the texts examined here, work by female professional artists recording their extended engagements in caregiving—work that lands disproportionately on female shoulders like theirs—Dana Walrath, Sarah Leavitt, Joyce Farmer, and Roz Chast deploy the often startling resources of graphic form to help us look properly at their (and all) aging m|others. Throughout, their texts reiterate the countercultural truth—that there is much to be *made*, aesthetically, and much to be *gained*, psychically, emotionally, relationally, and culturally, by challenging conventional representations of aging, dying, memory loss, and death.

"[S]howing the faces, the lived experience, and the daily reality of those with Alzheimer's and other altered, different states removes the stigma and restores their humanity," Walrath insists (6), while Stephen Katz reminds us that "good memory is not only about healthy cognitive capacity but also about how forgetting is crucial to both the sciences and the arts of life in the aging process." Katz and Walrath thus echo aspects of Gudmundsdottir's crucial insights that autobiography—and, with it, memoir and, with it, memoir about aging and death—is the genre in which memory and forgetting mingle inextricably. Instantiating Gudmundsdottir's claim, the four graphic memoirs examined here repeatedly balance remembering-forgetting with selective processes of remembering to forget.

Indeed, when Katz observes that "one of the benefits of human brain plasticity is that it allows us to filter, change, interpret, negotiate, and even forget our memories in order to create coherence and stability in our lives," he endorses the ways in which Chast, Farmer, Leavitt, and Walrath deploy the resources of graphic narrative to remember their mothers' increasingly complex aging bodies; to remember and sometimes gently forget the complex, fraught, gendered, frustrating, not infrequently life-giving processes by which they emerge as their mothers' caregivers; and to retune both their forgettings and their rememberings as elegiac compassion. By way of graphic narrative's "inventive textual practice," these female artists refuse lenses of "unspeakability or invisibility" (Chute, *Graphic* 26); prompt the sustained empathy, epiphanies, and increased emotional knowledge for which Gullette hopes (51–52); and tell deeply affecting, tacitly political feminist truths about caring for beloved (and difficult) elderly others.

Notes

1. Gudmundsdottir is working here with concepts developed by Marc Augé and Andreas Huyssen.
2. Chast's *Can't We Talk* and Farmer's *Special Exits* narrate stories of daughters who care for both parents, but even they focus primarily on the daughter's relationship with the (step)mother and the mother's decline.

3. In "Breaking Rules," for instance, Eakin wonders whether the "failed narratives" of people suffering from Alzheimer's disease reflect "failed identities" (113–14).
4. Two additional "autographics" of a (grand)mother's dementia not considered here are Roher's *Bird in a Cage* and Futerman's *Keeper of the Clouds*. As the male author of *Wrinkles*, Roca is an exception, though *Wrinkles* is a graphic novel, not an auto|biographical account, and does not specifically engage with the issues of caregiving by children.
5. Gudmundsdottir is developing concepts from Harald Weinrich's seminal work on forgetting, *Lethe: Kunst und Kritik des Vergessens*.
6. In one case, two sketches of the mother's face share a page (213).
7. Gullette attributes the epigraph to theater and film director and producer Michael Lessac.

Works cited

Åsberg, Cecilia. "Imagining Posthumanities, Enlivening Feminisms." *The Subject of Rosi Braidotti: Politics and Concepts.* Ed. Bolette Blaagaard and Iris van der Tuin. London: Bloomsbury, 2014. 56–64. Web. 4 Mar. 2015.

Baetens, Jan, and Hugo Frey. *The Graphic Novel: An Introduction.* Cambridge: Cambridge UP, 2015. Print.

Bercaw, Nancy Stearns. "Alzheimer's Disease as an Adventure in Wonderland." *New York Times,* 21 June 2016. Web. 12 Sept. 2017.

Chaney, Michael A. *Reading Lessons in Seeing: Mirrors, Masks, and Mazes in the Autobiographical Graphic Novel.* Jackson: UP of Mississippi, 2016. Print.

Chast, Roz. *Can't We Talk about Something More Pleasant?* New York: Bloomsbury, 2014. Print.

Chute, Hillary L. "Comics Form and Narrating Lives." *The Routledge Auto/Biography Studies Reader.* Ed. Ricia Anne Chansky and Emily Hipchen. London: Routledge, 2016. 295–99. Print.

—. *Graphic Women: Life Narrative and Contemporary Comics.* New York: Columbia UP, 2010. Print.

Cioffi, Frank L. "Disturbing Comics: The Disjunction of Word and Image in the Comics of Andrzej Mleczko, Ben Katchor, R. Crumb, and Art Spiegelman." *The Language of Comics: Word and Image.* Ed. Robin Varnum and Christina T. Gibbons. Jackson: UP of Mississippi, 2001. 97–122. Print.

Couser, G. Thomas. *Memoir: An Introduction.* Oxford: Oxford UP, 2012. Print.

—. *Signifying Bodies: Disability in Contemporary Memoir.* Ann Arbor: U of Michigan P, 2009. Print.

DeFalco, Amelia. "Graphic Somatography: Life Writing, Comics, and the Ethics of Care." *Journal of Medical Humanities* 37.3 (2016): 223–40. *Academic Search Premier.* Web. 25 Apr. 2017.

—. *Uncanny Subjects: Aging in Contemporary Narrative.* Columbus: Ohio State UP, 2010. Print.

Eakin, Paul John. "Breaking Rules: The Consequences of Self-Narration." *Biography* 24.1 (2001): 113–27. Print.

Farmer, Joyce. *Special Exits: A Graphic Memoir.* Seattle: Fantagraphics, 2010. Print.

Feil, Naomi. *The Validation Breakthrough: Simple Techniques for Communicating with People with Alzheimer's and Other Dementias.* 3rd ed. Towson, MD: Health Professions, 2012. Print.

Futerman, Liza. *Keeper of the Clouds.* Illus. Evi Tampold. N.p.: Tampold, 2016. Print.

Gallagher, Paul. "Such Small Increments: Joyce Farmer's *Special Exits* a Moving and Unique Graphic Novel on Old Age and Death." *Huffpost*, 17 December 2010. Web. 1 Nov. 2017.

Goldman, Marlene. "Aging, Old Age, Memory, Aesthetics: Introduction." *Arcade: Literature, the Humanities, and the World* Spec. issue of *Occasion* 4 (2012): 1–6. Web. 12 Mar. 2015.

Gudmundsdottir, Gunnthorunn. "Future's Memory." *a/b: Auto/Biography Studies* 32.2 (2017): 367–69. *Project MUSE*. Web. 27 Apr. 2017.

—. *Representations of Forgetting in Life Writing and Fiction.* Basingstoke: Palgrave, 2017. Print.

Gullette, Margaret Morganroth. *Ending Ageism, or How Not to Shoot Old People.* New Brunswick: Rutgers UP, 2017. Print.

Hatfield, Charles. *Alternative Comics: An Emerging Literature.* Jackson: UP of Mississippi, 2005. Print.

Kadar, Marlene. "Introduction: What Is Life Writing?" *Reading Life Writing.* Ed. Kadar. Oxford: Oxford UP, 1993. ix–xv. Print.

Katz, Stephen. "Embodied Memory: Ageing, Neuroculture, and the Genealogy of Mind." *Arcade: Literature, the Humanities, and the World.* Spec. Issue of *Occasion* 4 (2012): 1–11. Web. 12 May 2018.

Kontos, Pia, and Wendy Martin. "Embodiment and Dementia: Exploring Critical Narratives of Selfhood, Surveillance, and Dementia Care." *Dementia* 12.3 (2013): 288–302. *SAGE CRKN Collection.* Web. 12 Mar. 2015.

Kukkonen, Karin. *Studying Comics and Graphic Novels.* Hoboken, NJ: Wiley-Blackwell, 2013. Print.

Leavitt, Sarah. *Tangles: A Story about Alzheimer's, My Mother and Me.* Calgary: Freehand, 2010. Print.

Lock, Margaret. *The Alzheimer Conundrum: Entanglements of Dementia and Aging.* Princeton: Princeton UP, 2013. Print.

MacDonald, Tanis. *The Daughter's Way: Canadian Women's Paternal Elegies.* Waterloo: Wilfrid Laurier UP, 2012. Print.

McCloud, Scott. *Understanding Comics: The Invisible Art.* New York: Harper Collins, 1993. Print.

Mortimer-Sandilands, Catriona. "Landscape, Memory, and Forgetting: Thinking through (My Mother's) Body and Place." *Material Feminisms.* Ed. Stacy Alaimo and Susan Hekman. Bloomington: Indiana UP, 2008 265–87. Web. 1 Mar. 2018.

Prodromou, Amy-Katerini. *Navigating Loss in Women's Contemporary Memoir.* Basingstoke: Palgrave, 2013. Print.

Riegel, Christian. "Introduction: The Literary Work of Mourning." *Response to Death: The Literary Work of Mourning*, edited by C. Riegel. Edmonton: U of Alberta P, 2005. xvi–xxix. Print.

Rifkind, Candida. "Graphic Narratives." *a/b: Auto/Biography Studies* 32.2 (2017): 187–90. *Project MUSE.* Web. 27 Apr. 2017.

Roca, Paco. *Wrinkles.* N.p.: Fanfare, 2015. Print.

Roher, Rebecca. *Bird in a Cage.* Wolfville, NS: Conundrum, 2016. Print.

Sacks, Peter M. *The English Elegy: Studies in the Genre from Spenser to Yeats.* Baltimore: Johns Hopkins UP, 1985. Print.

Shildrick, Margrit. *Embodying the Monster: Encounters with the Vulnerable Self.* London: SAGE, 2002. Print.

Siebers, Tobin. *Disability Theory.* Ann Arbor: U of Michigan P, 2008. Print.

—. "Special Exits: My Parents—a Memoir." *Publisher's Weekly*, August 2010. Web. 21 Apr. 2017.

Swinnen, Aagje, and Mark Schweda. *Popularizing Dementia: Public Expressions and Representations of Forgetfulness*, Ed. A. Swinnen and M. Schweda. Aging Studies 6. Bielefeld: Transcript, 2015. 9–20.

Uppal, Priscila. *We Are What We Mourn: The Contemporary English-Canadian Elegy*. Montreal: McGill-Queen's UP, 2009.

Venema, Kathleen. "Untangling the Graphic Power of *Tangles*. "In *Canadian Graphic: Picturing Life Narratives*, Ed. Candida Rifkind and Linda Warley. Waterloo: Wilfrid Laurier UP, 2016. 45–74.

Walrath, Dana. *Aliceheimer's: Alzheimer's through the Looking Glass*. Graphic Medicine Ser. University Park: Penn State UP, 2016. Print.

Childhood Exile: Memories and Returns

By Leonor Arfuch

ABSTRACT

In the context of contemporary forced migrations, this essay deals with the problem of political exile. The author focuses on the experiences of children whose parents had to flee the repression of the Chilean (1973–89) and Argentinian (1976–83) dictatorships, and for whom living "outside the lines" was often a matter of life or death. From Verónica Gerber Bicecci's and Laura Alcoba's autobiographical and autofictional novels to Macarena Aguiló's and Virginia Croatto's autobiographical and testimonial films, this analysis focuses on recent works that lie "outside the lines" of canonical genres, in which personal experience interfaces with collective memory and has an important ethical and political impact.

The idea of lives "outside the lines" seems to describe a contemporary condition perfectly: forced migrations, thousands of people forcibly displaced from their homeland (Syria, Libya, Yemen); refugee camps located in "no-man's-land" without human rights or nationalities; exiles, deportations, and internal margins of inequality that exclude great majorities from their own countries; and a growing inequity in the global world where there is an increasing number of lives that "do not matter" (Butler 66). But also the intriguing title of the International Auto|Biography Association Chapter of the Americas 2017 conference incites us to think about the positive meaning of "outside the lines": the possible infraction of the diverse forms of biopower, in terms of transgression of conventions, restrictions, prohibitions, or moral commandments. And there is still another possibility for interpretation: the infraction of the limits of genres—academic, literary, memorial— and the freedom to rehearse new forms in writing, film, and artistic practices, and even to think theoretical issues beyond their canonical boundaries.

It is to the crossing of these perspectives, a territory *in between*, that I wish to address my subject: exile as a political cause of displacement, where the option to go "outside the lines" is often a game of life or death. But it is also

This article was originally published with errors, which have now been corrected in both the print and online versions. Please see Correction (http://dx.doi.org/10.1080/08989575.2019.1588530)

an exile that compromises the country of childhood: that of children whose parents were forced to escape the repression of the Chilean and Argentinean dictatorships. I am interested in children born in exile who were affected by family trauma, and so-called exiled children who moved with their parents—and sometimes with another family member—toward an uncertain destiny, carrying with them only a few objects as vestiges of home. Exile is, without any doubt, one of the great topics, both in literature and politics, across centuries and modalities, which can also express the will to go beyond, to cross borders and take new directions—through voluntary exile, the breakup of ties, or the quest for other identities. The corpus that I have selected for analysis offers a singular perspective of those who, as grown-ups, negotiate the traumatic past through artistic creation, without adjusting to the limits of genre or, as Régine Robin says, *outside of genre*. My choice also involves gender, as I look at women who narrate, at the thresholds of the autobiographical, a story that recognizes a self-fictional trace, the fantasy of souvenir—or the evanescence of memory—as impressions of an (un)certain experience of identity.

These women are Verónica Gerber Bicecci, a visual artist and author of the autofictional graphic novel *Conjunto vacío* (*Empty Set*); Laura Alcoba, author of the autobiographical novel *El azul de las abejas* (*The Blue of the Bees*); Macarena Aguiló, a filmmaker, with her autobiographical documentary *El edificio de los chilenos* (*The Chilean Building*); and Virginia Croatto, a filmmaker, with her testimonial documentary *La guardería* (*The Nursery*). These women, aged between thirty-six and fifty, have had unique experiences with exile that mark their lives and artistic works in unequivocal ways.

The Writers

Gerber Bicecci was born in Mexico, where her parents were exiled during the Argentinean dictatorship. The main idea of her book, as she expressed in interviews, was to take on the concept of "disappearance" from various perspectives—from the words that seem to blend into the narrative to the drawings that accompany the texts (see Figures 1 and 2). Pieces that are texts and texts that are pieces question the limit of what cannot be said or seen, and they would come to say what is missing while simultaneously presenting a mystery to the reader: Why are they there? What is their meaning? Why do they come to occupy the space that seeks to expand over a chasm?

Conjunto vacío is a self-fictional narrative,[1] in which the protagonist, Verónica, reveals the hardships of family relationships between herself and her brother, her father, and her mother, who has "disappeared" from the house she inhabited; we do not know whether she simply left one day without any warning or whether she cut ties with her family. It is the

Figure 1. From Verónica Gerber-Bicecci's *Empty Set.*

same house to which—symptomatically—Verónica has now returned. The author plays a subtle fictional game with the topic of exile and its everlasting mark on subjectivity through the fragility of loving bonds and the indeterminacy of the course to follow—the protagonist does not know what to do with her time and her work. The condition of a recurring

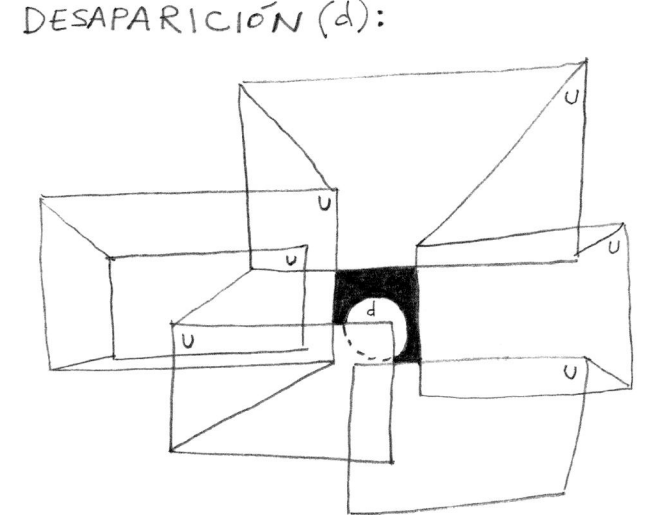

DESAPARICIÓN (d):

Figure 2. From Verónica Gerber-Bicecci's *Empty Set.*

circularity is also expressed through the drawings, which seem to return always to the same place—a beginning, an origin, an essential place that contains the fullness of home: "Argentina. Sometimes, I imagine myself ringing the doorbell of my grandmother's home (G) and my mother (M) is the one who opens the door, as if she had been there all this time (see Figures 3 and 4). We two are playing hide-and-seek inside that tiny house in a borough of Córdoba" (160).[2]

Thus, the past and the present are interwoven in an imaginary "return," although she never moved from there, as if one could return to a moment prior to the real departure, that of the parents—in this case, the author's true story—a departure that abruptly changed the family's destiny and left the protagonist in an intermediate position, with a divided identity and a tension between two hypothetical points, "here" and "there," those deictics that migrants always invest with exact meanings, which acquire a dreamlike character within exile. The "empty set" articulates itself with other emblematic signifiers that trace an unfortunate cartography— "excavations," "exposed foundations," "structures in ruins," an "interior necropolis"—as if the narrator has assumed the costs of a "damaged life," according to Theodor Adorno's celebrated concept, and attempted to work with them: "I have this nightmare: I want to speak but I cannot. I want to scream and I cannot" (98).

There is a certain equilibrium in the narrative with the invention of a parallel story: that of Marisa, an Argentinean exile whose archive of correspondence and photographs has to be organized after her death.

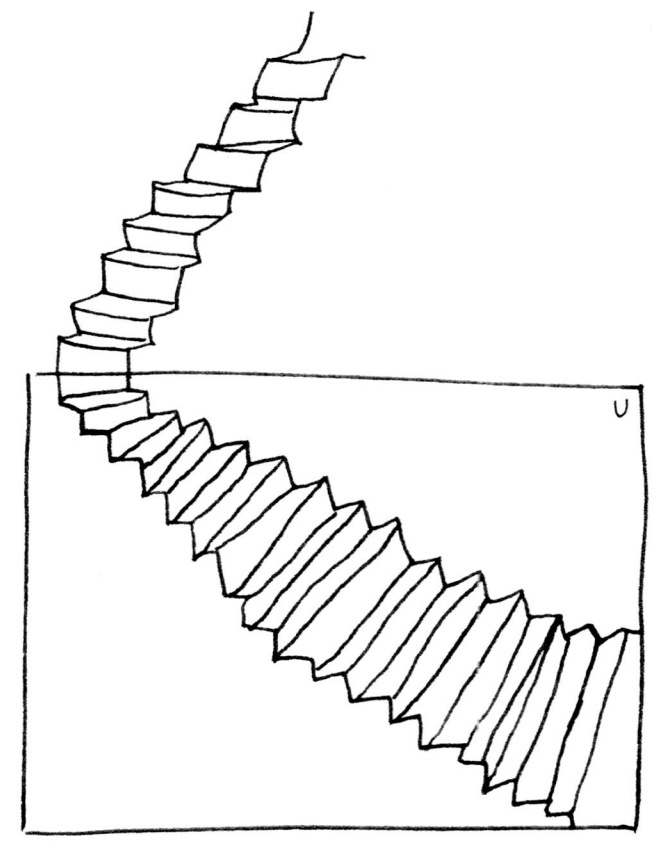

Figure 3. From Verónica Gerber-Bicecci's *Empty Set.*

ROMPIMIENTO DE a ∩ b :

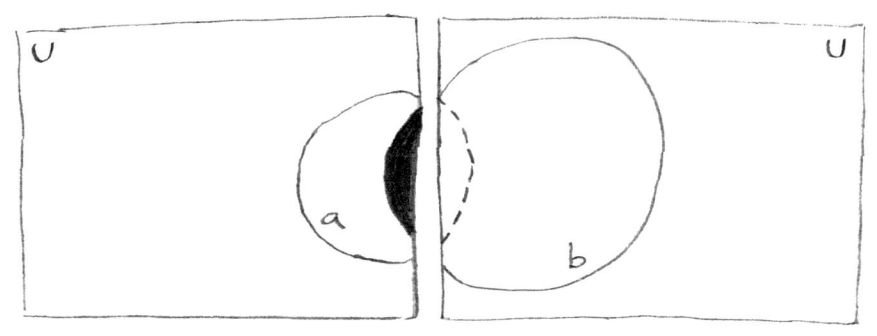

Figure 4. From Verónica Gerber-Bicecci's *Empty Set.*

The protagonist accepts the job and enters another "life outside the lines," attempting to discover Marisa's interior world, with its sensations, events, and relationships. A telescope, a rare object found within the house, allows Verónica to peek into the surrounding world in a hazardous search, a world that is always seen at a distance from a suspended window (see Figure 5). Then, the narrative turns to another autobiographical genre: collected letters, whose intimate register can combine the trifling day-to-day with profound reflections. There is something detective-like about the ordeal, the desire to discover what is hidden by the letters or the curious photographs that all have one person cut out of them, the mystery of that life, its evasive chronology, which is also shadowed by "disappearance." It is a confrontation between the void and the archive, the material registry of what remains, of objects that, according to Jorge Luis Borges, "will endure far beyond what we have forgotten | they will never know that we have left" ("Durarán más allá de nuestro olvido | no sabrán nunca que nos hemos ido"; lines 13–14).

The second writer, Laura Alcoba, moved to France at the age of eleven to meet her mother, who had been exiled three years earlier. Alcoba is an *exiled daughter*, according to the distinction that Eva Alberione proposes to consider this experience not as a "second-generation" one—as a daughter of exiled parents—but rather as the protagonist of her own story and identity, of which childhood exile is a part. Alcoba, in "real life," had previously lived with her mother, hiding in a house of militant Montoneros, which shortly after their departure was bombed by the Argentinean army, killing all of its occupants. Later, she lived with her grandparents in semi-normalcy, waiting for the legal documents that would permit her to leave

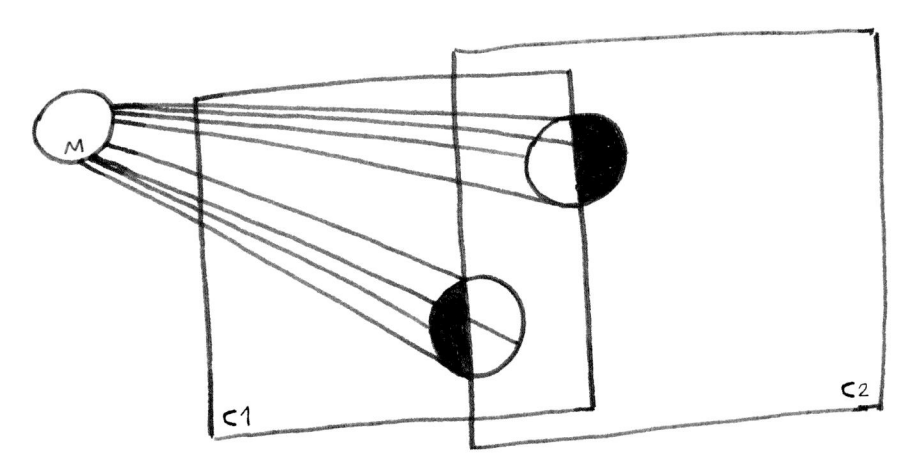

Figure 5. From Verónica Gerber-Bicecci's *Empty Set.*

the country. During that time, her father was in jail, and she was allowed to visit him every two weeks. Those life experiences "outside the lines" for such a young girl, configure the plot of Alcoba's first autobiographical novel, *La casa de los conejos* (*The House of the Rabbits*). In this book, she narrates her true story—the facts of living in a house whose residents hid an illegal printing press under the cover of a rabbit farm.

In *El azul de las abejas*, her third autobiographical novel, the author focuses on the everyday experience of exile, the slow adaptation to another environment, another language, and other people, places, and traditions that imply a radical difference. The narrative is made by small gestures, domestic scenes, journeys to school and inside the school, meetings with other children of exiled parents, arduous remembrances of a country that is further away with each passing day, conversations with her mother, and especially an epistolary relationship with her father, who is still in prison and proposes to her that they read jointly a book, *El azul de las abejas*, by Maurice Maeterlinck. It is this reading at a distance that articulates a suspended temporality between letters. Once again, the correspondence, a genre essential to narratives of exile, is where the fatherly relationship is consolidated precisely through the connection between the two languages—she reads the book in French—each with its own poetic resonance; it is a true story with a fictional plot, as is often the case in literature.

The deictic punctuates this everyday journey in the girl's voice, which becomes adult at times: "here" | "there"; "today" | "yesterday"—the names of the past and the present, spoken in a language that sometimes sounds *dérisoire* ("ridiculous," "insignificant"). The relevance of the place—the house, the borough, her discoveries within the city—and the anchoring in the domestic space, sometimes lived as "confinement," are remarkable. Disappearance also sneaks its way into the narrative, perhaps surreptitiously: "on one of two Thursdays [visiting days with her father] I disappeared [from school]: that was all" (12). Or rather, she worried about the "language-immersion" task, that foreign language whose mastery seemed to be an imperative: "I wish I could erase it, make it disappear, tear this Argentinean accent out of me" (34). It is quite symptomatic of the narrator's attempt to work on this register of the assimilation process, the additional trouble of an "exile from the mother tongue," that even her nightmares are related to the shame of having an accent and being exposed as someone who comes from somewhere else: "I am standing, at the very end of the bus, when I suddenly realize that I've forgotten to get dressed and that I am barefoot, and now I do not have any other clothes

Figure 6. The cover of Laura Alcoba's *El Azul de las Abejas* (*The Blue of the Bees*).

on besides my underwear … and I would like to disappear promptly from that place" (34).[3]

Other signifiers also allude to memory work: knitting and undoing, the scarf that can never be finished, that always requires of her to turn back, undo, thread the missing stitch that has been released from the chain and prevents the text from continuing. Voids of memory oscillate and demand certain lists—of the absent, the dead, and the missing—which other exiled friends insist on reviewing when they come to visit, and there are the abrupt silences that arise when, with her little friends, she summons some evocations of that *faraway* or *that time*: fears, anguish, and images that do not have to be named "because that's the way exile works: no need to say more" (78).

The Filmmakers

The two films I discuss, *El edificio de los chilenos* and *La guardería*, deal with the same topic: the tremendous decision taken by militants from armed organizations—the Movimiento de Izquierda Revolucionaria (MIR or Revolutionary Left Movement from Chile) and Montoneros (from Argentina)—to return to their countries at the end of the 1970s to confront their respective dictatorships, leaving their children in Cuba in the care of "social parents" to protect them from the agents of a fight that became devastating, especially for Argentineans. Both filmmakers have experienced that limit state of childhood exile—although their paths never crossed on the emblematic island—and they decided, possibly at the same age their parents had at the time of exile, to narrate their story by employing the "aesthetic apparatus" of cinema (Déotte 19), perhaps the most appropriate medium to imbue images of a historical era, both past and present, with a strong sense of authenticity.

Aguiló was nine years old and had been living in Paris when her mother, an MIR militant, decided to return to Chile, leaving Macarena in the care of colleagues especially chosen to be social parents. In the reenactment in the film, the mother explains that she cannot take her and that she will instead remain with other children in a community life project—the "Homes Project"—and that she will now become part of a great family.

The film is an autobiographical documentary—also referred to as a "subjective documentary"—where the filmmaker is present from the very beginning, and her warm voiceover accompanies the narration, tracing a great parable from fleeting Parisian images to the children's reunion in Belgium, before departing for Havana to life on the island, where the camera returns today. Then, we can see the tainted façade of what will always be, according to some nostalgic neighbors, "the Chilean building (see Figure 7)." The film also includes an urgent interrogation of the consequences of that past for subjectivities and historical perspectives. Old audio and film registers, photographs, contemporary images, animated drawings, and interviews are interwoven in a harmonic modulation of time and space, where letters—in a complete archive that the filmmaker has miraculously conserved—once again weave the plot of affection with its everyday details, where the separation between children and parents is justified, in the maternal emphasis, for the ideal of "creating a better country for our children (see Figures 8 and 9)." The film is not only a narrative of this story "outside the lines" with tenderness and admirable fortitude, without resorting to melodrama or sentimentalism, but it is also an inquisitive and critical challenge because Aguiló invites its protagonists—her own parents, the social parent, and her colleagues—to give testimony of this experience, to confront the past from their position in the

Figure 7. From Macarena Aguiló's *El Edificio de los Chilenos* (*The Chilean Building*).

Figure 8. From Macarena Aguiló's *El Edificio de los Chilenos* (*The Chilean Building*).

Figure 9. From Macarena Aguiló's *El Edificio de los Chilenos* (*The Chilean Building*).

present, and to bare the wounds, the weaknesses, the mistakes, and the failures of the way chosen to accomplish those ideals.

It is painful and sometimes devastating to watch: a father who recalls in tears how he left his baby of only few months; the social father who narrates how he welcomed a baby girl of just two at the Gare du Nord in Paris; Macarena's father, who expresses his grief for the loss of the life in common; another exiled child who will never forgive that loss. However, the film is not dyed with melancholy but rather with a certain nostalgia, and the narrator's character is defined through the recognition of the events as an affirmation of her own identity and the acceptance of the limits between what can be said and what can be shown. She shows the value of what is said in front of the intimidating camera and what remains unsaid and perhaps peeks out in a furtive tear, a grimace, an agitation of the body, or a look.

In a different tone, *La guardería*, by Croatto, focuses on the testimonies of colleagues with whom she shared the experience of living in Cuba. She had the fortune of having her birth mother working as the social mother in charge, after her father, a high-ranking Montonero leader, was killed in a confrontation with the army and the family was forced into exile. Those testimonies, punctuating the temporality of the narrative, evoke the config- uration of the group of about thirty children, ranging from the ages of six months to ten years, their everyday life, their games, their relationships with one another, and some memorable anecdotes. Unlike the Chilean film, the interviewees respond to a fixed camera without disclosing any- thing about their current lives. Since we do not know anything about them besides the impressions and the memories they evoke, their reiterated inter- ventions trace a one-dimensional arc, where the traumatic weight of this experience only shows up in a certain word or gesture.

Figure 10. From *La Guardería (The Nursery)* by Virginia Croatto.

Figure 11. From *La Guardería (The Nursery)* by Virginia Croatto.

With scarce archival materials, the camera turns back to the island and captures beautiful images in a narrative that puts space between the interviewees' voices. Regardless of the restraint of these stories—they are "pain-restrained," we might say—the political reality of that time appears through some unexpected expressions—in particular, the death of many of the militants who returned to Argentina. The incredible naturalization of childhood arises in the evocation of games such as "playing soldiers" and "games of death," where the figure of the "missing" is replaced by the "fallen"—to fall in the grasp of repressive forces—and where the news of a dead or missing parent is normalized and integrated into the daily routine. In this way, a child can tell another child who makes some comment about their father that "he will die like mine." Others want to invent a machine that "brings people back to life." Letters here also weave bonds, perhaps more unstable ones. Prompted to evoke that time, the interviewees oscillate between dream and reality. To some, Cuba was a "place of adventure"; to others, it was "a theme park." Yet they all value their community life and the state of normalcy that "the nursery" had on the island: the possibility to speak freely, "beyond the silence or the lies" that had marked their clandestine lives with false names, changes of address, separation from their family members, and more (see Figures 12–14).

Toward the end of the film, the interviewees meet up to have lunch in a garden with their children on a sunny day, where they evoke once again the shared good moments. There we can see some images of Virginia, the filmmaker, who does not appear in any other scene of the film. These idyllic images leave in suspense questions, experiences, sensations, and affections that perhaps had no expression, as if the goal of the film had been to dismiss the traumatic weight of that childhood exile, perhaps by

Figure 12. From *La Guardería (The Nursery)* by Virginia Croatto.

Figure 13. From *La Guardería (The Nursery)* by Virginia Croatto.

Figure 14. From *La Guardería (The Nursery)* by Virginia Croatto.

unconsciously repeating those old gestures and habits: not speaking, not telling, not revealing the lights and shadows of an experience that has, without a doubt, left a profound mark on their subjectivity.[4]

Temporalities of Memory

Why choose these works, which saw the light in different places—Mexico, Chile, France, and Argentina—and bring them today as my contribution to the discussion about "lives outside the lines?" First, I was interested in placing the problem of exile in the framework of present-day reflections on forced migrations, often involving the risk to life, which painfully mark the contemporary horizon, where thousands of children face brutal uprooting. Although they are not fully comparable, in some ways these contemporary migrations can also be considered childhood exiles. In fact, Gerber Bicecci, who lives in Mexico, correlates Argentinean exile with that of Mexicans, eternal migrants fleeing from the violent reality that harms them: the expansion of crime and miserable life conditions.[5]

Second, these recent narratives are part of a set—not an empty one—of other narratives where children of the disappeared, who did not have to go into exile themselves, have addressed their traumatic experiences from the standpoint of literature or artistic practices. If there are temporalities of memory, perhaps this is "the time of children," and art, in its multiple aspects, seems to be the most appropriate way to deal with that experience. However, my main interest in these narratives is how the past comes to life from the speaking present, and how new autobiographical and self-fictional forms give strength to memory work, outside the limits of canonical genres.

To make a symptomatic reading, it is, curiously, Verónica, the author's alter ego in *Conjunto vacío*, born in Mexico, who vividly expresses her attachment to the faraway land of her parents and the void that migration has left in her present, as she cannot find a definite point, or an anchor, in her everyday life. Words come and go, and drawings seek to express the inexpressible: a mother missing without any known reason; a brother and a father with whom all ties are unstable, who have almost no presence in the novel; fleeting love affairs and quests for identity that seem to be mirrored by an enigmatic parallel story, of which only letters and mutilated photographs remain. An emptiness prevails, as it surely must for those who have listened to the stubborn remembrances of parents away from their homeland; times turn disorderly, as is the true nature of the act of remembering, with its sudden, hazardous appearance.

By contrast, *El azul de las abejas* is a detailed construction of *place*— the place of arrival for an exiled daughter, whose daily task is precisely adaptation to a new home, leaving open questions of what home is, if it is the homeland, the mother, the language, or the place where a migrant can finally put down their baggage and dwell (see Figure 6). There is a notable will and effort on the part of this little girl to dominate the language of exile, to become other so as to be considered a member of that community. The narration of this effort takes up a large space within the novel, alongside the epistolary dialogue with the narrator's absent father and conversations with her mother, which perhaps explains why the author decided to write her story in French, at a distance from the mother tongue, to tackle different aspects of the traumatic experience. In some way, Laura's character, at the same time as she returns to the painful scars of exile, shows the possibility of opening up other horizons, discovering other directions, living other lives—those other possible ways that chance puts before us, even if we are not living far from home.

Similarly, Aguiló reconstructs the territory of her childhood with its emblematic objects—letters, drawings, photographs, and settings—poised between nostalgia for that time and the suspension of family life brought about by her stay in Cuba. Confronted with a present that could not simply proceed in silence or obscurity, the camera wisely interconnects two symbolic places of exile—Havana and Santiago de Chile—with their diverse light and the rhythm of current life. The ocean serves as the limit, its distance impossible to take on, with its threat of shipwreck, as is illustrated—even today—by animated drawings made by one of her colleagues, a fellow artist who receives her at his workshop. There are pressing questions, searches for the whys, inquiries about the militant subjectivity of that time (and still today?) that make this film, which won awards at different film festivals, the most political work of my corpus. It goes beyond a mere therapeutic exercise to provide testimony and allow others to speak, including various exiled children who recognize that they were not able to do so with their parents, in order to raise bold questions regarding the relationship between ethics and politics. In this sense, the film has been a great contribution to the debate on the past that has intense relevance in the filmmaker's country.

On a smaller scale, *La guardería* focuses on the impressions and memories of the group to whom the filmmaker belonged, sticking to more classical methods of testimony but without delving into singular stories (see Figures 10 and 11). We do not know who the interviewees are, what their present lives are like, or what happened to their parents. This distance is emphasized by the absence of questions probing the group's experiences in more depth. The film also eludes the political evaluation that appears in previous works by children of the disappeared. It is true that the difficulty of speaking about the Argentinean exile weighs on this film, given the fate of those who followed orders to return to their country while others remained abroad. Many feel guilty for having survived.[6] The truth is that the question of exile comes in fourth place, we could say, in the progression of the work on memory in my country, after the narratives of the victims, the militants, and other sons and daughters. It seems as if the experience of exile required more time to be processed. Moreover, the act of leaving one's children in the care of other parents, as shown in *La guardería*, was perhaps one of the most questioned aspects at the level of social sensitivity: it is difficult to accept that militancy could be put ahead of the family institution.

Finally, we could say that genre and gender are articulated in my corpus in a unique manner. The register of the biographical and autobiographical genres, which is my domain of interest (Arfuch, *El espacio* and *Memoria*), shows yet again its potential for the elaboration of traumatic experiences and the relevance of the concept of "biographical value" articulated by Bakhtin in the construction of collective memories (Bajtin).[7] With regard to gender, the works analyzed, far from the idea of "women's writing," or *écriture féminine*, have an unfolding subjectivity focused on the small details, on sensitivity's vibrations, on the tones and registers of voices at play, on the subtle relationship with the mother, on the ambiance in which words emerge, on the ways to say and listen—in short, on bringing the past to the present. Looks, images, appreciations, and intimate valuations configure the singular and common heritage—in contrast to epic tales or heroic profiles, more frequent in male narrations of that unfortunate past—but which, through different tones and hues, contribute to the highest degree to this "historian representation," which, according to the philosopher Paul Ricoeur, makes way to history, in its ethical and political dimensions.

Notes

1. Autofiction combines two apparently inconsistent narrative forms—namely, autobiography and fiction. Authors may decide to recount their lives, to modify significant details or "characters," using fiction in the service of a search for self. This is sometimes the best way to address traumatic experiences in the past, which is the case of the authors and filmmakers discussed here.
2. All quotations in this article are my translations.
3. At this point, a comment made to me by Mariana Wikinski, a psychoanalyst and author of an important book about testimony, seems illuminating: "in

Alcoba's dream, there is a mark similar to Laplanche's 'enigmatic signifier,' which seems to result from the effects of the prohibition to talk (experienced firsthand by her or by her parents?) the mark of a clandestine life that must not be shown. This mark of the forbidden and what must remain concealed in order to survive is present in exiles in an insidious manner because the mandate of silence is not easily lifted and leaves a nearly indelible imprint." Grateful for her contribution, I would answer her question as follows: in effect, Alcoba was constricted by the pact of silence throughout her life in secrecy, as narrated in her first autobiographical novel, *La casa de los conejos*.

4. Here we could also think about the insistence of the "enigmatic signifier."

5. "This is how this topic connects to Mexico, just now that we find ourselves in the epicenter of this problematic. Now we can think only about the consequences it will have for those children, survivors of violence; what will become of them in ten or twenty years?" (Talavera).

6. Back home, some of the exiled had to face silence or disapproval from the relatives of the disappeared or survivors of the repression. Maybe this explains why the subject of exile, in biographical genres or fiction, came up after another series of traumatic experiences.

7. "Biographical value," according to Bakhtin, implies "putting in order" the narrator's life and, correlatively, the receiver's life, with an obligatory ethical reference to "life" in general, but also we could speak of a "memorial value" that brings the evocation of the past to the present of narration, with its symbolic and often traumatic weight on the individual or collective memory. A memorial value also appears in visual surfaces and gives way to new genres, such as, for example, autofiction, subjective documentary, and the autobiographical novel.

Disclosure Statement

No potential conflict of interest was reported by the author.

Works Cited

Adorno, Theodor. *Mínima moralia: Reflexiones desde la vida dañada*. Madrid: Taurus, 2001. Print.

Aguiló, Macarena, Dir. *El edificio de los chilenos*, Aplapac, Les Films d'ici, Instituto Cubano de Cinematografía, 2010. DVD.

Alberione, Eva. "Narrativas contemporáneas de los *exiliados hijos*: Esa particular manera de contarse." 2016. TS.

Alcoba, Laura. *El azul de las abejas*. Buenos Aires: Edhasa, 2014. Print.

—. *La casa de los conejos*. Buenos Aires: Edhasa, 2010. Print.

Arfuch, Leonor. *El espacio biográfico: Dilemas de la subjetividad contemporánea*. Buenos Aires: Fondo de Cultura Económica, 2002. Print.

—. *Memoria y autobiografía: Exploraciones en los límites*. Buenos Aires: Fondo de Cultura Económica, 2013. Print.

Bajtin, Mijail. *Estética de la creación verbal*. Trans. Tatiana Bubnova. Mexico City: Siglo XXI, 1982. Print.

Borges, Jorge Luis. "Las cosas." *Elogio de la sombra* By Borges. Buenos Aires: Emecé, 1969. *Poemas del alma*, n.d. Web. 3 June 2018.

Butler, Judith. *Vida precaria*. Buenos Aires: Paidós, 2007. Print.

Croatto, Virginia, Dir. *La guardería*, 2015. Cuba -Argentina, 2016. 71', DVD.

Déotte, Jean Louis. *¿Qué es un aparato estético? Benjamin, Lyotard, Rancière*. Santiago: Metales Pesados, 2012. Print.

Gerber Bicecci, Verónica. *Conjunto vacío*. Mexico City: Almadía, 2014. Print.

Ricoeur, Paul. *La memoria, la historia, el olvido*. Buenos Aires: Fondo de Cultura Económica, 2004. Print.

Robin, Régine. "La autoficción: El sujeto siempre en falta." *Identidades, sujetos y subjetividades*. Ed. Leonor Arfuch. Buenos Aires: Prometeo, 2002. 45–59. Print.

Talavera, Juan Carlos. "Verónica Gerber Bicecci hace al lector un detective en su novela 'Conjunto vacío.'" *Imagen Digital*, 4 Aug. 2015. Web. 13 May 2018.

Women Making Freedom: Locating Gender in Intra-Caribbean Migration from a Curaçaoan Perspective

By Rose Mary Allen

Introduction

Historically, neoclassical economic theories have explained migration as a predominantly male endeavor, and the economics of labor migration has neglected women as independent participants and autonomous decision-makers in the migratory process (Cerrutti and Massey; Baldwin and Mortley). While men have been recognized as active decision-makers in migration, women who play the same role have been stigmatized, rendered invisible, or excluded (Huq). In the Caribbean, too, even though migration is deeply rooted in the region's history, migration has been conceptualized as a largely male worker affair. The scholarly research on migration has long sidelined gender and made women nearly invisible. Historiography has sometimes subsumed women's participation in migration under the category of family reunification and has paid very little attention to women's autonomous migration. Yet, like men, women in the Caribbean have emigrated on their own and left their households behind to seek employment or fulfill other ambitions abroad.

Curaçao, an island[1] of 444 square kilometers in the southern Caribbean, near the coast of Venezuela, fits in this general picture of the region. The historian W. E. Renkema, in his study on Curaçaoan migration in the nineteenth century, points to a correlation between drought and migration. He notes that the number of people leaving the country in search of work would increase dramatically after a year of drought. The scope of his study is limited to male migration. Although Curaçaoan women did not always migrate in numbers as large as men, they represented a proportion of the population that, by emigrating, stepped outside the boundaries set by the Curaçaoan society for their gender. As for scholarly attention, most studies about past emigration from Curaçao

This article was originally published with errors, which have now been corrected in both the print and online versions. Please see Correction (http://dx.doi.org/10.1080/08989575.2019.1588530)

have hinted at the presence of women but have not explored their role sufficiently as part of a gender-sensitive analysis of migration. Renkema's study helps us to understand the circumstances that encouraged men to migrate but does not answer why Curaçaoan women also migrated. In the last four decades, Caribbean studies have seen a significant shift toward a more gendered approach to research on past and present waves of migration (Green). Given this recent development in Caribbean social historiography, Curaçao should not remain behind, should also employ a gender perspective, and should include women in studies of past (and present) intra- and extra-regional migration.

However, when one wants to understand gender-specific migration movements and in that sense also recover the experiences of women in migration, in particular working-class women, one must address issues related to the process of data collection. It is here that one can clearly see how colonialism, race, and class intersect with gender and sexuality. The patriarchal social structure of inequality that has historically relegated women to an inferior status in society and the consequent disadvantages has impacted women of all races and classes. Nevertheless, in the colonial Caribbean, some women were more affected than others, since women belonged both to the enslaved and slave-owner groups, to the oppressed and the oppressors, to the colonized and the colonizers. After the abolition of slavery, freed working-class women in particular continued to suffer oppression based upon gender, race, and class (Beckles; Shepherd; Scully and Paton). Curaçao shares this history with the rest of the Caribbean: the wretchedness of slavery, the trials of postemancipation, and the continuing struggle against racist and patriarchal ideologies and forms of economic subjugation. Feminist scholarly historical research addresses these issues and concerns and recognizes power as a central factor in the lives of the research subjects. It takes into account that gender intersects with race, sexuality, and class, and it is also an important aspect of the differential power relations that determine what the dominant groups in societies want people to remember and forget. Consequently, what kinds of data are available to scholars of gender-specific migration is related to history and intersectionality.

Connecting Archival and Oral History Data to Engender Migration Historiography: The Case of Curaçao

Applying a feminist approach in the present paper means looking at what past emigration has meant for Curaçaoan working-class women in particular and asking what is missing in the authoritative records of historiography. Archives are a complex cite of influences and representations and are in most cases fragmented and unfixed (Kadar and Buss 115). For a long while, archival documents have tended to represent the official colonial view or other dominant views, in most cases defined by "the metropolitan eye; the white, male gaze" (Brereton 3). There exists this coloniality in the production of information: colonial, racial, patriarchal, and other hegemonic forms of producing data erase certain events and experiences (Grosfoguel 220). Arturo Escobar has introduced the concept of "coloniality of knowledge," which he defines as the state of knowledge production in a (post)colonial setting based on Eurocentric epistemologies that claim to be objective, scientific, neutral, universal, and truthful while replacing local modes of knowing and producing meaning.

Any writer of a critical analysis of archival data should keep in mind that alternative views have been "silenced" in the sense of Michel-Rolph Trouillot's *Silencing the Past*. Caribbean women were even more absent in historiography, and the Jamaican historian Lucille Mathurin Mair points out that therefore, researchers should revisit the archival records in order to open up "new emphases and new interpretations relating to the black Jamaican woman, and to decode the real world of enslaved and free women so as, eventually, to shift the parameters of traditional historiography" (234–35). The sociologist Latoya Lazarus adds another dimension to this in her article "Working with Marginalized" and 'Hidden' Populations: Researchers' Anxieties and Strategies for Doing Less Harmful Research regarding the unsilencing of gender and women's inclusion in historiography. She states that in a Caribbean context, a feminist approach entails, first, decentering white, heterosexual, high- and middle-class males in research as well as privileged, nonwhite, heterosexual, middle-class males. Archival texts, in a similar way as conventional literary texts, lend themselves properly to feminist modes of thinking by deconstructing and reclaiming existing patriarchal considerations (Kadar and Buss 115). Brereton underscores that such an approach of decoding, deconstructing, and reading against the grain will not only "put women into history" but will redefine and reconstruct gendered historical narratives as well (2).

I argue that in addition to this new gendered approach to archival documents, oral history—the so-called "bottom-up" approach—offers great potential for the reconstruction of history by giving voice to those whom historiography has rendered voiceless (Allen, "'Nothing'"). Oral history has been defined as the testimonies and personal recollections of people who have experienced certain events firsthand or who were sufficiently close to these events to recollect them. Also, in the case of Curaçao, where orality has been a dominant form of communication by the Afro-Curaçaoan working-class population, oral history has often been used for the collection of folklore material as well. These folkloric materials refer to stories, myths, songs, proverbs, and other information passed down by word of mouth from generation to generation. Eyewitness accounts sometimes become stories as they are transmitted orally from the older generations to the younger ones, beyond people's lifetimes. As a research practice, oral history is also called biographical research because when narrators recall their personal past, they engage in a review of their life story. In addition to its emphasis on factual statements to provide historical data, oral history is also a vehicle of biographical memories, expressions of meaning, and representations of culture. Here, oral history is not primarily concerned with the accuracy of a person's recollection but with the manner in which and the reasons why people remember what they do. Oral history can be instrumental in revealing, contesting, challenging, and reversing the aforementioned coloniality of knowledge, framed by class, race, and gender. It can be used to foreground the testimony of those normally excluded from hegemonic discourse production: those who might be spoken about, but not spoken with (Hoagland). What makes oral history so interesting to researchers is that it produces data that can often lead to new interpretations of history.

By exploring women's migration in a Dutch Caribbean context, this paper challenges the near erasure of the Dutch Caribbean from Caribbean scholarship, not only in migration studies but generally. Postcolonial Caribbean scholarship still displays a form of "coloniality of knowledge" whereby the colonial habit of dividing the region into language areas is maintained in much the same way as during colonial days. A "fragmented nationalism," as the historian Franklin Knight (*Caribbean*) calls it, still holds firm in Caribbean studies, including migration studies, notwithstanding the fact that the people participating in intra-Caribbean migration transgress the traditional subregional barriers and weave a web of connectedness between people of different Caribbean societies.

The sources I have used for my research on gender and migration are a cross-section of different forms of archival materials, both present in Curaçao as well in the countries where emigrations took place. Searching in foreign archives is not an easy task, as documents are not always accessible; however, digitalized documents obviously facilitate the search. In that way, I hope to avoid fragmented knowledge and one-sided views that usually come along when one uses only one type of document. For, according to Marlene Kadar and Helen Buss, archives, besides being a complex site of influence and representations, are also an incomplete as well as an unfixed and changing piece of knowledge that will grow as it is being built (Kadar and Buss 115). First of all, some of the archives of Curaçao are located at the National Archive of the Netherlands in The

Hague. Also, there are the Curaçao's passenger record books: the passports of people leaving the country since 1863 that provide information such as name, year of birth, place of birth, profession, and destination. I have examined protocols of notarial and secretarial deeds that include contracts migrants entered into with their foreign employers regarding their work conditions and the benefits that they would receive. The colonial accounts (*koloniale verslagen*) of the late-nineteenth and early-twentieth centuries have offered some statistical insight into the number of people who emigrated during a given year. I have also consulted editions of *De Curaçaosche Courant*, a weekly publication that between 1812 and 1870 was the only newspaper in circulation on the island. It was the semi-official herald of government, publishing official government announcements, while also containing international news (Langenfeld 59). In the local Roman Catholic newspapers in the Papiamentu language, *La Cruz* and *La Union*, one could also find articles on migrations from Curaçao, in which Roman Catholic priests warned against venturing to unknown destinations. They feared that they would lose control over the Curaçaoan black working-class people when they migrated (Allen, *Di*).[2] For my research on the migration to Cuba, I have also consulted documents in the Archivo Nacional de la República de Cuba, Archivo Histórico Provincial de Las Tunas, Registro Civil de Manati, Registro Civil de Puerto Padre, and Archivo Histórico Provincial de Camagüey. Finally, oral history interviews as historical material helped to capture and unlock the expressions of subjective experience and historical imagination of working-class migrant women. By means of oral history, I was also able to "uncover" the near-invisible working-class Curaçaoan women as they moved as intra-Caribbean migrants and "unsilenced" their voices in this regard. By analyzing both archival documents and oral history material for traces of counternarratives, one could explore working-class women's participation in migration movements.

Emigration from Curaçao

Before the abolition of slavery, which occurred in the Dutch Caribbean in 1863, manumitted, working-class black Curaçaoans, affected by the poor economic conditions of the island, would often opt to become migrant workers elsewhere in the region. An example is the migration to Berbice and Demerara (in modern-day Guyana) that lasted until 1838, after which the local government enacted legislation prohibiting foreigners from coming and recruiting laborers for work elsewhere. Documents show that not only men but also a few single mothers rented themselves out to employers in Berbice and Demerara. In some cases, such as with Cathalina

Isenia, Anna Margaritha, and Maria Girigoria, mothers took along their infants. Their contracts stated that they would be responsible for the care of their children but that the employer could advance them needed monies for this purpose (Langenfeld 94). It is unclear whether it was common practice for Curaçaoan mothers to take along their children when they emigrated; there are also cases of women leaving their children behind, as I will discuss later in this paper.

After abolition, because of the persistent deteriorating economic situation in Curaçao, men and, to a lesser extent, women continued to emigrate to countries that offered work opportunities. So, together with other Caribbean migrant laborers, Curaçaoans helped constitute the necessary labor supply for postplantation agricultural economies in the region. Curaçao followed the general Caribbean model of temporary, circular labor migration, with people moving back and forth depending on the availability of work in a given territory. The most popular migration destinations for Curaçaoans were Puerto Rico, St. Thomas, Venezuela, the Dominican Republic, Panama, Colombia, Costa Rica, and Suriname (Van Soest 20; Koot 44, 54; Dekker 98; Pietersz; Allen, "Emigración" and *Ta Cuba*).

The reasons people chose to leave their country in search of work elsewhere were far more complex than what is usually assumed. People did not migrate at random; instead, when confronted with the opportunity of voluntary emigration, they would weigh their choices. Faced with the prospect of getting a job, or perhaps even earning a higher income as a migrant than in their country of origin, they based their migration choices on factors such as the proximity of the job location, the fluidity of the border in relation to their island of origin, and the personal costs of separation from their loved ones. This explains the emigration of many generations of Afro-Curaçaoans to Venezuela and Colombia, located near the island. Because of its proximity, Venezuela served during the time of slavery as a destination of emigration for people from Curaçao: the enslaved escaped primarily to the Coro region in northwest Venezuela.

However, emigration also occurred to Puerto Rico in the north, which cannot be explained by geographical nearness. Kathryn R. Dungy explains that ships from Curaçao often had to tack against strong trade winds to reach Puerto Rico, which made the voyage a long and tedious event (93). This means that there were other factors that determined the decision to leave. Beside the expectation of earning a higher wage, kinship proved to be another decisive factor in emigration. One example from the nineteenth century may help to elucidate this. In 1862, two months after she gained freedom, a young Curaçaoan woman named Maria requested permission from the colonial authorities to leave Curaçao for Puerto Rico.

She wished to go there with her two sons to join other members of her family who were already working in the Spanish colony (Nationaal). It should also be mentioned that before abolition, in times of economic hardship, Curaçaoan slave-owners would often sell their enslaved workers to buyers in Puerto Rico, such as Pablo Bettini from Ponce and Buenaventura Quiñones (Langenfeld 89). This case of the recently manumitted Maria wanting to join her relatives in Puerto Rico shows that family reunification was an important motive for emigration and that manumission from slavery enabled some people to reestablish kinship ties across the islands of the Caribbean. Also, freed working-class people, both men and women, left for Puerto Rico.

Studies conducted in Puerto Rico provide additional details about who these Curaçaoan migrant women were and what they did for a living.[3] In *Women and Urban Change in San Juan Puerto Rico, 1820–1868*, Félix V. Matos Rodríguez uses listings of foreigners residing in the capital, San Juan, and mentions some Curaçaoan women (called females of color) who lived there and held professions such as street vendor, *dulcera* (maker of sweet candy), seamstress, laundress, and hat maker. Some of them had arrived as enslaved people; it is not clear whether all of them did. Dungy cites the 1830 register of Aguadilla and the neighboring town of Aguada that also identifies colored female Curaçaoan immigrants in Puerto Rico. Aguadilla was a new town, founded in the late 1770s, where many free people of color as well as immigrant free people of color lived (Dungy 92). For example, the thirty-three-year-old Vuelemina [or Wilhelmina] Ferrer had arrived from Curaçao in 1830 with her three young children. This register also shows that some colored female migrants from Curaçao ran their own businesses in Puerto Rico. Such was the case of Catalina Ricardo, who, along with her daughter, Constanza Henrique, owned a small grocery store and a small inn (Dungy 95). It shows that these women changed from serving people to becoming more autonomous.

Curaçaoan women in the role of small merchants could also be found in the then-Danish island of St. Thomas, another popular destination for Curaçaoan emigrants. Both elites and nonelites emigrated to St. Thomas in the third decade of the nineteenth century. According to Els Langenfeld (89), some Jewish merchants from Curaçao moved to St. Thomas and took along their enslaved. Neville Hall states that a large portion of St. Thomas's freed population was of foreign origin; among them were people from Curaçao but also from another Dutch island: St. Eustatius (180–81). In his master's thesis, *Een vergeten parel in de Deense Kroon* (*A Forgotten Pearl in the Danish Crown*), Tim Deahl emphasizes that more freed women from Curaçao than men emigrated to St. Thomas

(66). Deahl quotes a report by Von Walterstorff, who maintains that women outnumbered men in the migration from Curaçao to St. Thomas: 108 women versus forty-six men (66). According to Deahl, the reason was that in the Dutch colonies, more women than men received their freedom (66).

Most of these women were engaged in commerce. They would buy goods in Puerto Rico and sell them in St. Thomas. This behavior was condemned by the white elite in St. Thomas, who complained that these women imported worthless goods from Puerto Rico and sold them at a higher price. In practice, however, it proved difficult to get these merchants off the island. The detailed description of these women is striking. The historian Julia Clancy Smith concludes that, indeed, women traveling without men or kin guardians were often ignored in historical data except when they were accused of illegal activities such as smuggling, theft, or prostitution (38). Reading the archival texts about these women carefully and against the grain points to how this group was ideologically stereotyped by the dominant class of St. Thomas and how these Curaçaoan women made use of their acquired freedom to improve their social position and status while transcending colonial geographical frontiers as well as racial, class, and gender stereotypes.

In Their Own Words

The migration of Curaçaoans to Cuba in the early-twentieth century was the last massive migration of Curaçaoans in the immediate postemancipation era. Alejandro Paula described this migration as an overwhelmingly male working-class event in *Problemen Rondom de Emigratie van Arbeiders uit de Kolonie Curaçao naar Cuba 1917–1937* (*Problems around the Emigration of Workers from the Colony of Curaçao to Cuba 1917–1937*). This book was based on the vast amount of existing written archival documents, and Paula identified the problems the male workers faced in Cuba as they were reported to the local colonial government.

In the case of my own work in the 1980s on this particular migration from Curaçao to Cuba, I was just in time to find a few elderly returnees from Cuba still alive in Curaçao as well as some others or their families who had remained permanently in Cuba. In my project, alongside archival research in Curaçao and in Cuba, I was able to include their voices as counternarratives to the written documents. Names of these informants could be obtained by appealing to homes for the elderly, daycare centers for senior citizens, and people who dealt with senior citizens on a daily basis, as well as by asking these sources whether they knew other people who had also gone to Cuba and were still alive. Through this snowball effect I was able to identify a fair number of informants, including women who had migrated from and returned to Curaçao and children whose migrant mothers had left them behind in the care of a grandmother and never returned to Curaçao. Archival documents do not mention female emigration to Cuba, and the statistics about these women are not accurate. Through oral history, I have been able to acquire additional information concerning women's participation in this migration through the voices of migrant women themselves and to compare their experiences with those of the men.

Most of the male Curaçaoans were drawn to Cuba by stories of earning a lot of money. Stories that "even the lizards there rustled around with dollars" influenced many to leave for Cuba. This labor-migration movement from Curaçao to Cuba commenced in 1917 and reached its peak in 1919. There is official data stating that in 1919, at least 1,900 men went to work as cane cutters for the *colonias* owned by the American Chaparra and Manati sugar companies in the eastern part of Cuba. A large part of Cuba's sugar production was financed by US capital, which at that time controlled an important part of the Cuban economy. The men worked in the vicinity of factories situated in Delicias, Chaparra, and Manati, and many of them settled in the port of Cayo Juan Claro, the city of Puerto Padre, and the town of Vazquez in the province of Las Tunas. There they met other migrants from Haiti, Jamaica, and the smaller English-speaking countries. Never before had men emigrated from Curaçao in such large numbers, even when economic conditions had not been favorable on the Dutch island. Although it is not clear how many male migrants from Curaçao left for Cuba at the beginning of the twentieth century, it is likely that about fifty percent of men in their prime working years emigrated to work in the Cuban cane fields (Allen, "Emigración" and *Ta Cuba*). This massive move consisting predominantly of men had an impact on Curaçaoan society, in particular the women who were left behind to survive on the bare minimum. Documents and oral history both support this assessment. The departure of so many men resulted in a double workload for the women who stayed behind. Many women went to seek help from the government to ascertain the whereabouts of their husbands, sons, or other family members (Allen, "Curaçaoan"). In addition to experiencing this migration as a relative, wife, or partner of a male migrant, women also took part. However, they remained in the shadow of the men and were not present in the official statistics of the time. In interviews with Curaçaoan returnees such as Andres (Didi) Sluis, Raymundo Emelina, and Angel Martina, the names of women were also provided, and I was able to interview some of these female migrants.

Women migrated to Cuba in response to gender-specific employment in the service of Curaçaoan elite families who bought land in Cuba in the beginning of the twentieth century. Some of them went to work either as nannies or cooks for these Curaçaoan families. One of them, whose pseudonym is Petra in this paper, told the following story of her migration experience. Petra left Curaçao for Cuba around 1913, while she was in her early twenties, to work for a family, leaving her only child with her mother. Her principal motive for going to Cuba was the poor socioeconomic conditions on Curaçao. As she recounted, in Cuba she earned US$40 a month as a nanny, compared to the five Antillean guilders (approximately US$2.80) she could earn in Curaçao as a domestic servant, plus the one guilder per straw hat she could earn making hats. Petra stated, "You went through a lot of trouble to get just one guilder per hat." By immigrating, Petra provided a steady income for her family. Every month she sent some of the money she earned to her mother to take care of her daughter, and she also sent gifts, such as dresses, for her daughter. She remembered that when it was her daughter Merelda's birthday, she asked a Cuban seamstress to sew clothes for her to send to Curaçao (Allen, "Curaçaoan" 68–69).[4]

Compared to male emigrants, who upon leaving knew only that they were going to Cuba to cut cane, Petra knew the family for whom she was going to work before she left; in fact, she herself had requested to work for this family in Cuba. Petra's story gives us a clear impression of a nanny's life and her life as an immigrant. She shared with the employing family the daily stress of family life in a foreign country and functioned as a form of psychological release for the family, who, being migrants themselves, had to cope with an unfamiliar sociocultural setting. For example, she would help them to overcome a common fear of Cuba in that time of white children being abducted. She was someone they could trust and to whom they could turn with certain problems. In an evocative way, she described her presence in their lives by saying, "when you are a nanny, you are involved in everything [*Ora bo ta yaya, bo ta den tur kos*]." Even though in an unequal power relationship based on her skin color and class position, she presented herself as a worthy woman who contested existing religious, class, racial, and ethnic divisions.

Another female interviewee who had gone to Cuba as a cook for a Jewish family, some of whose members lived in Curaçao and whom she already knew, recounted a similar story to me.[5] The family branch in Cuba wanted to change their former cook, who had also come from Curaçao but who had grown old. The Jewish family she had gone to work with had asked her to join them so that they would have someone they could trust to prepare their food in a Kosher manner. She was also handpicked for security purposes, based on foreign rich families' fear of being poisoned by Cuban cooks. Juanita left for Cuba in 1924 and stayed there with the family for about ten years. By migrating, she was able to earn a better salary and to help out the rest of her family at home. Her story tells us what it meant to be a cook at that time and to be one in a foreign country. She recounted how she had to take into account religious food prescriptions as well as food customs based on products that were not always to be found there. Consequently, she remembered the moments she would cook local Curaçaoan food such as *kòmkòmber chikí stobá* (cucumber stew) and *kalbas largu stobá* (green calabash stew), much to the enjoyment of the family. In the course of time, she also learned to cook Cuban food, such as the popular *tostones.* Both Juanita's and Petra's stories focused on the economic gain of migration. However, both lived in a familial context and stressed the fact that they were important in the lives of the principally Jewish Curaçaoan female family members and their children living in the exterior. In that way, their histories added a different perspective than those of the men.

Interviewees also stated that some men, after they had been to Cuba and seen the situation, returned to Curaçao and then took their legal or common-law wife and children back to Cuba. This was also confirmed by articles in the local newspaper, *La Cruz,* which provided some data of women leaving the island together with their partner and children (6 March 1918, 11 June 1919, 18 June 1919). These women would sometimes work as washer women (*lavar por la calle*) or cook for pay in Cuba.

During the exodus between 1917 and 1921, when about fifty percent of the Curaçaoan male labor force left Curaçao temporarily to work in the cane fields in Cuba, single mothers went to Cuba, not knowing their employer ahead of time the way the abovementioned Petra and Juanita had. They were also drawn, just like the men, by stories about a *riu di oro* (river of gold) in Cuba. I have not been able to interview this category of women about their journey, their motives for leaving home, and their travel as single women. Some of these women left their children with their mothers, went to Cuba, and never came back to Curaçao; I was able to interview some of these children in the 1980s and 1990s and found that they still remembered this traumatic episode in their lives of longing for their mother's love but never being able to experience it. Their stories can also be considered what Deborah Britzman calls "difficult knowledge," that causes pain to both those who have experienced it, as well as to the one who is doing the research about it (qtd. in Kadar and Warley 6).

This migratory pattern seems also to have occurred at other times in Curaçao's history; one indication is a local song in which children say that they want to go and see their moms. This traditional song, which expressed a traumatic experience of abandonment, used to be sung by fishermen in the village called Boka Samí when they pulled their boats onto land in the early- and mid-twentieth century (Allen, "Curaçaoan" 70; Zikinzá). A fisherman, who was seventy years old in 1991 when I interviewed him, recalled that as a child, he had heard of a woman named Virginia from his village, Boka Samí, who had gone to the Dominican Republic, where she sold peanut candy in the port. There are two versions of the song. The following version refers to migration to the Dominican Republic, also a popular country of emigration for Curaçaoans:

Awa na awa bati mayó
Mi t'ei bai Santo Domingo, bai mira mama.Si mi pagai kibra na kaminda.
Si mi pagai kibra na kaminda, lo mi rema ku mi man. Awa na awa bati mayó

Awa na awa bati mayó [untranslatable]
I am going to Santo Domingo to see mother If my oars break on the way.
If my oars break on the way, I will row with my hands
Awa na awa bati mayó [untranslatable]. (Allen, "Curaçaoan" 70)

Some Concluding Remarks

Emigration is one of the ways in which working-class Curaçaoans have tried to deal with economic challenges on the island. As both men and women participated in emigration, researching migration lends itself very well to gender analysis. Women have shown a pattern of migration that differs from that of men: there were usually fewer women migrants (although migration to St. Thomas appears to have been an exception in this regard); women often migrated alone (whereas men usually traveled in groups); and women performed other types of work in the country of destination.

To participate in the discipline of migration studies requires any scholar to pay attention to the selection and collection of different types of data. First, a combination of documents in the country of origin and in the country of destination is necessary. This necessitates creative ways of managing documents that transcend the geographical and linguistic borders originally set by the colonial powers, as well as scholarly cooperation across those boundaries to counteract the "coloniality of knowledge" still alive in Caribbean societies today. Modern technologies (such as making research data accessible online) can play a facilitating role in this regard. Second, transcending the traditional male gaze and looking at the female experiences also requires expanding the idea of information archive to one that is intersectional. Understanding gender in migration studies in particular must take into account the interconnectedness of gender with social class, religion, sexuality, ethnicity, and race in knowledge production in order to get traces and fragments to understand the social reality of those neglected in historical writings.

The utilization of oral history helps to better illustrate the complex and varied ways in which marginalized, excluded, silenced, and hidden people understand and interpret their own lives in relationships of unequal power by negotiating and contesting social categories of race and ethnicity, gender and sexuality. Their intimate and personal stories help us to understand their daily life experiences within existing social, political, and economic conditions and the role migration plays in this process. It is precisely the expressive dialogue between document archives and oral history that produces the richness of human experience.

Notes

1. Curaçao is situated in the southern Caribbean, between Aruba and Bonaire, north of Venezuela. Curaçao was one of the islands comprising the former Dutch Caribbean federation called the Netherlands Antilles (1954–2010). In 2010, this federation fell apart and Curaçao became an internally self-governing entity or "country" with direct ties to the Netherlands.
2. The Roman Catholic mission, in this case the Fathers of the Dominican Order, published various weekly newspapers from 1870.
3. The catalog compiled by Dra. Estela Cifre de Loubriel, *Catálogo de extranjeros residentes en Puerto Rico en el siglo XIX*, shows that of the 158 immigrants from Curaçao living in Puerto Rico at that time, thirty-six were women.
4. The interviewee was born in 1885, and I interviewed her on 14 May 1986.
5. Author interview in 1995 with Juanita Ilario-Tromp, who was born in Aruba (Dutch Caribbean) on 23 June 1909 and who came to Curaçao when she was nineteen years old.

Disclosure Statement

No potential conflict of interest was reported by the author.

Works Cited

Allen, Rose Mary. "Curaçaoan Women's Role in the Migration to Cuba." *Mundu Yama Sinta Mira: Womanhood in Curaçao*. Ed. Richenel Ansano et al. Curaçao: Fundashon Publikashon, 1992. 59–75. Print.
—. "Emigración Laboral de Curazao a Cuba a Principios del Siglo XX: Una Experiencia." *Revista Mexicana del Caribe* 5.9 (2000): 40–103. Print.
—. *Ta Cuba Mi Ke Bai: Testimonio di Trahadónan ku a Emigrá for di Kòrsou bai Cuba na Kuminsamentu di Siglo XX*. Zaltbommel, NE: ICS Nederland/Curaçao, 2001. Print.

—. *Di Ki Manera: A Social History of Afro-Curaçaoans, 1863–1917*. Amsterdam: SWP, 2007. Print.

—. "'Nothing About Us, Without Us': Constructing Women's Historical Knowledge: A Case Study of Curaçao." *Yearbook of Women's History/Jaarboek voor Vrouwengeschiedenis*. Ed. Noortje Willems and Sylvia Holla. Hilversum: Verloren, 2017. 93–102. Print.

Baldwin, Andrea Natasha, and Natasha K. Mortley. "Reassessing Caribbean Migration: Love, Power and (Re) Building in the Diaspora." *Journal of International Women's Studies* 17.3 (2016): 164–76. Web. 4 May 2018.

Beckles, Hilary. *Centering Women: Gender Discourses in Caribbean Slave Society*. Kingston: Ian Randle, 1999. Print.

Brereton, Bridget. "Women and Gender in Caribbean (English-Speaking) Historiography: Sources and Methods." *Caribbean Review of Gender Studies* 7 (2013): 1–18. Print.

Cerrutti, Marcela, and Douglas S. Massey. "On the Auspices of Female Migration from Mexico to the United States." *Demography* 38.2 (2001): 187–200. Print.

Deahl, Tim. "Een Vergeten Parel in de Deense Kroon: De Ontwikkelingen van de Nederlandse Connecties met het Deense Eiland St. Thomas, 1770–1807." MA Thesis. U of Leiden, 2012. Print.

Dekker, Jeroen J. H. *Curaçao zonder/met Shell. Een Bijdrage tot Bestudering van Demografische, Economische en Sociale Processen in de Periode 1900–1929*. Zutphen: De Walburg Pers, 1982. Print.

De Loubriel, Estela Cifre, *comp. Catálogo de Extranjeros Residentes en Puerto Rico en el Siglo XIX*. Río Piedras: Ediciones de la Universidad de Puerto Rico, 1962. Print.

Dungy, Kathryn R. "Live and Let Live: Native and Immigrant Free People of Color in Early Nineteenth Century Puerto Rico." *Caribbean Studies* 33.1 (2005): 79–111. Print.

Escobar, Arturo. "Worlds and Knowledges Otherwise: The Latin American Modernity/Coloniality Research Program." *Cultural Studies* 21.2 (2007): 179–210. Print.

Green, Nancy L. "Changing Paradigms in Migration Studies: From Men to Women to Gender." *Gender & History* 24.3 (2012): 782–98. Print.

Grosfoguel, Ramón. "The Epistemic Decolonial Turn: Beyond Political Economy Paradigms." *Cultural Studies* 21.2–3 (2007): 211–23. Print.

Hall, Neville A. T., and B. W. Higman. *Slave Society in the Danish West Indies: St. Thomas, St. John, and St. Croix*. Mona, Jamaica: U of the West Indies, 1992. Print.

Hoagland, Sarah Lucia. "Giving Testimony and the Coloniality of Knowledge." *U of West Indies*. U of West Indies, n.d. Web. 5 May 2018.

Huq, Shireen. "Gender and Development in Brief." *Bridge Bulletin* 14 (2004): 1–6. Print.

Kadar, Marlene, and Helen M. Buss. *Working in Women's Archives: Researching Women's Private Literature and Archival Documents*. Waterloo: Wilfrid Laurier UP, 2001. Print.

Kadar, Marlene, et al. *Tracing the Autobiographical*. Waterloo: Wilfrid Laurier UP, 2006. Print.

Knight, Franklin W. *The Caribbean: The Genesis of a Fragmented Nationalism*. 1978. New York: Oxford UP, 2011.Print.

Koot, Willem Cornelius Jozef. *Emigratie op de Nederlandse Antillen. Een Sociaalwetenschappelijk Onderzoek naar Omvang en Achtergronden van de Emigratie,* in *het bijzonder op Aruba en Curaçao.* Amsterdam: U of Amsterdam P, 1979. Print.

Langenfeld, Els. *Verhalen uit het Verleden, deel 2.* Curaçao: De Curacaosche Courant, 2010. Print.

Lazarus, Latoya. "Working with Marginalized and 'Hidden' Populations: Researchers' Anxieties and Strategies for Doing Less Harmful Research." *Caribbean Review of Gender Studies* 7 (2013): 1–22.

Mair, Lucille Mathurin. *A Historical Study of Women in Jamaica, 1655–1844.* Ed. and intro. Verene A. Shepherd and Hilary McD. Beckles. Kingston: U of the West Indies P, 2006.

Nationaal Archief (National Archives), Den Hague. Algemeen Rijksarchief. Minister van Kolonie, nr. 6734 (1850–1900), nr. 701, National Archives of the Netherlands.

Paula, Alejandro F. *Problemen Rondom de Emigratie van Arbeiders uit de Kolonie Curaçao naar Cuba, 1917–1937.* Curaçao: Centraal Historisch Archief, 1973. Print.

Pietersz, Jorge A. *De Arubaanse arbeidsmigratie 1890-1930: drie studies over de trek van arbeiders in het Caraibisch gebied voor de Tweede Wereldoorlog.* Leiden: Caraïbische Afdeling KITLV, 1985. Print.

Renkema, Willem E. "De Export van Curaçaose Slaven 1819–1847." *Exercities in ons Verleden.* Ed. W. J. Wieringa, et al. Assen: van Gorcum, 1981. 188–208. Print.

Rodríguez, Félix V. Matos. *Women and Urban Change in San Juan Puerto, 1820–1868.* Gainesville: UP of Florida, 1999. Print.

Scully, Pamela, and Diana Paton, eds. *Gender and Slave Emancipation in the Atlantic World.* Durham: Duke UP, 2005. Print.

Shepherd, Verene, et al. *Engendering History: Caribbean Women in Historical Perspective.* New York: St. Martin's, 1995. Print.

Smith, Julia Clancy. "Locating Women as Migrants in Nineteenth-Century Tunis." *Contesting Archives: Finding Women in the Sources.* Ed. Nupur Chaudhuri et al. Champaign: U of Illinois P, 2010. 35–55. Print.

Trouillot, Michel-Rolph. *Silencing the Past: Power and the Production of History.* Boston: Beacon, 1995. Print.

Zikinzá, No. T. 38. Tapes Zikinzá collection. Interviews collected by Paul Brenneker and Elis Juliana, 1958–1960. Stored at the National Archives, Willemstad (NatAr).

The Process

Rejecting Objectivity: Reflections of a Black Feminist Researcher Interviewing Black Women

By Keila D. Taylor

"My dad was sixty-eight so it's not like he was super young. He already had a few health issues but apparently, something failed, his stomach or something. It happened really quick. My brother called me. I just got back from a charity event. He was like, 'Well, Dad's in the hospital.' Then an hour later he called back and said 'They [the doctors] don't think he's going to make it.' Then he died maybe five hours later. They said when they were trying to resuscitate him, blood was coming out of different places."

Her story trails off, and she pauses to prevent her voice from breaking while simultaneously trying to stop the tears that have been welling in her eyes for the past fifteen minutes. I am conducting an interview with Marie Smith,[1] a twenty-eight-year-old writer from Austin, Texas, for my thesis in sociology. Her story of her father dying never made it into my published thesis, but the emotional intensity of the moment replayed in my mind weeks after our meeting concluded. The most memorable detail Marie shares with me is the date of her father's death, July 24. When I hear the date, my thoughts become muddled and I cannot focus. July 24 is the same day of my younger brother's death in 2013.

Immediately, I am transported to the anguish I felt three years ago, and I am no longer a sociologist; I am a secular Black woman empathizing with another secular Black woman who has also experienced tremendous loss. These moments of compassion happened repeatedly throughout my interviews. Every participant's story provided me with new insight into the multiple trajectories to nonreligion, and all of them shared the common theme of forcing a hyperawareness of my positionality as a qualitative researcher.

Marie identifies as a secular Black woman, and one goal of my thesis was to illuminate this misrepresented demographic's unique experiences. Furthermore, my thesis examined the manner in which self-identified

This article was originally published with errors, which have now been corrected in both the print and online versions. Please see Correction (http://dx.doi.org/10.1080/08989575.2019.1588530)

nonreligious (atheist, agnostic, secular humanist, irreligious, freethinker) Black women navigate their social lives and shape their social identity without the direct influence and guidance of traditional Black theology. In the course of my project, I conducted twenty interviews. The questions focused on the development of interviewees' nonreligious identity, from childhood to present, with an emphasis on their current beliefs, where those beliefs stem from, and how they embody those beliefs through action.[2]

The purpose of this methodological essay is to discuss what I learned through conducting qualitative interviews with secular Black women. From my perspective as a Black feminist qualitative researcher, I explore what I discovered about Black women's vulnerability, secrets, and overall (un)willingness to share their experiences as persons managing a secular identity that is further stigmatized because it is compounded by the marginalizing of all Black women's experiences in the United States. Ultimately, I use both my scholarship and my activism to illustrate that empathy is a powerful and vital component of collecting Black women's stories.

I used to feel ashamed to admit my personal longing to seek other secular Black women. It was a desire I hid from my mentors and colleagues. In sociology, one of the first things we are taught is objectivity. We learn about the scientific method and how imperative it is not to allow your personal biases and beliefs to influence your research practices. Fortunately, I had never quite acquired the ability to completely set aside my opinions or ignore my lived experiences as a Black woman.

When I first began the interviews, this empathy felt antithetical to my burgeoning identity as a social scientist. However, once the interviews commenced it proved to be vital in crafting a climate where my participants felt comfortable enough to share their deeply intimate stories about life, love, and sometimes, like Marie, deep personal loss. After hearing participants' stories, qualitative researchers frequently reflect on their relationship to the communities they study and how it affects their research. This process is called reflexivity. Reflexivity involves introspection and a constant mindfulness of the relationship dynamics between the researcher and the participant (Bourke 1). While my identity as a sociologist allows fluidity, meaning I can step in and out of that role as necessary, my identification as a Black woman is not afforded that same flexibility, and because of the nature of my topic, in almost every interview I worried that I regularly obscured the lines between researcher and Other.

It was our mutual interest in the topic of secular Black womanhood that allowed my participants and me to connect, academically and personally. We both wanted to craft biographies centered on this understudied identity. The final question I ask in the interview is, "Can you tell me why you agreed to participate in this research study?" Many of these women told me they agreed because they wanted to help me, another Black woman. Others mentioned that they participated because of the nature of the topic; they expressed frustration at rarely or never having the opportunity to talk candidly about being secular or a nonbeliever in a setting without judgment, and my thesis presented them an opportunity to do so. Jennifer Brown, an athletic coordinator at a high school in Houston, viewed her interview as a platform to tell her story in her own words:

> I feel like no one's ever asked how we [secular Black women] felt about anything, and when we do I feel like there are whitewashed answers sometimes. I know sociologically at an interview y'all do probe because you want the real answer … . I'm sick and tired of having the mis-connotation we don't believe in God. I think we need to speak up. No, we are very spiritual people. If we don't speak up someone else is going to speak up and they are probably going to fuck up what we got to say. I rather you hear from me than somebody else.

I left this quote out of my published thesis as well, but I use it here as an example of how Jennifer trusted that I would communicate her story with respect and honesty. Additionally, Jennifer's comment reveals her acknowledgment of the continuous exploitation of Black women and our experiences, nonreligious and religious. Our experiences are frequently represented inaccurately and rooted in noxious stereotypes such as the Mammy, Sapphire, or Jezebel (Collins 69). Other times, our experiences are simply not shared at all.

It is my responsibility as a sociologist and a Black feminist scholar to engage in a research methodology that reveres the unique challenges Black women combat every day in the face of combined racial, gendered, and, in this case, religious bias. Qualitative studies provide biographies of the communities they study and allow me to "introduce a different type of person as worthy of biographical treatment" (Benjamin 16). Jennifer and numerous other participants understood how susceptible they (Black women) are to misrecognition and felt confident enough to trust that I would handle their truths with dignity because I share that vulnerability with them. They supposed that if I was studying a topic most people did not even care to think about, I may be worth speaking to. That's where our trust started.

The more they revealed to me, the more I noticed we were uniquely bound by our shared experiences of iconoclastic Blackness and womanhood, and for roughly two hours, my participant and I no longer had to "shift" our secular identities. In the United States, many view nonreligious individuals as outsiders and consider them to be the most distasteful of all social groups (Ecklund and Lee 729). This can mean concealing or "shifting" their identity to mitigate the stigma of living their life outside of religious norms.

The principle of shifting for Black women has been internalized since slavery, but it has evolved over time. During enslavement and the Jim Crow era, shifting was external as much as it was internal, such as physically moving to the back of the bus or not making eye contact with a white person. In the contemporary era, shifting has become subtler. Black women shift when they mitigate their anger to placate their white co-workers or downplay their abilities or skills to soothe the Black men in their lives who also encounter racism. The consequences of continual shifting include a range of psychological problems, such as "anxiety, low self-esteem, disordered eating, depression, and even outright self-hatred" (Jones and Shorter-Gooden 8). Thus, as secular Black women shift to negotiate the challenges of sexism and racism, they also shift to manage the social stigma associated with being a religious outsider.

Interviews act as more than merely a dialogue between two individuals. The work we are doing, the stories we document, the analysis we apply, take on lives of their own. They raise the question, "What does it mean to conduct an interview with a Black woman?" or more specifically, what does it mean when we, Black women, are allowed to tell our stories unapologetically? There are many ways Black feminist scholars can answer those questions, but as I continue to evolve as a Black feminist researcher, it means this work (my writings, my collected data, my conference presentations) is a form of social activism. In a society where for secular Black women it is difficult to find community and where Black women are often forced to hide their nonreligious identity even from their loved ones, my interview practice briefly served as a moment of healing. A brief moment in time, when we did not need to shift, led both Marie and me to share the pain of losing important men in our lives and bond in our grief in a way neither of us expected. When Black women are allowed to tell our stories unapologetically, it creates, like for Marie and me, the possibility of healing. It was the first time I realized how powerful and transformative an interview had the potential to be.

From this research process, I learned that in-depth interviews can be as radical as a political protest. It had never occurred to me that activism can be embodied through intellectual production within academic institutions. I was taught the two could not coexist. Not only is that untrue, but activism and scholarship can enhance one another. The groundbreaking Black feminist theorist and sociologist Patricia Hill Collins categorizes this work as "intellectual activism" (11). She challenges scholars to question the role of their research and how social issues are communicated to the public. Interviews can serve as a means of connecting scholars to the populations we study and permit us to tell their stories in their voices.

Documenting my subjects' stories has become a Black feminist mission and personal intervention. Writer and critic Gloria Hull experienced similar feelings during her process of researching Alice Dunbar-Nelson. She states, "For black women being face to face with another Black woman makes the most cruel and beautiful mirror" (Hull 319). My own insights and experiences of oppression were articulated and addressed in unexpected ways as I spoke with the interviewees. These interviews acted as a space affirming my participants' experiences and, unexpectedly, mine too. Memories of abandoning Christianity resurfaced but no longer with the same amount of shame or guilt I once felt. I never expected the validation of my own experiences and my identity to come forward in this process. The completion of my thesis served as a project I believed in both as a scholar in transition from master's to doctorate in my academic career and as a secular Black woman dedicated to making space for secular Black women to feel valid and secure.

The comfort of the interviewee is frequently at the center of how to conduct a successful interview. Before I began my thesis, I encountered a plethora of advice on how to properly ask the correct probing questions, build rapport, guide the interviewee to stay on topic, and most importantly, remain neutral. This supposedly guarantees the data is rich. Outside of recommending the interviewer dresses comfortably and appropriately, I have received very little advice or preparation for interviewers that would ensure that I am prepared for the mental and emotional work required for an in-depth interview. I have learned that my personal investment in conducting research is an advantage when building rapport between researchers and participants, not a hindrance. I have learned it is the first step in ensuring there is a space for a decolonized relationship to form, where power is shared, and every voice has a chance to be heard. A space where Black women temporarily no longer have to shift and hide some of the most unique parts of themselves.

Ethical critical practice involves self-assessing your comfort and openness as a researcher before you ever step into the room to do an interview. Are you prepared for the stories you may hear? Are you prepared for the responsibility that comes with hearing those stories? Black feminist researchers must incorporate their activist perspectives through knowledge, consciousness, and empowerment, but we must also practice maintaining an informed reflexive consciousness (Few et al. 210). This includes contextualizing our own subjective experiences and assessing how we can utilize them to connect with our participants, not hiding them or pretending they are not there. The process of opening ourselves up to our interviewees grants us access to richer data because it builds empathy. Our motivations are no longer solely tethered to the academic obligations of being a successful scholar. Richer data means we have better tools to tell the unheard stories that reflect the lives of the participants more authentically; it also means a more participant-driven method where interview subjects have more control over how they are represented to the larger academic community. Here, in a space of possibility, we can begin to trouble a wide range of institutions (religious or otherwise) harmful to or apathetic about nontraditional narratives.

Notes

1. The participants were asked to create a pseudonym at the end of our interview. Any personal information mentioned, including names, was changed during transcription.
2. The interview questions were divided into five sections: religious background, life experiences as a non-religious Black woman, coming out as nonreligious, social support networks, and coping.

Disclosure Statement

No potential conflict of interest was reported by the author.

Works Cited

Benjamin, Shanna Greene. "Black Women and the Biographical Method: Undergraduate Research and Life Writing." *a/b: Auto/Biography Studies* 32.1 (2017): 15–26. Taylor and Francis Online. Web. 16 Dec. 2016.
Bourke, Brian. "Positionality: Reflecting on the Research Process." *The Qualitative Report* 19.3 (2014): 1–9. Nova Southeastern University, n.d. Web. 20 Apr. 2016.
Brown, Jennifer. Personal interview. 24 Jan. 2017.
Collins, Patricia Hill. *Black Feminist Thought: Knowledge, Consciousness, and the Politics of Empowerment*. New York: Routledge, 2000. Print.
Collins, Patricia Hill. *On Intellectual Activism*. Philadelphia: Temple UP, 2013. Print.
Ecklund, Elaine Howard, and Kristen Schultz Lee. "Atheists and Agnostics Negotiate Religion and Family." *Journal for the Scientific Study of Religion* 50.4 (2011): 728–43. Wiley Online Library. Web. 6 Apr. 2016.
Few, April L., et al. "Sister-to-Sister Talk: Transcending Boundaries and Challenges in Qualitative Research with Black Women." *Family Relations* 52.3 (2003): 205–15. Wiley Online Library. 28 Apr. 2016.
Hull, Gloria T. "Researching Alice Dunbar-Nelson: A Personal and a Literary Perspective." *Feminist Studies* 6.2 (1980): 314–20. *JSTOR*. Web. 10 May 2017.
Jones, Charisse, and Kumea Shorter-Gooden. *Shifting: The Double Lives of Black Women in America*. New York: Perennial, 2004. Print.
Smith, Marie. Personal interview. 17 Jan. 2017.

How Would You Teach It?

A|B

The Work of Teaching Women's Auto|Bio Comics

By Candida Rifkind

Introduction: on Swimming with Marlene Kadar

Many of us who work in the expansive field of life-writing studies are swimming in Marlene Kadar's wake, but I feel a particular buoyancy thanks to my relatively brief contact with her as a doctoral student at York University, where she was a genuinely inquisitive (albeit formidable) examiner on my Women and Literature comprehensive exam committee. In person and in her writing, I have always felt that Marlene asks the unexpected, and that throwing the rest of us a bit off our course is the way she calls us to be more accountable for our own work, to ask different and more difficult questions of ourselves as well as our objects of study. Ultimately, it is Marlene's close attention to texts—to words, images, and their multivalent meanings—and the lived contexts they represent that I hope to channel in my teaching of graphic life narratives. Marlene's interest in the traces of people's lives, her scholarly methods of tracing these traces, and her feminist commitment to lives lived on the margins and forced into the shadows is an important model for studying women's graphic life narratives. After all, auto|bio comics[1] trace lives literally, through the ink marks on the page that outline the person and imply the persona. The fragmented form of comics divides the narrative into the units and moments of panels, encouraging each reader to project meaning into the gaps between them, so that we at once trace the meaning of the story and leave our own traces in these gutters. Teaching women's graphic life narratives is important and gratifying work, and in what follows I hope to channel some of what I have learned from Marlene by combining the theoretical with the practical, the serious with the playful.

Like Marlene, I wear many critical hats. I am trained in literary methods of close analysis, historicist approaches to the moments and movements of textual production, Bourdieusian theories of cultural production and aesthetic value, life-writing theory's questions about the self and the

This article was originally published with errors, which have now been corrected in both the print and online versions. Please see Correction (http://dx.doi.org/10.1080/08989575.2019.1588530)

social, and comics studies' attention to form, medium, and format. All of these frameworks appear in my classrooms, sometimes explicitly but more often implicitly. I teach at the University of Winnipeg, Canada, which is a primarily undergraduate, urban university proud of its high percentage of first-generation scholars from working-class and immigrant backgrounds, its commitment to increasing the representation of Indigenous students, and a long history of social justice in education. I have the luxury of being at a small university that does not have large lecture classes, so I can experiment with all kinds of alternate pedagogies and assignments in ways I am aware are very difficult for colleagues teaching larger classes in departments with more rigid curricula and assessment rubrics. I teach comics and graphic narratives in undergraduate lecture courses at the first-year level in a reading-culture course that focuses on the alternative graphic novel and at the third-year level in a topics in comics and graphic narratives course for which I have developed several iterations, including graphic life narratives, women and comics, and Canadian comics. I also teach seminar courses at the honors and graduate level, usually on graphic witness or graphic biography. In some ways, the day-to-day work of teaching auto|bio comics is not that different from teaching any kind of literary or cultural production: it involves close reading and attention to literal and figurative language, contextualizing the work in its histor-ical, geographic, ideological, generic, and aesthetic moments and commit-ments, and listening to students' verbal or written responses to gauge how the text does or does not resonate with them and the other texts in the course. There are plenty of resources available now on the study and teaching of graphic narratives, and I have listed a few I find helpful at the end. Having worked in comics studies, with a focus on auto|bio comics, for over a decade now, I want to use this opportunity to think reflexively about what this teaching has taught me and how I try in turn to feed this new knowledge back into my evolving pedagogy.

Methodologies: Visual Literacies and Cultural Frames

Since I teach in an English department, I stress the building of visual liter-acy skills alongside the students' training in language and literary genres in their other courses. I emphasize that comics is[2] a unique form, created across print and digital media, for which there is a specific yet still develop-ing analytical toolkit. Given the newness of comics studies, I point out how much of our terminology comes from literature, film, and media studies, and I encourage students to draw on their own backgrounds and even risk coining new terms to describe what they see. In one sense, teaching comics comes down to two fundamental yet very difficult questions I pose time and again to my students: "What do you see?" and "How do you know?" I want students to understand that they already possess many of the skills to study comics, even if they need to transition from the role of fan to critic. But I also want students to interrogate the act of seeing itself and their habitual ways of knowing or constructing meaning too. Once we have reviewed the basic elements of the comics page (panel, gutter, speech balloons, and caption or narrative boxes), I introduce students to the now widely accepted notion, popularized by Scott McCloud's *Understanding Comics*, that comics depend on closure. Readers insert themselves in the gaps, called gutters, between panels in order to construct a narrative out of fragmented units of meaning. I often give students an exercise to practice conscious closure. I might give them a series of seemingly disconnected panels and ask them to generate as many stories as possible from the sequence; I have used a variation of Scott McCloud's "Five Card Nancy" game with some success; and I have used Matt Madden's online *Exercises in Style* to show students the nearly infinite number of page compositions available to break down the same template narrative.

Then I complicate the idea of closure, because these formalist games have sometimes misdirected students to the idea that the gutter is a neutral space into which a reader can project any, or an infinite number of, meanings. I like to start classes with critical quotations on the board that form epigraphs to the discussion. The following important statement on comics reading by Christina Meyer is always a good discussion generator: "Frames serve as perspectival and directional coordinates as well as guiding lines in the reading process; in other words, frames set the parameters of looking and guide the interpretation of a graphic narrative ... . Yet, the reader's gaze, evoked through frames, is already culturally determined and enframed upon the entering of the reading process" (Meyer 54).

Visual literacy, to me at least, is not just teaching students how to read comics, it is also teaching them to interrogate the formal and cultural framing that occurs at the nexus of cartoonist, text, and reader.

This is especially important when studying women's auto|bio comics because so many female-identified cartoonists draw the taboo, unspoken, unrepresented, undocumented, ignored, overlooked, derided, repressed, and suppressed experiences of their lives. The comics page combines the presence of panels with the absence of gutters, and women's auto|bio comics often mobilize this tension for serious play around problems in representation already familiar to life-writing scholars: the perceived authenticity of the first-person narrator, the imposed divide between fiction and nonfiction, the autonomy of the narrating-drawing subject, and the instability of memory, among others. So I try to balance my desire, as a comics-studies scholar, to train students in terminological precision and formalist methodologies with my commitments, as a feminist life-writing scholar, to nudge students toward an analysis of the politics of literary, cultural, and social production and reproduction and the social construction of meaning.

Marianne Hirsch puts this another way in her brief discussion of witnessing trauma in visual texts when she asks, "What kind of visual-verbal literacy can respond to the needs of the present moment?" (1212). Most long-form narrative comics are not only recent, but they document present moments—and past moments that resonate in the present—of personal and collective conflict, displacement, trauma, and survival. As Hirsch and many others note, comics have become a productive form to represent these destabilizing individual and collective experiences precisely because the form itself is structured around the seen and the unseen, the known and the unknowable. Therefore, when my students become conscious of performing the act of closure, they can recognize that comics are, as Hirsch puts it, "biocular": words function as images and images "demand to be read" in ways that foreground "the impossibility of seeing and the impossibility of not looking" (Hirsch 1213). The compulsion to look at the intimacies of lives drawn on the page is part of the pleasure of comics reading; the recognition that our gaze is at once framed by the cartoonist and enframed by our cultural, gendered, racialized, classed, religious, linguistic, and other standpoints is part of the seriousness of comics reading.

Pedagogies: The Classroom and Stranger Sociability

How we read comics is related to much larger questions around reception, and so I also want students to understand the politics of comics, starting with the ways that comics and even graphic novels—much like life writing—have historically been dismissed, sidelined, scorned, and censored by cultural tastemakers and the academy. However, this ignoble history of the form has also been enabling for female-identified cartoonists to push against the ideologies and borders of gendered identities entrenched in more prestigious literary and cultural forms. In addition to their centrality in comics studies, auto|bio comics are steadily finding their way into life-writing courses, and for good reasons. They have proliferated since the first wave of contemporary alternative comics emerged in early 1970s Europe and North America. Jared Gardner begins his impressive survey essay, "Autography's Biography, 1972–2007," by quoting celebrated cartoonist Alison Bechdel musing, "there is something inherently autobiographical about cartooning" (1). Bechdel insists that the form of comics itself compels its practitioners toward the genres of autobiography, memoir, diary, and other genres of writing the self. Gardner positions Justin Green's pioneering, iconoclastic, and confessional auto|-biographical comic, *Binky Brown Meets the Holy Virgin*, within a broader field of subversive underground US comix by R. Crumb, Spain Rodriguez, and Kim Deitch, each of whom to different degrees combines gross-out humor, explicit sexual material, and political critique to shock readers and challenge the status quo.

As much as these early US autographers reinvented comics as a sociopolitical form for adults, their highly personal and revealing self-representations were also a way to construct the kind of counterpublic organized by textual circulation that Michael Warner, working in a very different context, terms "stranger sociability." According to Warner, the circulation of texts sutures individuals to each other when their private reading acts enter them into a social imaginary. Warner emphasizes that this stranger sociability produces a counterpublic when the social imaginary produced by textual circulation is aware of its subordinate status to a dominant public, and this is manifested in the content as well as the forms of its speech genres and modes of address (119). Green claims that the surprise of publishing *Binky Brown* for him was the way readers saw themselves in it, that others shared experiences he thought were unique to him. Gardner then connects Brown's comments to reports that Bechdel's highly personal coming-out stories spoke to queer readers in a similar experience of "collective self-revelation" (Green, qtd. in Gardner 13). This conversation reveals how auto|bio comics have always been about the interactions between self and text, and between self and other, that produce the stranger sociability of the counterpublic.

Reading and teaching auto|bio comics about women's lives pushes on the boundaries of this counterpublic that was, at least in its first formations around US countercultural comix, highly masculine. Teachers of women's auto|bio comics need to understand that their students will often participate in this collective self-revelation as well. Because so many of the texts I teach contain narratives of coming of age, coming out, coming to feminist consciousness, and creative struggle and fulfillment, I often encounter students responding to them on a personal level. They find that these works speak to them in new ways, and students across the gender spectrum often identify with the outsider, marginalized, rebellious women they see on the pages. I hope to harness this stranger sociability organized by women's auto|bio comics into a critical engagement with the texts and their contexts. I ask my students to register their initial emotional responses to the texts in roundtables and journal entries, and then we work to unpack how their affective relationships to the course texts are produced in the collaboration between cartoonist, comic, and reader.[3] Teaching women's auto|bio comics challenges me to push students to more critical engagement with the style and content of the course texts and to acknowledge the significance of this stranger sociability in our collective reading practices. I hope that students leave my classes asking challenging questions about the craft of cartooning the self, about the techniques and strategies these cartoonists use to construct an affective response of identification and recognition, and about the role of life narratives in producing new social relationships and new cultural forms.

Teaching the Stories of Women's Auto|Bio Comics

There are several starting points for a genealogy of women's auto|bio comics. I could start with pioneering strip cartoonists writing their lives into syndicated newspaper comics and cite Lynn Johnston's family serial, *For Better or For Worse*, as a landmark of popular and comics culture. Or women's auto|bio comics might begin with Aline Kominsky Crumb, Trina Robbins, Diane Noomin, and the other pioneers of the radical feminist *Wimmen's Comix* collective (Robbins). As in the broader field of comics studies, serial, satiric, and short comics remain understudied in contrast to the book-length, prestigious auto|bio comics that are often marketed as "graphic novels." An emerging canon in this subfield includes titles that have garnered significant scholarship from life-writing and comics scholars, among them Marjane Satrapi's *Persepolis*, Phoebe Gloeckner's *A Child's Life and Other Stories*, Alison Bechdel's *Fun Home*, and Lynda Barry's *One! Hundred! Demons!*—some of which use avatars for semiautobiographical representations but are nevertheless received as auto|bio comics. Questions of prestige and the emerging comics studies canon have been taken up by Bart Beaty, Benjamin Woo, Ariella Freedman, and others, and I agree with them that the dominance of English departments and literary criticism in the formation of comics studies has reproduced modernist standards of the well-made text to the detriment of popular, serial, ephemeral, funny, web, and collaborative comics that defy traditional definitions of authorship and the autonomous literary text. When I assembled my reading list for a third-year lecture course on women and comics, I wanted to teach some more canonical works and also introduce students to lesser-known cartoonists and less prestigious forms of auto|bio comics, including serial and web comics.

Teaching these works demands a lot, as my comments above suggest. Instructors need to balance students' openness to a popular form with the difficult knowledge it often represents. We need to teach students to read gaps, elisions, and the unrepresentable in ways that remain accountable to what is present and represented on the page. And we need to encourage visual literacy skills that often require training in the much broader histories of art, photography, film, painting, dance, and so on, often from multiple cultural, regional, and national traditions. But this is why teaching graphic life narratives, especially women's auto|bio comics, is so gratifying: there is always something new to learn from each text, whether it is a new layout strategy to challenge the conventional comics grid, a disorienting way of visualizing the self that challenges gendered beauty ideals and comics stereotypes, an innovation in lettering that pushes the boundaries between word and image to blur sign systems, or an incorporation of other media and creative practices, such as photography, painting, quilt-making, scrapbooking, doodling, or diagramming, all of which then invite us to learn about their own histories and contexts. In the decade that I have been reading, teaching, and writing about graphic life narratives, I feel that these unruly, sometimes disorienting, and often captivating texts have pushed me toward the condition of polymathy, and that it is an ever-receding horizon. I have studied the "femmage" art movement to understand Barry's self-representation in *One! Hundred! Demons!*; I have learned about Persian portraiture and Iranian political posters to teach Satrapi's *Persepolis*; I have sourced photographs and film footage from the civil rights archive to see how Lisa Quintero Weaver redraws them in *Darkroom: A Memoir in Black and White*; I have learned about the debates over ASL in the deaf community from Cece Bell's *El Deafo*; I have read up on the history of Chinese magicians in the West to teach Ann Marie Fleming's *The Magical Life of Long Tack Sam*; I have studied the history of Vietnamese refugees' complicated journeys to the US to contextualize Thi Bui's *The Best We Could Do*; and the list goes on. Teaching auto|bio comics is about what they teach us, what new knowledge we gain from these life narratives themselves and from the homework they ask us to do, and what we learn from our students' affective and intellectual responses to them. This is the work of teaching women's auto|bio comics.

Notes

1. Although I often use "graphic life narratives" and Whitlock and Poletti's "autographics," I am lately more drawn to the term "auto|bio comics" because it is commonly used by cartoonists, publishers, fans, and critics outside the academy. I want my practice as a comics scholar to recognize and be in conversation with the broader comics community that produces important, and all too often undervalued, knowledge about these texts.
2. It is standard in comics studies to use the plural (comics) to refer to the form in the singular.
3. In an earlier reflection for this journal on teaching failure, I wrote about how I have learned from my students to recognize and respond to the affective power of graphic life narratives in my classrooms.

Disclosure Statement

No potential conflict of interest was reported by the author(s).

Works Cited

Barry, Lynda. *One! Hundred! Demons!* Seattle: Sasquatch, 2005. Print.

Beaty, Bart, and Benjamin Woo. *The Greatest Comic Book of All Time: Symbolic Capital and the Field of American Comic Books.* New York: Palgrave Macmillan, 2016. Print.

Bechdel, Alison. *Fun Home: A Family Tragicomic.* Belmont, CA: Wadsworth, 2007. Print.

Bell, Cece. *El Deafo.* New York: Abrams, 2014. Print.

Bui, Thi. *The Best We Could Do.* New York: Abrams, 2017. Print.

Fleming, Ann-Marie. *The Magical Life of Long Tack Sam.* Toronto: Riverhead, 2007. Print.

Freedman, Ariella. "Comics, Graphic Novels, Graphic Narrative: A Review." *Literature Compass* 8.1 (2011): 28–46. *Wiley Online Library.* Web. 20 Apr. 2016.

Gardner, Jared. "Autography's Biography 1972–2007." *Biography* 31.1 (2008): 1–26. *Project Muse.* Web. 4 May 2012.

Gloeckner, Phoebe. *A Child's Life and Other Stories.* New York: Penguin Random House, 2000. Print.

Hirsch, Marianne. "Editor's Column: Collateral Damage." *PMLA* 119.5 (2004): 1209–15. *JSTOR.* Web. 5 Nov. 2017.

Johnston, Lynn. *For Better or For Worse.* Entercom Canada Inc. Web. 5 Nov. 2017.

McCloud, Scott. "Five Card Nancy." *ScottMcCloud.com.* Scott McCloud, n.d. Web. 18 Apr. 2018.

—. *Understanding Comics: The Invisible Art.* New York: HarperPerennial, 2004. Print.

Meyer, Christina. "Teaching Visual Literacy through 9/11 Graphic Narratives." *Teaching Comics and Graphic Narratives: Essays on Theory, Strategy and Practice.* Ed. Lan Dong. Jefferson: McFarland, 2012, 53–65. Print.

Rifkind, Candida. "Graphic Life Narratives and Teaching the Art of Failure." *a/b: Auto/Biography Studies* 32.1 (2017): 104–06. Taylor and Francis. Web. 20 May 2017.

Robbins, Trina, ed. *The Complete Wimmen's Comics.* Seattle: Fantagraphics, 2016. Print.

Satrapi, Marjane. *The Complete Persepolis.* New York: Pantheon, 2007. Print.

Warner, Michael. *Publics and Counterpublics.* New York: Zone, 2002. Print.

Weaver, Lisa Quintero. *Darkroom: A Memoir in Black and White.* Tuscaloosa: U of Alabama P, 2012. Print.

Whitlock, Gillian, and Anna Poletti. "Self Regarding Art." *Autographics.* Ed. Whitlock and Poletti. Spec. issue of *Biography* 31.1 (2008): v–xxiii. *Project MUSE.* Web. 10 Sept. 2013.

Getting Started: Teaching Resources

Baetens, Jan, and Hugo Frey. *The Graphic Novel: An Introduction.* New York: Cambridge UP, 2015. Print.

> A textbook overview of the "graphic novel" (including comic strips, autographics, and other forms) divided into three sections: "Historical

Context," "Forms," and "Themes." The chapters "Understanding Panel and Page Layouts" and "Drawing and Style, Word and Image" are particularly helpful resources for students learning to write about comics.

Barry, Lynda. *Syllabus: Notes from an Accidental Professor.* Montreal: Drawn & Quarterly, 2014. Print.

As the title suggests, this is a book full of exercises, notes, and prompts for visual creativity. I use some of these exercises based on Barry's teaching (some of which you can also access through her Tumblr and online lectures) when I want students to experience for themselves how memory, the imagination, and the senses contribute to the creation of auto|-bio comics.

Bonner Online Comics Research Bibliography. University of Bonn. Web. http://www.comicforschung.uni-bonn.de/

The Bonner Online is the most comprehensive international database for scholarly literature about comics, graphic narratives, manga, and related fields.

Kukkonen, Karin. *How to Study Comics and Graphic Novels.* New Jersey: Wiley-Blackwell, 2013. Available in print and ebook.

This is a relatively short, accessible textbook that provides practical and theoretical frameworks for teaching and studying graphic narratives.

Madden, Matt. *99X: Exercises in Style.* Web. http://mattmadden.com/comics/99x/

I use the online examples from Madden's book *Exercises in Style*, in which he draws the same story in ninety-nine different comics styles, to show students how comics form and content operate together.

"Teaching Comics." *The Center for Cartoon Studies.* Web. http://www.teachingcomics.org/copy.php

The Center for Cartoon Studies provides a variety of resources for teaching comics that are free to use and adapt, including helpful handouts on comics form and study guides on specific texts.

"The Comics Artists Challenge." *New York Times Sunday Book Review.* 13 Oct. 2015. Web. https://www.nytimes.com/interactive/2015/10/12/books/review/18roundup.html

Seven established cartoonists responded to the challenge, "Can the power of graphic storytelling be communicated in one comic panel?" I use these at the beginning of a course as examples of how comics can convey meaning through the complex relationship between the visual and verbal tracks.

Further reading (scholarly books)

See the Bonner Bibliography for journal articles and book chapters.

Chaney, Michael. *Reading Lessons in Seeing: Mirrors, Masks, and Mazes in the Autobiographical Graphic Novel*. Jackson: U of Mississippi P, 2016. Print.

Chaney, Michael, ed. *Graphic Subjects: Critical Essays on Autobiography and Graphic Novels*. Madison: U of Wisconsin P, 2011. Print.

Chute, Hillary. *Disaster Drawn: Visual Witness, Comics, and Documentary Form*. Cambridge: Harvard UP, 2016. Print.

—. *Graphic Women: Life Narrative and Contemporary Comics*. New York: Columbia UP, 2010. Print.

Dong, Lan, ed. *Teaching Comics and Graphic Narratives: Essays on Theory, Strategy and Practice*. Jefferson: McFarland, 2012. Print.

El Rafaie, Elisabeth. *Autobiographical Comics: Life Writing in Pictures*. Jackson: UP of Mississippi, 2012. Print.

Hatfield, Charles. *Alternative Comics: An Emerging Literature*. Jackson: UP of Mississippi, 2005. Print.

Kunka, Andrew J. *Autobiographical Comics*. London: Bloomsbury, 2018. Bloomsbury Comics Studies.

Mickwitz, Nina. *Documentary Comics: Graphic Truth-Telling in a Skeptical Age*. London: Palgrave, 2017. Palgrave Studies in Comics and Graphic Novels.

Rifkind, Candida, and Linda Warley, eds. *Canadian Graphic: Picturing Life Narratives*. Waterloo: Wilfrid Laurier UP, 2016.

Index

Note: Page numbers followed by "n" denote endnotes.